CHEVROLET VEGA 2300 1970-71 AUTOBOOK

Workshop Manual for
Chevrolet Vega 2300 1970-71
Chevrolet Vega Panel Delivery 1970-71

by

Kenneth Ball G I Mech E

and the

Autopress team of Technical Writers

AUTOPRESS LTD   GOLDEN LANE   BRIGHTON   BN1 2QJ   ENGLAND

The AUTOBOOK series of Workshop Manuals is the largest in the world and covers the majority of British and Continental motor cars, as well as all major Japanese and Australian models. For a full list see the back of this manual.

CONTENTS

Acknowledgement

Introduction

ISBN 0 85147 262 1

First Edition   1972

© Autopress Ltd 1972

J55989

Printed and bound in Brighton England for Autopress Ltd by G Beard & Son Ltd

ACKNOWLEDGEMENT

My thanks are due to General Motors Corporation for their unstinted co-operation and also for supplying data and illustrations.

I am also grateful to a considerable number of owners who have discussed their cars at length and many of whose suggestions have been included in this manual.

Kenneth Ball G I Mech E
Associate Member Guild of Motoring Writers

Ditchling Sussex England.

INTRODUCTION

This do-it-yourself Workshop Manual has been specially written for the owner who wishes to maintain his car in first class condition and to carry out his own servicing and repairs. Considerable savings on garage charges can be made, and one can drive in safety and confidence knowing the work has been done properly.

Comprehensive step-by-step instructions and illustrations are given on all dismantling, overhauling and assembling operations. Certain assemblies require the use of expensive special tools, the purchase of which would be unjustified. In these cases information is included but the reader is recommended to hand the unit to the agent for attention.

Throughout the Manual hints and tips are included which will be found invaluable, and there is an easy to follow fault diagnosis at the end of each chapter.

Whilst every care has been taken to ensure correctness of information it is obviously not possible to guarantee complete freedom from errors or to accept liability arising from such errors or omissions.

Instructions may refer to the righthand or lefthand sides of the vehicle or the components. These are the same as the righthand or lefthand of an observer standing behind the car and looking forward.

CHAPTER 1

THE ENGINE

1:1 Description

The engine is available in two versions; a basic 90 h.p. unit and one giving an output of 110 h.p. achieved by the fitting of a dual barrel carburetter, larger inlet and exhaust valves and a modified camshaft. Both are of four cylinder in-line overhead camshaft construction with a capacity of 140 cu inch and both use the same main mechanical components.

The cylinder head is an iron casting in which the camshaft operates the valves through adjustable tappets. Drive to the camshaft is by toothed belt direct from the crankshaft. Adjustment is effected by moving the water pump body thus pressihg the fan hub against the back of the belt.

An aluminium alloy containing 17 per cent silicon and 4.5 per cent copper is used for the cylinder case die casting. After boring and honing, the surface of the cylinder bores is electrochemically etched to expose the silicon. The iron plated aluminium pistons run against this surface; no liners are fitted. When excessive wear makes the bores unserviceable, the cylinder case is renewed, no reboring is possible. Chrome plated or molybdenum treated top rings are fitted to the pistons as standard.

The oil pump consists of a gear fitted to the front of the crankshaft meshing with a ring gear in the engine front cover. Oil is delivered via galleries and drillings to all bearings through an externally mounted fullflow filter. The electric petrol pump is supplied with current from a connection on the oil pressure sensor except when the ignition key is in the 'start' position. If the oil pressure drops below 2 p.s.i. the current is cut off and the petrol pump stops.

FIGS 1:1 and **1:2** show side and end views of the engine.

1:2 Removing the engine

All major overhaul operations except crankshaft and flywheel removal can be carried out without removing the engine. However, it is often quicker and more convenient to work on the engine if it is out of the car. When working on a vehicle equipped with air conditioning

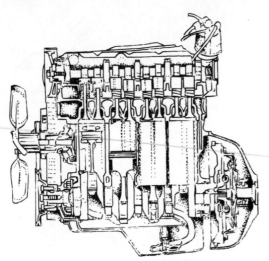

FIG 1:1 Side view of engine

do not disconnect any hoses or interfere with the system except to release the compressor supports and remove the drive belt. Rest the compressor on the frame forward brace and secure the rear of the compressor to the engine compartment. This arrangement will not hinder removal of the engine.

Remove the engine as follows:

1 Depending on the lifting tackle available, either open the hood and install a bolt in the strut (see **FIG 1:3**), or remove the hood entirely.
2 Disconnect and remove the battery.
3 Drain the engine cooling system, remove the radiator hoses and disconnect the heater hoses at the water pump and heater inlet (lower hose).

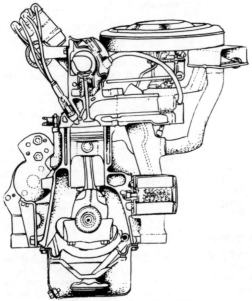

FIG 1:2 End view of engine

4 Disconnect all the emission control system hoses taking careful notes so that replacement is facilitated.
5 Remove the radiator shroud, radiator, fan and spacer then take off the air cleaner, disconnecting the vent tube at the base of the cleaner.
6 Detach all electrical leads, carefully marking each one ready for reconnection.
7 Disconnect the automatic transmission linkage at the manifold bellcrank (if fitted), remove the fuel line at the carburetter, the transmission vacuum modulator and air conditioning vacuum line from the inlet manifold and then the accelerator cable at the bell-crank.
8 If power steering is fitted, dismount the pump but do not disconnect the hoses. Secure the pump out of the way.
9 From below the car, disconnect the exhaust pipe at the manifold and remove the flywheel dust cover or convertor underpan as applicable. Drain the engine oil.
10 On automatic transmission models scribe a line across the converter and drive plate then remove the retaining bolts. Make sure the converter is free of the engine drive plate then arrange a piece of strong wire between the converter and drive plate with the ends secured to the transmission case so that the converter is held back in its housing and cannot fall out as the engine is removed.
11 Remove the engine to flywheel or converter housing bolts. Place a jack under the transmission and just take the weight. Protect the transmission pan by a piece of soft wood on the jack head.
12 Loosen the engine to frame mounting bolts.
13 Place a sling round the engine, one loop under the rear main bearing and the other loop under the oil pump cover, forward of the oil pan. Attach the sling to a suitable lifting tackle and just raise the engine enough to take the weight from the engine mountings. Remove the mounting bolts. Raise the engine slightly more and pull towards the front of the car. See that the convertor (if fitted) is not moving out of the housing, lift the engine clear of the car.

Refit the engine as follows:

1 Raise the engine on the lifting tackle and position it over the engine compartment. Lower carefully until the engine and transmission are in alignment.
2 On synchromesh transmission models slide the engine towards the transmission making sure that the splines of the first motion shaft enter the clutch friction plate. It may be necessary to rotate the crankshaft slightly to achieve this.
3 If automatic transmission is fitted, align the scribed marks on the convertor and engine drive plate, remove the retaining wire and fit the drive plate to convertor bolts. Tighten to 30 to 35 lb ft.
4 Fit and tighten the engine mounting bolts finger tight.
5 Fit and tighten the convertor housing to engine bolts to 35 lb ft or if dealing with synchromesh transmission, the clutch housing to engine bolts to 25 lb ft. It is important that all bolts fitted to the aluminium engine block have clean threads coated with anti-seize compound. Tighten the clutch dust cover bolts to 80 lb inch or the convertor underpan to 95 lb inch.

6 Check that the engine mountings are aligned as shown in **FIG 1 : 4** then fully tighten the bolts.

Complete the refitting by reversing the dismantling procedure.

1 : 3 Removing the cylinder head

The cylinder head can be removed without disturbing the camshaft. If it is intended to decarbonize the head or service the valve gear, the camshaft must eventually be withdrawn. Service tool J.23591 is essential for camshaft removal, no make-shift tool will be acceptable. For compressing the valve springs, service tool J.23591 is equally essential.

Proceed as follows:

1 Drain the coolant and detach the hose from the thermostat outlet. Disconnect the battery.

2 Unbolt and remove the fan and spacer.

3 Slacken the two lower screws holding the top part of the timing belt cover, remove the two upper retaining screws and lift the cover away.

4 Remove the air cleaner and Positive Crankcase Ventilation (PCV) valve from the camshaft cover then remove the cover. Preserve the gasket for reuse unless damaged.

5 Loosen the alternator, air conditioning compressor or power steering pump mountings as applicable and remove the drive belts. Remove the centre bolt from the drive pulley then the four pulley to timing belt sprocket bolts. Remove the pulley and damper or washer as applicable.

6 Loosen the four water pump bolts so that tension on the timing belt is released.

7 Remove the four screws holding the timing belt lower cover and lift the cover from the engine.

8 Slip the timing belt from the sprockets. **Do not rotate the crankshaft until the head is removed or a piston will contact a valve causing serious damage.** Similarly, do not rotate the camshaft unless certain that all pistons are well down the cylinder bores.

9 The water pump, once disturbed, must be removed, the mating surfaces between pump and block cleaned, a new gasket installed and the pump refitted but with the bolts left loose at this stage. Coat the bolt threads with anti-seize compound.

10 See paragraph 8, then rotate the camshaft so that a socket can be inserted through a hole in the camshaft sprocket and fitted to the head of one of the cover bolts to restrain the sprocket from turning. Undo the sprocket retaining bolt and remove the sprocket. **FIG 1 : 5** shows the sprocket and belt drive in detail.

11 Disconnect the throttle linkage, fuel lines and vacuum lines at the carburetter.

12 If fitted, disconnect the power steering pump strut at the manifold. Release the alternator to thermostat housing through-bolt and swivel the alternator sufficiently to obtain access to the inlet manifold bolts. Remove the four bolts arrowed in **FIG 1 : 6** and withdraw the manifold complete with the carburetter.

13 Disconnect the exhaust pipe from the exhaust manifold, undo the oil dipstick bracket then release the bolts arrowed in **FIG 1 : 7**. Remove the manifold complete with the carburetter heater.

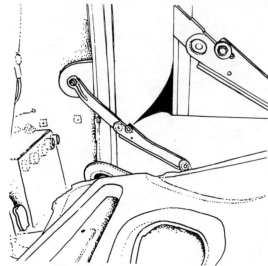

FIG 1 : 3   Bolt installed in hood strut

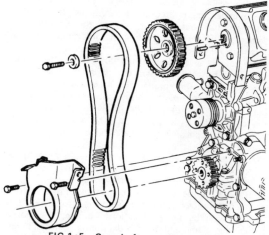

FIG 1 : 4   Engine mounting details

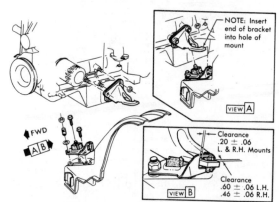

FIG 1 : 5   Camshaft sprocket removal

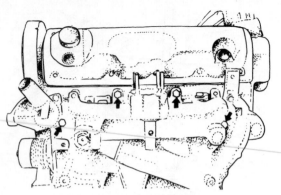

FIG 1 : 6   Inlet manifold bolts

FIG 1 : 7   Exhaust manifold bolts

14 Release the cylinder head bolts evenly, then lift the cylinder head clear of the engine. Support on two wooden blocks so that the valves held open are not in contact with the bench. Discard the cylinder head gasket.

1 : 4 Removing the camshaft

It is possible to remove the camshaft without removing the cylinder head. Proceed generally as described in **Section 1 : 3** but do not remove the manifolds or carburetter. Disconnect the fuel line and remove the idle solenoid. Remove the carburetter choke coil, cover and rod assembly and the camshaft cover. Turn the crankshaft until the pistons are well down the bores clear of the valves. Release the engine forward mounting brackets, jack the engine up and insert blocks $1\frac{1}{2}$ inch thick between the mounts and the body frame. Ensure that the coolant hoses and exhaust pipe are not strained. Remove the camshaft sprocket. The procedure is now the same whether the head is installed or not.

1 Refer to **FIG 1 : 5**. Remove the three bolts holding the top piece of the timing belt cover to the head. This will release the seal and retainer plate.

2 Release the vacuum line at the distributor then remove the distributor cap and plug leads after labelling each lead with its proper location. Remove the clamp bolt and clamp and pull the distributor from the head. The timing will need to be reset when the camshaft is

reinstalled and the drive connected, therefore there is little point in attempting to mark the camshaft and distributor drive at this stage.

3 Install service tool J.23591 to the cylinder head as shown in **FIG 1 : 8**. Ensure that the attachment holes in the tool line up with the camshaft cover lower attachment holes and that the tappet depressing levers are seated squarely over every tappet. The screws in the bottom of the tool must not contact the head at this stage. Bolt the tool to the head with the special hardened bolts supplied then rotate the screws in the bottom of the tool until they just contact the cylinder head. Lubricate the ball end of each of the four lever bolts and screw each one down until the tappets are completely depressed. Use a torque wrench for the last few turns to check that the tool is operating properly. If more than 10 lb ft are required, check the installation.

4 With all tappets held down by the service tool, the camshaft can be withdrawn forwards taking care not to damage the bearings.

1 : 5 Fitting new bearings for camshaft

If service tool J.23638 is available it is an easy task to fit new bearings; failing this, the work must be entrusted to a Chevrolet Agent.

1 With the camshaft removed and the tappets held down as described in **Section 1 : 4**, use tool J.23638 to tap each bearing from its housing (see **FIG 1 : 9**). Be careful to drive the rear bearing into the distributor housing gently so that the end plug is not disturbed. Crush the bearing with a screwdriver then withdraw it through the housing with a pair of pliers.

2 Using tool J.23638, install the new bearings as shown in **FIG 1 : 10**. Commence with the rear bearing and align the oil feed holes as indicated by the arrows in **FIG 1 : 10**. The oil groove in No. 1 bearing must face the front of the engine to lubricate the thrust plate.

1 : 6 Removing the valves

Remove the head and camshaft as described in **Sections 1 : 3** and **1 : 4** then release the pressure on the tappets. Do not remove tool J.23591.

1 Lift out each tappet and place in sequence ready for reassembly. Use small boxes or marked compartments on the work bench so that all the valve components can be identified and kept in sets. Number them from 1 to 8 commencing at the front of the engine for Number 1.

2 Compress each valve spring in turn commencing at No. 1 using service tool J.23592 as illustrated in **FIG 1 : 11**. Remove the valve locks, cap, seal, damper and spring. Withdraw the valve. Repeat for all remaining valves. **FIG 1 : 12** shows the component parts of the valve with the tappet removed. Remove tool J.23591.

1 : 7 Servicing the cylinder head

Apart from fitting new camshaft bearings, other major work on the cylinder head involves the removal of carbon and the reseating or renewal of valves and springs. Remove the cylinder head, **Section 1 : 3**, the camshaft

Section 1:4, and the valves **Section 1:6.** Remove all spark plugs. Plug all oilways using hard wood plugs rather than rag. Thoroughly clean all carbon from the combustion chambers and ports with a wire brush and electric drill or a blunt scraper. Do not use emerycloth. Scrape the head gasket face clean then wash the head thoroughly in clean fuel and allow to dry. Scrape all carbon from the valves and polish on a buffing wheel. Wash all the valve components in clean fuel.

Inspection:

Examine all the head surfaces for cracks, the valve seats for pitting and burning and the valve guide bores for excessive wear. Check the condition of the valves, springs and tappets. Inspect the camshaft for wear or misalignment. Detailed inspection procedures are as follows:

Valve guides:

Ensure that the valve guide bore is clean and dry, then insert a new valve and check for sideways movement. If this exceeds .001 inch inlet and .002 inch exhaust the guides must be reamed oversize and valves with oversize stems fitted. These are available in .003 inch, .015 inch and .030 oversizes; Chevrolet Agents have the necessary reamers under part Nos. J.5830-1, 2 and 3 respectively.

Valves:

Check the stem for straightness using a Vee block and dial indicator against the head. Scrap the valve if the indicator shows more than .010 inch full scale deflection. This is the limit beyond which refacing will thin the head excessively. Examine the head and stem very carefully for cracks or scoring. Reject any valve which shows a reduction of more than .001 inch between the bearing and non-bearing surfaces of the stem. If the valve head edge is less than $\frac{1}{32}$ inch thick, this also involves rejection since the valve would quickly overheat and burn out.

Tappets:

Remove the adjusting screw and wash the parts in clean fuel. **FIG 1:13** shows the tappet and screw in section. Note that when reassembling the screw to the tappet it is entered in the hole nearest the tappet top face so that the flat ground on the screw becomes parallel to the valve stem. Renew if wear is apparent on the tappet face or the screw bearing surface. If a new tappet is fitted on a used camshaft, polish the top face with No. 600 grade wet or dry abrasive paper before installation.

Valve springs:

These are best checked against a new spring. Any reduction in the free height of 2.03 inch must involve rejection. It is good practice to renew springs at every decarbonization in any case.

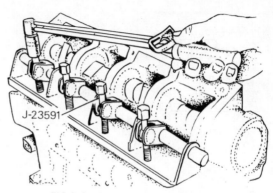

FIG 1:8   Service tool J.23591 in use

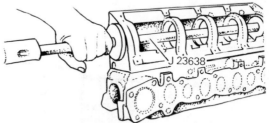

FIG 1:9   Removing camshaft bearings

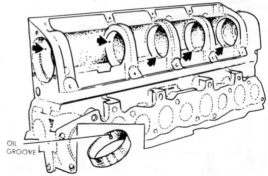

FIG 1:10   Position of oil holes in camshaft bearings

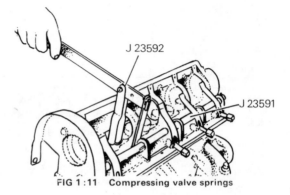

FIG 1:11   Compressing valve springs

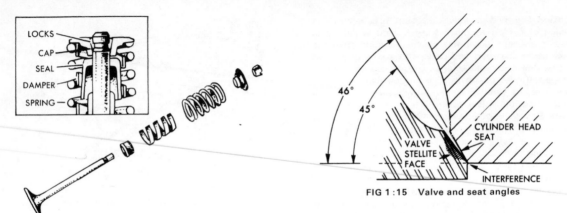

FIG 1:12   Valve spring and cap assembly

FIG 1:15   Valve and seat angles

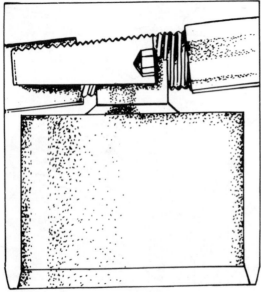

FIG 1:13   Tappet and adjusting screw

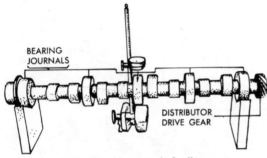

FIG 1:14   Checking camshaft alignment

Camshaft:

Measure the journals with a micrometer. If more than .001 inch out of round exists, replace the shaft. Mount the camshaft as shown in **FIG 1:14**. More than .0015 inch full scale deflection of the indicator must involve rejection. Examine the cam lobes for scuffing and the distributor gear for wear.

Valve and seat reconditioning:

1 Unless the valve has only the slightest pitting it should be refaced on a purpose built refacing machine. Attempts to hand lap excessively pitted valves are timewasting and damaging to the cylinder head seats. Refacing by machine will automatically remove any eccentricity between the valve stem and face. The face angle should be 45 deg. as shown in **FIG 1:15.**

2 If the valve guide bores have been reamed oversize, the seats in the head must be recut to 46 deg. with a piloted cutter. This is best done by a Chevrolet Agent who will have the correct equipment.

3 Ensure that all grinding dust has been removed then make pencil marks across the valve face at $\frac{1}{4}$ inch intervals. Insert it in the head and, holding the valve firmly against its seat, rotate it half a turn in each direction. Remove the valve and check that all pencil marks have been removed at the point of contact between valve and head. If not, locate the cause of the eccentricity and rectify it.

4 The manufacturers do not recommend any further work on the valves and seats such as hand lapping if the valves and seats have been refaced and recut as specified in preceding paragraphs. Only if the components are in such good condition that a few light rubs with fine paste will restore the seat should this practice be allowed.

5 The width of contact between the valve face and the seat should be $\frac{3}{64}$ inch to $\frac{1}{16}$ inch intake and $\frac{3}{64}$ inch to $\frac{5}{64}$ inch exhaust.

Reassembly:

Check that all components are perfectly clean, particularly see that no foreign matter has entered the oilways.

1 Fit the service tool J.23591 to the head, tappets fingers free.

2 Lightly coat No. 1 valve stem with clean engine oil and install it in the head.

3 Fit a new oil seal to the valve stem then the springs and cap as shown in **FIG 1:12**. Compress the spring with service tool J.23592 as shown in **FIG 1:11** and fit the two locks. Be very certain that these are correctly seated. Remove the tool.

4 Repeat operations 2 and 3 for the remaining valves.

5 Check the installed spring height on all valves as shown in **FIG 1:16**. Measure from the spring seat on the cylinder head to the spring locating face under the valve cap. This should be $1\frac{3}{4}$ inch. If more than this by $\frac{1}{16}$ inch dismantle the valve assembly and put a $\frac{1}{16}$ inch shim on the cylinder head face. Never shim to less than $1\frac{3}{4}$ inch.

6 Coat the tappet bores in the cylinder head with clean engine oil and the face of the adjusting screws and top surface of the tappets with 'Molykote' or similar anti-scuffing compound. Insert all tappets and depress with tool J.23591.

1:8 Refitting the camshaft

Cylinder head removed:

The tappets must be depressed as instructed in **Sections 1:4** and **1:7**. Coat the bearings with clean engine oil and slide the camshaft right home. The end float of the camshaft must be checked and adjusted, proceed as follows:

1 Check the oil seal in the retainer plate. If it is damaged or shows signs of wear, prise it from the retainer plate and press in a new one. Smear the bearing surface of the seal with oil so that it is not fitted dry to the camshaft. These instructions apply to the fitting of the original camshaft and retainer. If new components are being fitted check the end float (paragraph 2) before fitting a seal in a retainer.

2 Fit a new gasket, and the retainer plate. While tightening the three bolts, continually move the camshaft endways to ensure that the retainer is not jamming the camshaft. Tighten the bolts to 15 lb ft. With a dial indicator against the face of the camshaft as shown in **FIG 1:17** ensure that the end play is within .004 inch to .012 inch; if not, a retainer with a greater or less spigot depth must be fitted. These are available in increments of .004 inch from .226 inch to .238 inch. When correct, remove the bolts, fit the timing belt upper cover and refit the bolts. Remove tool J.23591.

Cylinder head installed:

Proceed as for 'cylinder head removed' but see that the pistons are well down the bores before depressing the tappets. After fitting the camshaft remove the $1\frac{1}{2}$ inch packing blocks from below the engine mounts and fit the engine mount bolts.

Instructions for refitting the distributor are given in **Chapter 3**.

1:9 Refitting the cylinder head

See that the cylinder head, cylinder case surfaces and threaded holes are perfectly clean then place a new cylinder head gasket on the cylinder case with the smooth side of the gasket uppermost. No jointing compound is necessary. The pistons must be positioned down the bores to avoid interference with an open valve. If the crankshaft timing sprocket mark is set 90 deg. before

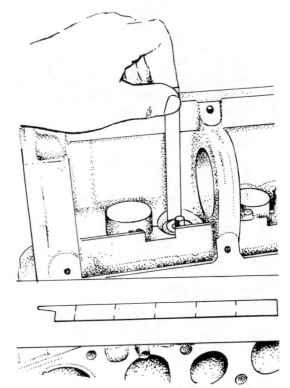

FIG 1:16   Measuring valve spring installed height

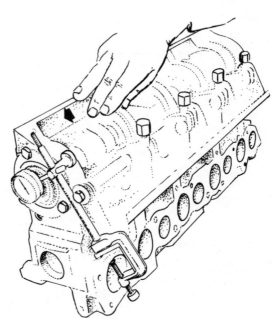

FIG 1:17   Checking camshaft end play

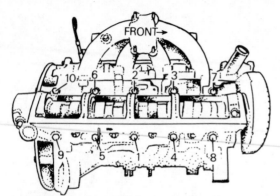

FIG 1 : 18   Cylinder head bolt sequence

TDC the pistons will automatically be in a safe position. With the aid of an assistant place the head on the cylinder case then fit the head bolts with their threads coated with anti-seize compound. The long bolts (6¾ inch) belong on the manifold side, the short (5⅝ inch) bolts on the spark plug side. Tighten all the bolts finger tight then tighten each a little at a time in the sequence shown in **FIG 1 : 18** until a torque of 60 lb ft is reached.

Fit the exhaust manifold using the 1½ inch long bolts in the upper holes and the 2¼ inch long bolts in the lower holes. Tighten evenly to 30 lb ft.

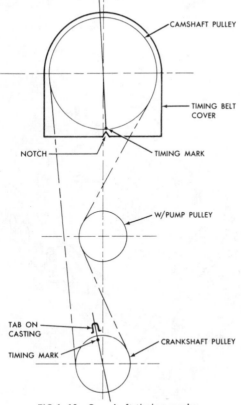

FIG 1 : 19   Camshaft timing marks

Fit a new gasket then position the inlet manifold over the dowels. Fit the bolts and tighten evenly to 30 lb ft. All bolts must have their threads coated with anti-seize compound before assembly.

Refit the timing belt and sprocket, carburetter and other accessories in the reverse order to dismantling. Refer to the next **Section, 1 : 10,** for instructions for fitting the timing belt and timing the engine.

1 : 10   Refitting the timing belt

The camshaft and cylinder head must be refitted as described in **Sections 1 : 8** and **1 : 9.** The crankshaft must be in the position quoted in **Section 1 : 9.**

1 Fit the camshaft sprocket with the dowel inserted in the camshaft. Tighten the centre bolt to 80 lb ft using a socket through one of the sprocket holes and fitting over a retainer bolt to prevent the sprocket from moving.

2 Align the camshaft sprocket timing mark with the notch in the timing belt upper cover as shown in **FIG 1 : 19.** Turn the crankshaft clockwise 90 deg. to bring the crankshaft sprocket mark in line with the cast rib on the oil pump cover.

3 Fit the belt to the crankshaft sprocket first, pass it behind the water pump drive grooves then slip it over the camshaft sprocket. See that it is correctly seated in the water pump drive grooves and that neither sprocket has moved from its timing mark.

4 Fit the timing belt lower cover.

5 The water pump bolts must be finger tight and a new gasket must have been installed between the pump and cylinder case. Fit tool J.23654 in the hole at the side of the cylinder case as shown in **FIG 1 : 20** and apply 15 lb ft of torque to the pump. Hold this pressure and tighten the pump bolts evenly to 15 lb ft.

6 Refit the timing belt front cover and the fan. Tighten the fan bolts to 20 lb ft. Refit the accessory drive pulley. Tighten the pulley to sprocket bolts to 15 lb ft and the pulley to crankshaft bolt to 80 lb ft.

1 : 11   Adjusting the tappets

Remove the air cleaner and cam cover unless the engine is being rebuilt in the sequence of previous **Sections.**

1 Turn the crankshaft by using a wrench on the accessory drive pulley nut or by an auxiliary starter switch. If using the latter method, disconnect the low-tension lead between the coil and distributor at the coil and turn the ignition switch 'ON'. **Failure to do this will cause the ground circuit in the switch to be wrecked.** Bring No. 1 piston to TDC on the firing stroke, both valves closed.

2 In this position adjust the tappets with a feeler gauge and Allen key as shown in **FIG 1 : 21.** The tappet screw must always be turned one full revolution to bring the flat in contact with the valve stem. Each revolution alters the clearance by .003 inch, a smaller adjustment is not possible. Turn the screw clockwise to decrease clearance and vice versa.

3 With the engine cold the intake tappet clearance should be .014 inch to .016 inch and the exhaust .029 inch to .031 inch.

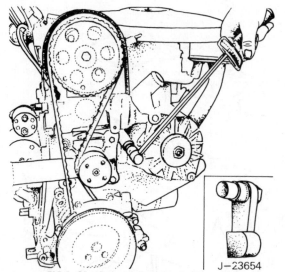

FIG 1 : 20   Adjusting timing belt tension

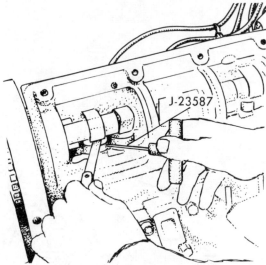

FIG 1 : 21   Adjusting tappet clearance

4 Adjust the tappets in the following sequence:
   Number 1 cylinder, both valves closed on firing stroke, TDC
   Number 1, both valves
   Number 2, intake
   Number 3, exhaust
   Number 4 cylinder, both valves closed on firing stroke, TDC
   Number 2, exhaust
   Number 3, intake
   Number 4, both valves
   Refit the cam cover and air cleaner.

1 : 12   Removing oil pan and oil strainer

The engine need not be removed from the vehicle.

1 Drain the engine oil, support the engine so that no weight rests on the engine forward mountings then unbolt and remove the frame crossmember and both braces (see **FIG 1 : 22**).

2 Disconnect the steering idler arm at the frame side rail unless air conditionihg is fitted. In that case, disconnect the arm at the relay rod. Mark the pitman arm to pitman shaft position then pull the arm from the shaft. Do not turn the steering wheel when the pitman arm is removed.

3 Remove the flywheel cover or convertor under pan then undo the oil pan bolts and lower the oil pan from the engine.

4 Remove the screw from the centre of the oil strainer then the strainer to baffle support bolts. Remove the support. Turn the baffle 90 deg. towards the lefthand side of the vehicle and remove. **FIG 1 : 23** shows the oil pan assembly.

5 Remove the two self-locking screws holding the oil pick-up tube to the cylinder case then tap the U-shaped section of the tube gently until it is free of the casting. **Use the greatest care not to damage the tube bore in the cylinder case. Do not work the**

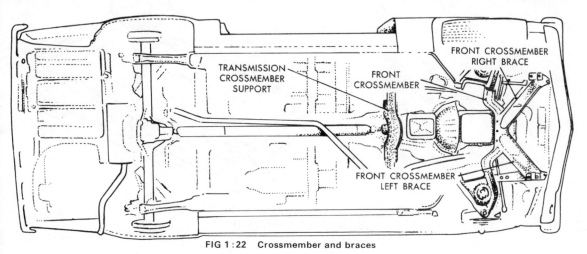

FIG 1 : 22   Crossmember and braces

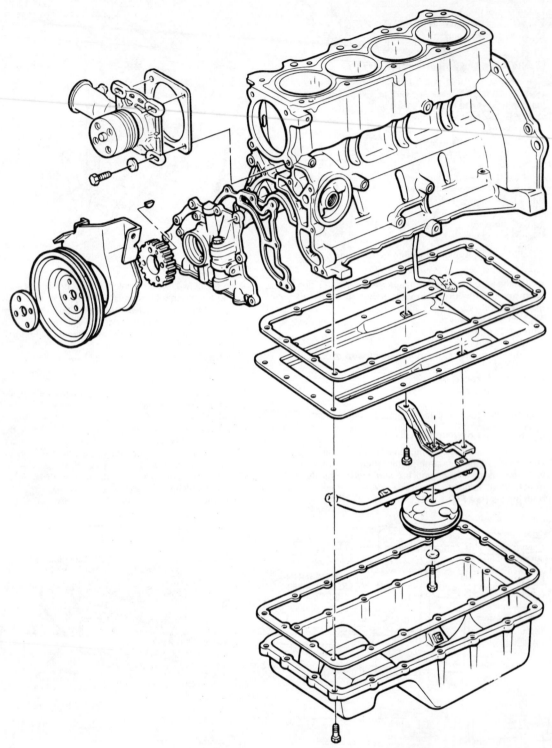

FIG 1 : 23   Oil pan and baffle

tube up and down to free it. If this bore is elongated, the oil pump will be ineffective due to air leaking into the suction side and the cylinder case will be scrap. No repair is possible.

6 Clean all surfaces and threaded holes.

1 :13 Refitting the oil pan and oil strainer

1 The oil pick-up tube and strainer must be renewed; do not refit a used assembly due to the danger of air leaks at the tube to cylinder case bore.

2 Apply a thin coat of jointing compound to the tube from the end to the boss which seats against the mouth of the bore in the cylinder case. Put a ring of compound round the boss.

3 Fit the tube as shown in **FIG 1 :24** using an open-ended wrench against the rear of the boss and tapping it with a soft-faced mallet. Refit the two self-locking bolts, tightening them to 25 lb ft.

4 Use new gaskets and apply jointing cement to that part of the gasket which fits between the baffle and the oil pump cover surface. Apply anti-seize compound to all bolt threads.

5 Refit the baffle and oil pan by reversing the removal procedure (see **Section 1 :12**). Torque the oil strainer support bolts to 50 lb inch and the oil pan bolts to 15 lb ft. Pull these up equally so that the gaskets are evenly compressed.

6 Replace the oil pan drain plug and refill the engine with oil.

1 :14 The oil pump and external filter

The oil pump is fitted to the crankshaft nose and consists of a drive gear on the shaft meshing with an eccentrically mounted ring gear. Refer to **FIG 1 :25** for a view of the arrangement and **FIG 1 :26** for the lubrication circuit diagram. Oil is sucked from the sump to the lower side of the gear cavity, carried past the cast crescent by the gear teeth and then forced through the filter to the engine from the upper side of the gear cavity as the gear teeth come into mesh. A pressure relief valve releases excessive pump pressure and a bypass valve relieves pressure in the filter should this become choked.

Removing the oil pump seal :

Leakage of oil from the front of the engine will be due to a worn seal. This can be renewed without removing the engine.

1 Remove the timing belt cover, accessory drive pulley, timing belt and lower cover as described in previous **Sections.**

2 Install sprocket puller J.23523 as shown in **FIG FIG 1 :27** and pull the crankshaft sprocket from the shaft.

3 Prise the old seal carefully out of the engine front cover.

4 Lubricate the lips of a new seal with engine oil, coat the outer circumference with jointing compound and pull into place using tool J.23624 or by tapping gently with a suitable hollow mandrel, being careful to enter the seal squarely into the seating.

5 Use a $\frac{1}{2}$ inch x 13 bolt, nut and washer as shown in **FIG 1 :28** to replace the crankshaft sprocket.

6 Refit the remaining components as described earlier.

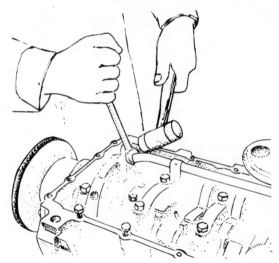

FIG 1 :24   Fitting new oil pick-up tube

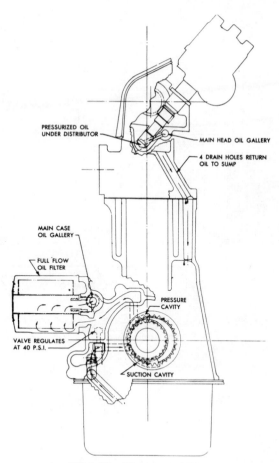

FIG 1 :25   Oil pump and filter

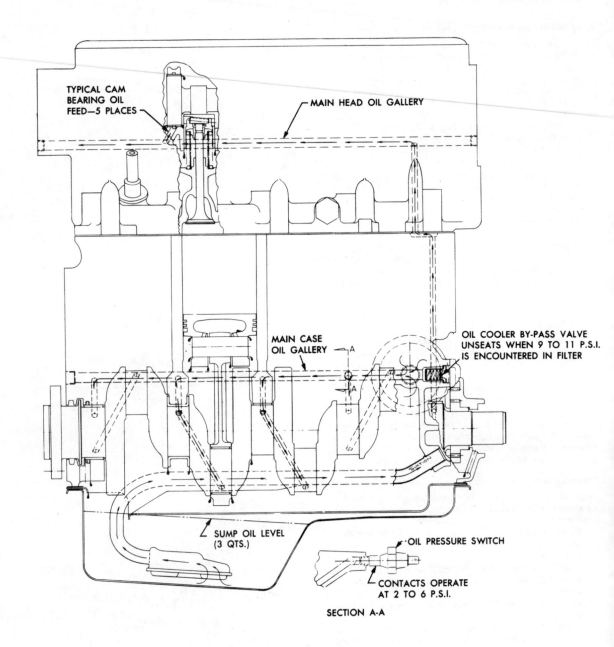

TYPICAL CAM
BEARING OIL
FEED—5 PLACES

MAIN HEAD OIL GALLERY

MAIN CASE
OIL GALLERY

OIL COOLER BY-PASS VALVE
UNSEATS WHEN 9 TO 11 P.S.I.
IS ENCOUNTERED IN FILTER

SUMP OIL LEVEL
(3 QTS.)

OIL PRESSURE SWITCH

CONTACTS OPERATE
AT 2 TO 6 P.S.I.

SECTION A-A

FIG 1:26   Lubrication diagram

Removing the pump:

This can be accomplished without removing the engine. Remove the timing belt, crankshaft sprocket, oil pan and baffle as described earlier. Carefully ease the sprocket key from the crankshaft then undo the bolts and stud holding the oil pump to the cylinder case. Pull the pump forwards free of the cylinder case. **FIG 1 : 23** shows the attachment of the pump and gasket.

Inspection of pumps:

The pump gears and housing are not supplied separately, only the pressure relief valve components and seal can be renewed.

1 With all parts scrupulously clean, check the pressure relief valve for damage or wear. See that it operates freely, if not, renew valve and springs. Check the valve seat.
2 Examine the gears for damage, any chipping or broken gears means rejection.
3 With the pump assembled as shown in **FIG 1 : 29** measure the clearances and compare with the following table, reject if these are exceeded.
Outside diameter of ring gear and housing
.0038 inch to .0068 inch
Outside diameter of drive gear and crescent
.0023 inch to .0093 inch
Inside diameter of ring gear and crescent
.0068 inch to .0148 inch
Face of gears below housing surface
.0009 inch to .0023 inch
4 If necessary, fit a new seal as described earlier.

Refitting the pump:

1 Lubricate all bearing surfaces including gears and seal with engine oil.
2 Fit a new gasket between housing and cylinder case, align the drive gear with the crankshaft key and fit the housing to the case.
3 Coat threads of bolts and stud with anti-seize compound; tighten the bolts to 15 lb ft and the stud to 30 lb ft. The stud fits in the upper righthand location when facing the engine.
4 Continue the reassembly of components as described in earlier Sections.

The external filter bypass valve:

When the pump is removed examine the valve to see that neither the fibre valve or the spring are jammed or broken. If any doubt exists remove and renew the parts as shown in **FIG 1 : 30**.

The external filter:

This is an AC·Type PF.25 self-contained can and element. Unscrew with a strap wrench but use hand pressure only to fit. Unscrew anticlockwise looking on the outer end of the filter.

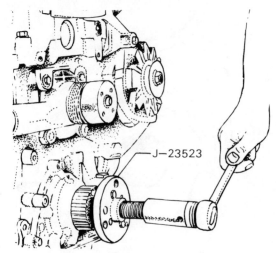

FIG 1 : 27   Removing crankshaft sprocket

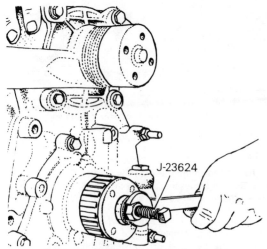

FIG 1 : 28   Refitting crankshaft sprocket

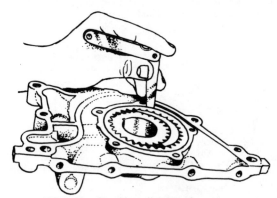

FIG 1 : 29   Checking oil pump clearances

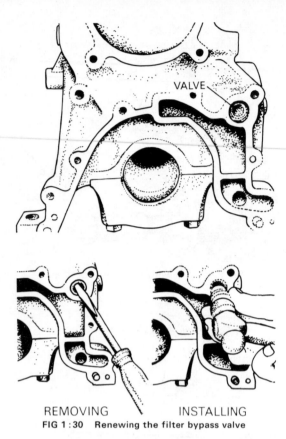

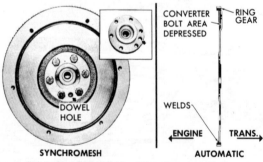

REMOVING   INSTALLING

FIG 1:30   Renewing the filter bypass valve

1:15 Removing and refitting the clutch and flywheel

Remove the engine as described in **Section 1:2** or the transmission as described in **Chapters 5** and **7**. Remove the clutch cover and driven plate as described in **Chapter 5.**

Undo the bolts and pull the flywheel or converter drive plate from the crankshaft.

Refit the flywheel or converter drive plate to the crankshaft ensuring that the mating surfaces are perfectly clean and dry. Refer to **FIG 1:31** for correct convertor drive plate attitude. Tighten the bolts for both types of transmission to 60 lb ft.

FIG 1:31   Flywheel or drive plate installation

1:16 Servicing connecting rods and pistons

The pistons can be removed with the engine installed in the car. Remove the cylinder head, oil pan and baffle as described in earlier **Sections**.

1 Rotate the crankshaft so that the piston is at the lower part of its stroke. Put a wad of rag in the cylinder bore. Use a ridge reamer or very sharp scraper and remove any deposits or ridge from the top of the bore. Bring the piston to the upper part of its stroke and remove the rag complete with swarf and dirt. Repeat for the other cylinders.

2 Mark each big-end cap and rod so that they can be correctly identified for refitting if necessary.

3 Undo the big-end bolts and remove the cap. Push the piston and rod assembly very carefully up the bore and remove from the top face of the cylinder case. **Remember that the bores are comparatively soft and that the big-end could cause a disastrous score if care is not exercised.**

4 Put each pair of big-end bearing shells together and identify them with a chalk mark for replacing in the engine if found to be suitable for further service.

5 The piston pin and rod are a press fit together and are not supplied separately. An arbor press and special tools are necessary to remove the pin; therefore if a piston and rod are to be dismantled the work must be entrusted to a Chevrolet Agent (see **FIG 1:32**). The pin is fitted with all components cold.

6 Measure the cylinder bore with an internal micrometer at a point $2\frac{1}{2}$ inch from the top face. Measure the skirt diameter of the piston at right angles to the piston pin. Subtract the piston diameter from the bore diameter to obtain the clearance figure. If this exceeds .005 inch it may be possible to fit an oversize piston. If only one bore is oversize it is permissible to replace one piston and rod assembly. Similarly, a different size of piston can be selected to suit each individual cylinder. If the bore is too worn to respond to piston replacement then a new cylinder case must be fitted together with new pistons. No cylinder reconditioning is possible. If the pistons are to be used again be careful not to scratch the surfaces when cleaning away carbon or oil deposits.

7 Insert a piston ring in the cylinder bore and square it up by pressing it in $\frac{1}{4}$ inch from the top face with a piston head. Use feeler gauges to measure the gap. If the figures exceed the following limits, renew the ring.
Top ring   ..   ..   .025 inch
Second ring   ..   ..   .025 inch
Oil ring rails   ..   ..   .030 inch
When fitting new rings the gap must not be less than .009 inch for compression and .010 inch for oil ring rails.

8 The side clearance between ring and groove must lie within .001 inch to .003 inch for compression and nil to .005 inch for oil rings.

9 When assembling the piston rings to the piston ensure that all components are absolutely clean and that the rings will roll smoothly round the grooves. The compression rings are marked on one side; this side must be towards the top of the piston. Arrange the ring gaps as shown in **FIG 1:33**.

10 Lightly coat the cylinder bore and piston with engine oil, fit a ring compressor and insert the rod and piston

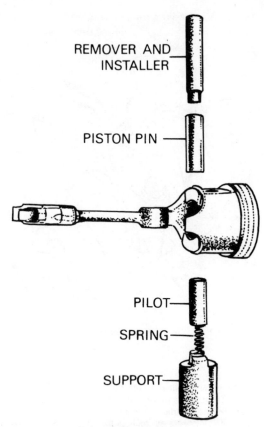

REMOVER AND INSTALLER

PISTON PIN

PILOT

SPRING

SUPPORT

FIG 1 : 32 Piston pin tools

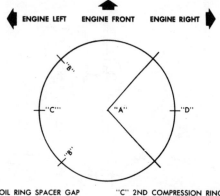

ENGINE LEFT   ENGINE FRONT   ENGINE RIGHT

"A" OIL RING SPACER GAP   "C" 2ND COMPRESSION RING GAP
"B" OIL RING RAIL GAPS   "D" TOP COMPRESSION RING GAP

FIG 1 : 33   Ring gap position

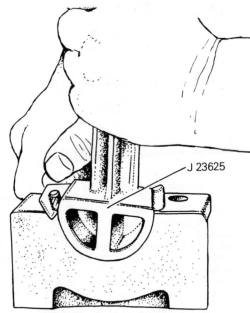

J 23625

FIG 1 : 34   Cutting oil seal to length

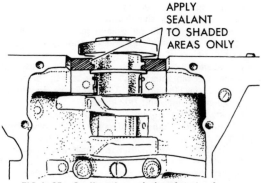

APPLY
SEALANT
TO SHADED
AREAS ONLY

FIG 1 : 35   Sealing the main bearing cap faces

assembly carefully into the bore. Again take great care not to damage the bore. The letter 'F' stamped on the piston pin boss must face the front of the engine. Use a hammer handle to tap the piston through the ring compressor into the cylinder.

11 Install the big-end bearings as described in the next Section.

12 Refit the oil pan and cylinder head.

1 : 17 Servicing the crankshaft and bearings

The crankshaft cannot be removed with the engine in the car. It is however possible to renew all bearings and the rear main oil seal without removing the crankshaft. The front oil seal is renewed as described in **Section 1 : 14, Oil pump.**

Renewing bearings and oil seal, crankshaft installed:

Remove the oil pan and baffle, **Section 1 : 12,** disconnect the battery and remove the spark plugs.

1 If a big-end bearing is to be renewed, remove the cap after suitably marking it for reassembly and push the rod just far enough up the bore to enable the top half bearing shell to be removed when necessary.

2 Measure the crankpin diameter. This should be between 1.999 inch to 2.000 inch and must not be

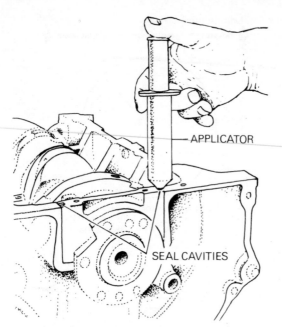

APPLICATOR

SEAL CAVITIES

FIG 1:36 Sealing the main bearing cap sides

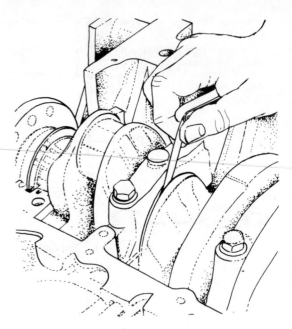

FIG 1:37 Measuring crankshaft end play

oval more than .001 inch. Bearing shells are available in .001 inch and .002 inch undersize to take up slight wear and .010 inch and .020 inch undersize for reground crankshafts.

3 Wipe the bearings and shaft clean and dry. Refit the bearings and cap with a piece of 'Plastigage' on the journal. Tighten the cap bolts to 35 lb ft then release them and remove the cap. Measure the flattened 'Plastigage' according to the instructions on the packet. If the clearance exceeds .004 inch either fit undersize shells or regrind the shaft. Never file the cap faces.

4 When a correct fit has been obtained, coat the shaft and bearings with engine oil and tighten the bolts to 35 lb ft.

5 If a main bearing is to be checked, first remove the bearing cap and wipe the bearing surfaces clean and dry. See that the letter 'F' on the cap faces the front of the engine before dismantling.

6 Place jacks under the flywheel (or converter drive plate) and the front pulley and raise sufficiently to hold the shaft hard up against the cylinder case bearing halves.

7 Use a piece of 'Plastigage' as described earlier and tighten the cap bolts to 65 lb ft. Release the bolts and measure the 'Plastigage'. The clearance should be between .001 inch and .003 inch.

8 Bearing shells are supplied in .001 inch, .002 inch, .010 inch and .020 inch undersizes. To fit a new upper half shell release the jacks, insert a splitpin in the crankshaft oil hole so that the head just protrudes. Turn the shaft carefully clockwise as seen from the front of the engine and the shell will be pushed out. Fit a new shell by the same method. Oil the bearing

surfaces and refit the cap, tightening the bolts to 65 lb ft. To obtain a perfect fit, shims are available which can be fitted under the main bearing caps. Make sure that the shaft rotates freely before proceeding to work on another bearing.

9 To renew a rear bearing oil seal, release all main bearing cap bolts one or two turns and remove the rear cap completely. The shaft will now have slight clearance between itself and the upper seal. Push the seal round the shaft until it can be gripped and pulled out. Cut a new seal to length by using the bearing cap and tool or a piece of suitable bar or pipe (see **FIG 1:34**).

10 Firmly attach a piece of wire to one end of the seal and push the wire round the shaft in the seal cavity. Pull on the wire and push the seal until it has passed over the shaft and into position. Remove the wire.

11 Tighten all bearing bolts except the rear main bolts to 12 lb ft at this stage.

12 Fit a new seal to the rear bearing cap. Coat the faces of the cap and crankcase with jointing cement as shown in **FIG 1:35**. Lightly oil the shaft and fit the cap, tightening these bolts also to 12 lb ft at this stage. Push the shaft hard to the rear then repeat by pushing it forward. This will align the bearing caps. Now tighten all cap bolts evenly to 65 lb ft. Ensure that the shaft still rotates freely.

13 Mix the special sealant according to the instructions on the pack and force it up between the sides of the bearing cap and crankcase. **FIG 1:36** shows the method with the engine out of the car; with the engine installed, a small piece of bearing sealing cord can be pushed into the gap to prevent the sealant running out before it sets.

Renewing bearings and rear oil seal, crankshaft removed:

The methods of measuring bearing clearance, fitting bearing shells and oil seal are similar, but with the shaft removed, the journals can be measured for ovality and taper. If more than .001 inch of either condition exists on the journals or crankpins, the shaft must be reground.

Crankshaft end play must not exceed .007 inch. Push the shaft forward and measure between the shaft and the front of No. 4 main bearing as shown in **FIG 1 : 37**. If the clearance is excessive a new shaft must be fitted.

1 : 19 Fault diagnosis

(a) Engine will not start

1 Lack of fuel
2 Discharged battery
3 Defective starter
4 Ignition failure (see **Chapter 3**)
5 Automatic transmission selector incorrectly set
6 Damp electrical connections
7 Carburetter flooded
8 Ignition timing incorrect
9 Valve timing incorrect

(b) Engine stalls

1 Low oil pressure (cutting off petrol pump electrical supply)
2 Ignition retarded
3 Carburetter incorrectly adjusted
4 Valve clearance incorrect

(c) Engine idles badly

1 Carburetter incorrectly adjusted or air leak
2 Ignition timing incorrect
3 Defective sparking plug
4 Unequal cylinder compressions
5 Choked air cleaner
6 Valve clearance incorrect

(d) Compression low

1 Worn piston rings
2 Scored cylinder
3 Burnt valve
4 Incorrect valve clearance
5 Blown gasket

(e) Engine lacks power

1 Ignition timing incorrect
2 Valve timing incorrect
3 Carburetter jets restricted
4 Air cleaner choked
5 Air leaks in induction system
6 Blocked exhaust
7 Burnt valves or incorrect clearance
8 Worn cylinders or piston rings

(f) Excessive oil consumption

1 Excessive clearance between piston rings and sides of groove
2 Valve stem oil seal failed
3 Worn cylinders or pistons
4 Broken piston rings
5 External leaks, oil pump seal defective

CHAPTER 2

THE FUEL SYSTEM

2:1 Description

The rear mounted fuel tank has a capacity of 11 gallons and incorporates an electric pump, fuel gauge metering unit and connections for the Evaporation Control System.

Two basic carburetters are available, the Rochester Monojet MV (1bb1) single barrel design and the Rochester 2 GV dual barrel (2bb1). In practice there are two types of each carburetter, one for manual and one for automatic transmission equipped vehicles. The differences between the manual and automatic versions are slight, being mainly confined to internal calibrations.

Provision is made for control of fumes caused by the evaporation of fuel from the tank and carburetter bowl. The complete air cleaner is intended to be discarded and renewed at 50,000 mile intervals.

2:2 The fuel pump

Refer to **FIG 2:1**. This illustrates the situation of the pump inside the fuel tank and also the cam plate which holds the assembly in place. A special tool is required to remove the cam plate (J.22554). Should the pump fail it must be renewed, no repair is possible. Note that the pump receives electrical power via the oil pressure switch except when the ignition key is in the start position. If the oil pressure drops below 2 p.s.i. the pump is cut off. In any case of pump failure check the electrical supply circuit thoroughly before removing the pump.

Removing the fuel pump:

Warning. Before commencing any operation involving fuel and fuel vapour always disconnect the battery so that there is no chance of an electrical spark causing an explosion and fire.

1 Drain the fuel tank by syphoning. No drain plug is fitted.
2 Lift the rear of the vehicle and support on stands or wooden blocks.
3 Disconnect the meter feed cable at the harness connector and the ground wire at the floor pan.
4 Disconnect the fuel and vapour lines identifying them for re-attachment.
5 Remove the strap bolts and lower the tank.
6 Undo the cam lock holding the pump and metering unit as shown in **FIG 2:2**. Lift the pump and metering unit from the tank. Discard the gasket.

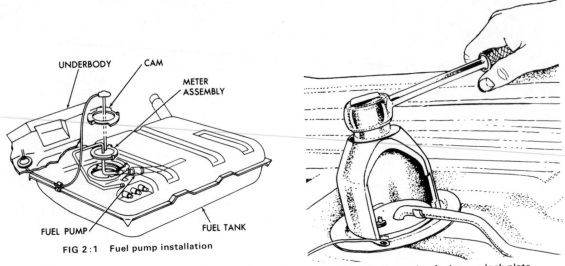

FIG 2:1 Fuel pump installation

UNDERBODY CAM

METER
ASSEMBLY

FUEL PUMP

FUEL TANK

FIG 2:2 Removing fuel pump lock plate

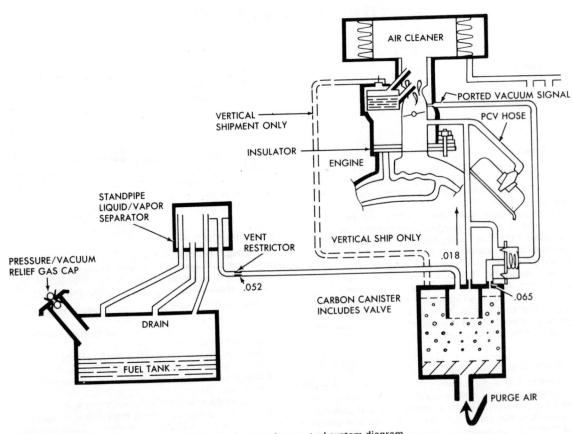

AIR CLEANER

PORTED VACUUM SIGNAL

PCV HOSE

VERTICAL
SHIPMENT ONLY

INSULATOR

ENGINE

STANDPIPE
LIQUID/VAPOR
SEPARATOR

VENT
RESTRICTOR

VERTICAL SHIP ONLY

.018

PRESSURE/VACUUM
RELIEF GAS CAP

.052

CARBON CANISTER
INCLUDES VALVE

.065

DRAIN

FUEL TANK

PURGE AIR

FIG 2:3 Evaporation control system diagram

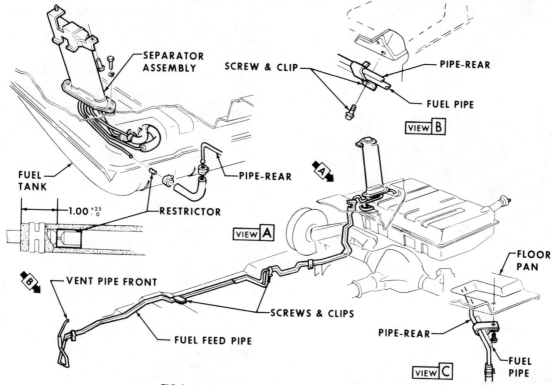

FIG 2:4 Fuel/vapour separator and connections

7 Remove the flat wire electrical conductor from the fuel tube. Squeeze the clamp and pull the pump back $\frac{1}{2}$ inch.

8 Remove the wires from the pump terminals. Squeeze the clamp again and pull the pump straight back to remove it from the tank unit.

Fitting a new fuel pump:

1 Slide the new pump through the support bracket up to the rubber coupling. See that it has the rubber isolator and saran strainer attached. These should be supplied with the pump in the maker's pack.

2 Connect the electrical leads to the pump terminals; the flat conductor to the terminal on the side away from the float arm.

3 Squeeze the clamp and push the pump into the rubber coupling then replace the flat conductor in the clip on the fuel tube.

4 Refit the pump and metering unit to the tank using a new gasket and tightening the cam lock ring with the special spanner.

5 Remake the electrical connections, replace the fuel and vapour lines and re-install the tank. Lower the car and refill the tank.

Note that if the metering unit (fuel gauge sending unit) fails, the procedure for removing the fuel pump applies since the metering unit is part of the fuel pump installation.

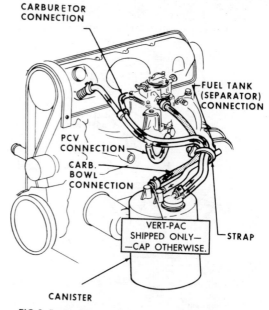

FIG 2:5 Vapour canister to engine connections

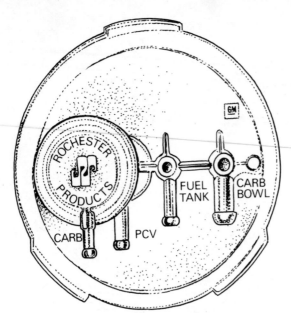

FIG 2:6　Canister top face

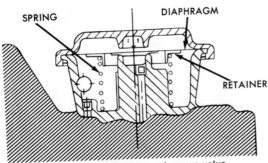

FIG 2:7　Section through purge valve

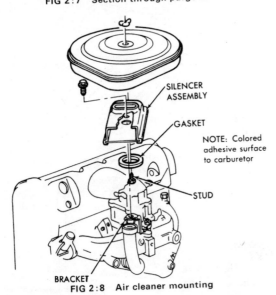

NOTE: Colored
adhesive surface
to carburetor

FIG 2:8　Air cleaner mounting

2:3 Evaporation control system

This consists of two components and the necessary hoses and lines. **FIG 2:3** shows the system diagrammatically while **FIGS 2:4** and **2:5** show the fuel/vapour separator above the tank and the connections between the activated carbon canister and the engine respectively. **FIG 2:6** shows the connections to be made to the canister.

In operation, vapour from the tank and carburetter bowl passes to the canister where it is either stored by the activated carbon if the engine is not running or drawn straight into the engine by the positive crankcase ventilation (PCV) system when the engine is running.

Servicing the system is confined to seeing that all hoses and lines are undamaged and unrestricted and giving attention to the canister at the recommended intervals. The separator is unlikely ever to give trouble but if it does it must be renewed as a unit.

Servicing the canister:

1 Identify the hoses then disconnect from the canister top.
2 Undo the clamp and remove the canister.
3 Every 12 months or 12,000 miles, renew the filter. Pull the old one from the bottom of the canister and install the new one under the wire retainer.
4 Check the operation of the purge valve by applying vacuum to the small pipe leading to the cap on the canister. This is the lefthand pipe marked 'CARB in **FIG 2:6**. A good valve will hold vacuum. If in doubt, obtain a service kit containing a new cap, diaphragm and spring assembly. Push the old cap off gently since spring pressure exists below the diaphragm. Refer to **FIG 2:7** and replace the internal components. Fit the new cap.
5 Replace the canister in the vehicle and reconnect the hoses.

General:

1 When renewing hoses, use only hose marked 'EVAP'. No other type of hose is to be used.
2 The tank filler cap incorporates pressure/vacuum valves and is an essential part of the system. No other cap is suitable.

2:4 The air cleaner

FIG 2:8 illustrates the air cleaner mounting details. It is intended that the complete air cleaner unit is discarded and a new one fitted every 50,000 miles. To remove the air cleaner, release the wing nut, rotate the cleaner clockwise a short distance to free the vent pipe from the cam cover then lift it straight up. If the grommet between the air cleaner and carburetter is in good condition it can be reused with a new unit.

2:5 The Rochester MV Monojet Carburetter—single barrel

Description:

This carburetter, illustrated at **FIG 2:9** is a single barrel, downdraught design using fixed jets and a main well air-bleed system. An automatic choke is fitted and a

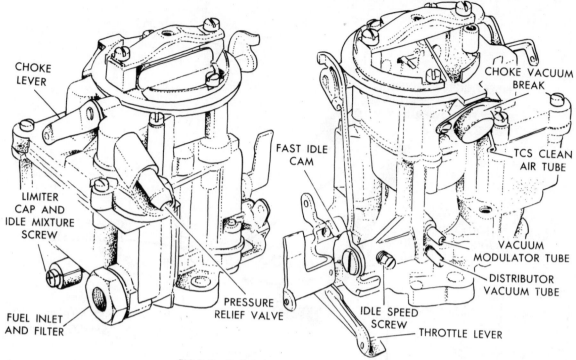

FIG 2:9   Rochester MV monojet carburetter

Labels in figure:
CHOKE LEVER
LIMITER CAP AND IDLE MIXTURE SCREW
FUEL INLET AND FILTER
PRESSURE RELIEF VALVE
FAST IDLE CAM
CHOKE VACUUM BREAK
TCS CLEAN AIR TUBE
VACUUM MODULATOR TUBE
DISTRIBUTOR VACUUM TUBE
IDLE SPEED SCREW
THROTTLE LEVER

throttle closing solenoid overrides the conventional idle stop screw. When the ignition is off the solenoid is de-energized and the throttle can close further preventing the engine from running on at high temperatures.

Adjustments:

All vehicles have an instruction decal attached to the underside of the hood which gives details of the latest procedures for tuning and adjusting the carburetter fitted to that particular vehicle. The following instructions must be read in conjunction with those on the decal.

General:

The engine must be at operating temperature; from cold it should be run for at least 15 minutes. See that all bolts and nuts holding the manifold and the carburetter are at the correct torque and that no air leaks exist. The manifold heat control valve (if fitted) must be operating freely.

Slow idle adjustment:

The idle mixture screw is fitted with a limiter (sealing) cap by the manufacturer when the initial adjustment is made so that the emission of CO is held at 2 per cent. This limiter cap must not be broken unless equipment is available to analyze the exhaust gas or if adjustment by engine rev/min as described later is considered adequate to meet the local traffic authority requirements. The idle

mixture screw is illustrated in **FIG 2:9**. If the idle mixture screw is disturbed proceed as follows:

1 Screw the idle mixture screw in until it bottoms then unscrew four turns. Disconnect the distributor vacuum hose and plug the carburetter connection. Disconnect the 'Fuel Tank' hose at the canister. Disconnect the solenoid electrically.

2 Start the engine and adjust the throttle idle speed screw until the engine is running at 730 rev/min

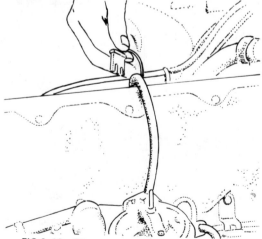

FIG 2:10   Disconnecting the TCS solenoid MV

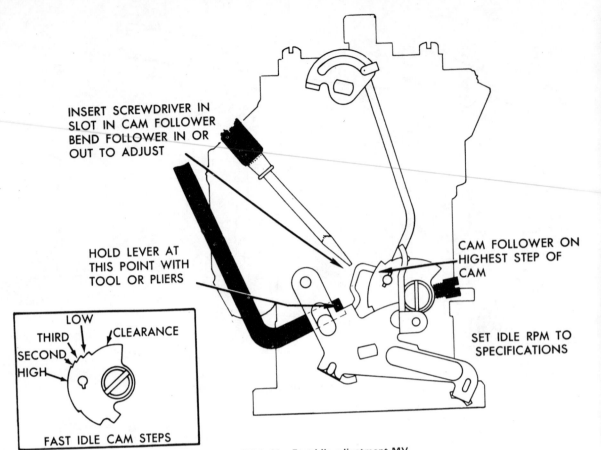

INSERT SCREWDRIVER IN
SLOT IN CAM FOLLOWER
BEND FOLLOWER IN OR
OUT TO ADJUST

HOLD LEVER AT
THIS POINT WITH
TOOL OR PLIERS

CAM FOLLOWER ON
HIGHEST STEP OF
CAM

SET IDLE RPM TO
SPECIFICATIONS

LOW
THIRD   CLEARANCE
SECOND
HIGH

FAST IDLE CAM STEPS

FIG 2:11   Fast idle adjustment MV

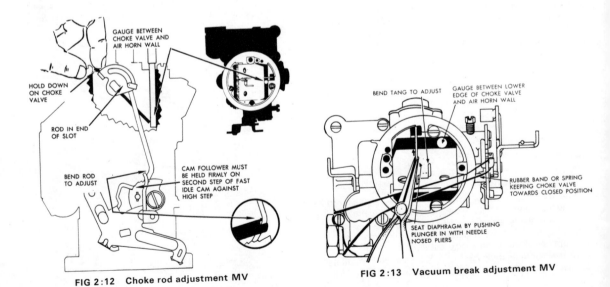

GAUGE BETWEEN
CHOKE VALVE AND
AIR HORN WALL

HOLD DOWN
ON CHOKE
VALVE

ROD IN END
OF SLOT

BEND ROD
TO ADJUST

CAM FOLLOWER MUST
BE HELD FIRMLY ON
SECOND STEP OF FAST
IDLE CAM AGAINST
HIGH STEP

FIG 2:12   Choke rod adjustment MV

BEND TANG TO ADJUST

GAUGE BETWEEN LOWER
EDGE OF CHOKE VALVE
AND AIR HORN WALL

RUBBER BAND OR SPRING
KEEPING CHOKE VALVE
TOWARDS CLOSED POSITION

SEAT DIAPHRAGM BY PUSHING
PLUNGER IN WITH NEEDLE
NOSED PLIERS

FIG 2:13   Vacuum break adjustment MV

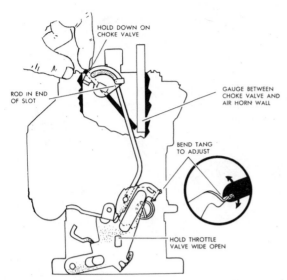

FIG 2:14   Choke unloader adjustment MV

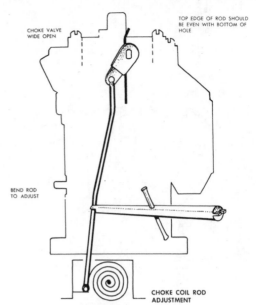

FIG 2:15   Automatic choke rod adjustment MV

(manual transmission) or 570 rev/min (automatic, in drive, parking brake on and wheels chocked).

3 Slightly adjust mixture screw inwards if necessary to achieve these rev/min figures.

4 Screw the idle mixture screw in to weaken the mixture until the engine slows to 700 rev/min (manual) or 550 rev/min (automatic).

5 Fit a new limiter cap and refit the vacuum and vapour hoses, reconnect the solenoid.

It is recommended that the emission of CO should be checked by analysis as soon as possible if the rev/min method of setting is used.

Fast idle adjustment:

1 Disconnect the Transmission Controlled Spark (TCS) Solenoid cable (see **FIG 2:10**), and see that the transmission is in neutral. Refer to Chapter 3 for details of this system of control.

2 Move the fast idle cam so that the follower is on the highest step (see **FIG 2:11**). The engine should now run at 2400 rev/min, if not, insert a screwdriver in the follower slot and bend the follower until the speed is correct.

3 Stop the engine and reconnect the TCS solenoid.

Choke rod adjustment:

1 Position the fast idle cam so that the follower is on the second highest step and hold it in place (see **FIG 2:12**).

2 Move the choke valve towards the closed position. The gauge gap between the lower edge of the choke and the air horn wall must be .080 inch for automatic transmission and .120 inch for manual transmission.

3 If necessary, bend the rod where indicated in **FIG 2:12** to obtain the specified gap.

Vacuum break adjustment:

1 With the air cleaner removed, hold the choke valve closed with a rubber band positioned as shown in **FIG 2:13**.

2 Push the vacuum break plunger rod into the diaphragm as far as it will go.

3 The gauge clearance between the choke valve and air horn wall should now be .200 inch manual and .140 inch automatic transmission.

4 Adjust to the proper figure by bending the tang illustrated in **FIG 2:13**.

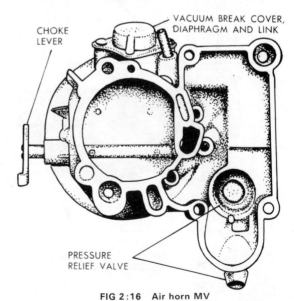

FIG 2:16   Air horn MV

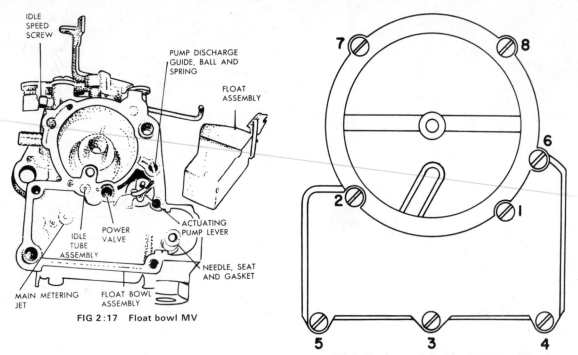

IDLE
SPEED
SCREW

PUMP DISCHARGE
GUIDE, BALL AND
SPRING

FLOAT
ASSEMBLY

ACTUATING
PUMP LEVER

POWER
VALVE

NEEDLE, SEAT
AND GASKET

IDLE
TUBE
ASSEMBLY

MAIN METERING
JET

FLOAT BOWL
ASSEMBLY

FIG 2:17   Float bowl MV

FIG 2:19   Screw tightening sequence MV

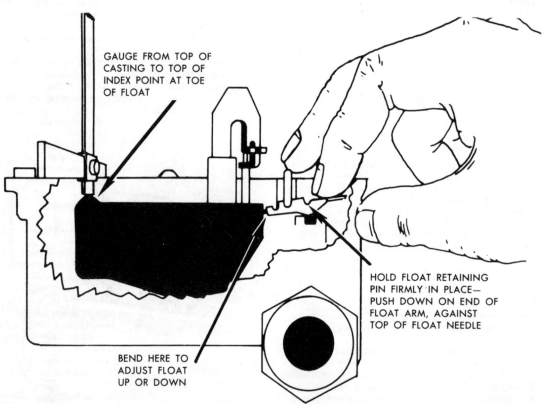

GAUGE FROM TOP OF
CASTING TO TOP OF
INDEX POINT AT TOE
OF FLOAT

HOLD FLOAT RETAINING
PIN FIRMLY IN PLACE—
PUSH DOWN ON END OF
FLOAT ARM, AGAINST
TOP OF FLOAT NEEDLE

BEND HERE TO
ADJUST FLOAT
UP OR DOWN

FIG 2:18   Float position adjustment MV

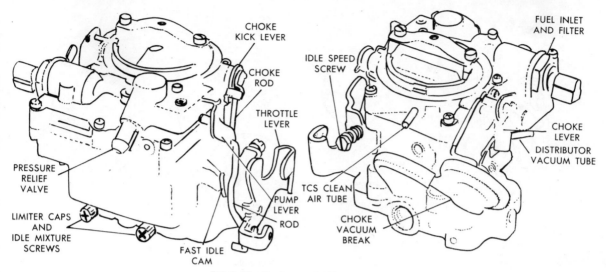

FIG 2:20   Rochester 2 GV carburetter

Choke unloader adjustment:

1 Refer to **FIG 2:14**. Hold the choke valve towards the close position.
2 Hold the throttle wide open.
3 Bend the tang as shown in **FIG 2:14** to adjust the choke to air horn wall gauge clearance of .350 inch for both manual and automatic transmission.

Automatic choke rod adjustment:

1 Refer to **FIG 2:15**. Disconnect the rod at the choke lever and hold the choke valve wide open.
2 Push the rod downwards as far as possible. The top of the rod should now coincide with the bottom edge of the hole in the choke lever. Bend the rod to adjust length.
3 Reconnect the rod.

Solenoid adjustment:

1 Run the engine to operating temperature. The choke must have fully opened, the air cleaner must be clean and in place and, if so equipped, the air conditioning system on.
2 Disconnect the fuel tank hose from the vapour canister and the vacuum hose from the distributor. Plug the latter hose so that no extra air is fed into the carburetter.
3 Disconnect the solenoid electrically.
4 If necessary set carburetter idle speed screw to achieve the specified slow idle rev/min. See previous paragraph.
5 Reconnect the electric lead to the solenoid and snap the throttle open momentarily.
6 Adjust the screw in the end of the solenoid armature until the engine rev/min rise to 850, manual transmission, and 650 automatic.
7 Stop the engine, unplug and reconnect the distributor vacuum hose and the fuel vapour hose.

Dismantling the carburetter:

1 Remove the fast idle cam, choke rod and automatic choke lever from the choke shaft.
2 Remove the six air horn to bowl screws and lift the air horn straight up. **FIG 2:16** shows the air horn in detail.
3 Undo the two screws and carefully remove the vacuum break diaphragm cover retainer.
4 Hold the choke wide open and manoeuvre the diaphragm rod from the choke valve. Remove the diaphragm rod through the hole in the air horn. Unless the choke valve is sticking it is not advisable to remove it. If it is removed see that the plastic washers between the valve and air horn wall are not lost.
5 The air horn need not be dismantled further. If the pressure relief valve disc is damaged the air horn must be renewed.
6 Remove the air horn to float bowl gasket then release the float from the hinge pin.
7 Remove the float needle, seat and gasket (see **FIG 2:17**).
8 Remove the fuel inlet nut, gasket, spring and filter element. Discard the filter element.
9 With a pair of long-nosed pliers remove the pump discharge guide, invert the bowl and the spring and ball will drop out. The idle tube and power valve will also be released.
10 Remove the actuating lever from the throttle shaft, hold the accelerator pump plunger down and release the actuating link and pump lever from the plunger shaft. Remove the plunger assembly from the float bowl and lift the return spring clear.
11 Remove the main metering jet and if necessary the idle stop screw. No further dismantling of the bowl is needed.
12 Remove the two throttle body to float bowl screws and part the body and bowl. Do not tamper with the

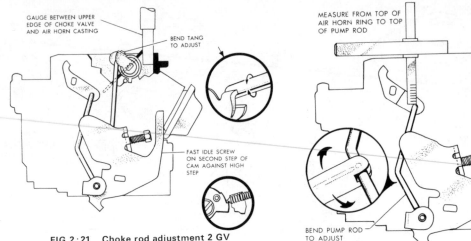

FIG 2:21   Choke rod adjustment 2 GV

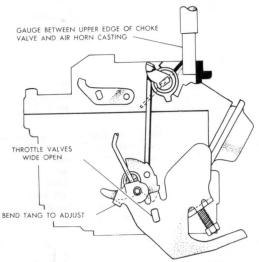

FIG 2:22   Choke unloader adjustment 2 GV

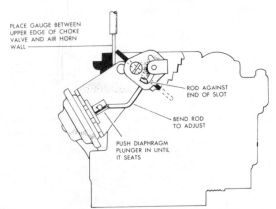

FIG 2:23   Vacuum break adjustment 2 GV

FIG 2:24   Accelerator pump rod adjustment 2 GV

idle mixture needle unless absolutely necessary due to damage. If the needle is to be removed, first count the number of turns necessary to seat the needle home from the set position. A new needle can be seated home and then unscrewed to the same position as the needle which it replaces. This will give a good starting point for subsequent adjustment.

13 Do not remove the throttle valve from the body; see that the screws are tight and staked in place.

Cleaning and inspection:

The castings and metal parts should be cleaned in a carburetter cleaning fluid of the cold immersion type. Do not clean any diaphragms, rubber components, plastics or the pump plunger in this way. The vent valve in the air horn can be cleaned in the fluid. Blow out all fuel and air passages with compressed air, never poke wire or bristle through the jets. Examine the float needle and seat assembly for wear, renew if ridges or burrs can be seen. See that all rods, levers and other moving parts are not worn or distorted. Check all springs for collapse or distortion.

Reassembling the carburetter:

Reverse the dismantling process but see that all new gaskets are fitted and that the new fuel filter is installed with the open end facing the inlet nut hole.

Set the float position by referring to **FIG 2:18**. The distance from the casting face, gasket removed, to the high point on the float must be $\frac{1}{16}$ inch.

Tighten the air horn to float bowl screws in the sequence shown in **FIG 2:19**.

2:6 The Rochester 2 GV Carburetter—dual barrel

Description:

The carburetter is illustrated in **FIG 2:20**. It is a dual barrel downdraught type similar in basic theory of fixed jets and air bleeds to the MV type. It has a similar solenoid control of throttle closing and automatic choke. An accelerator pump is fitted for rapid acceleration fuel supply.

The paragraphs dealing with engine condition during adjustment, temperature, etc., and the note concerning the individual turning decal under the engine compartment hood refer to this carburetter as well as the MV single barrel type (see **Section 2:5**).

Adjustments:

Choke rod adjustment:

1 Refer to **FIG 2:21**. Turn the idle stop screw in until it just touches the bottom of the fast idle cam, move the cam and turn one more full turn.
2 Reset the screw on the second step of the cam against the shoulder of the high step.
3 Hold the choke valve towards the closed position and measure the clearance between the upper edge of the valve and the air horn wall. It should be .080 inch for manual and automatic transmissions. If not, bend the choke lever as shown.

Unloader adjustment:

1 Refer to **FIG 2:22**. Hold the throttle valves wide open.
2 Hold the choke valve towards the closed position and bend the tang on the throttle lever until the clearance between the upper edge of the choke valve and air horn wall is .180 inch.

Vacuum break adjustment:

1 Refer to **FIG 2:23**. Push the diaphragm plunger home and start engine to hold diaphragm in place with vacuum if necessary.
2 Hold the choke valve towards the closed position.
3 Bend the diaphragm rod until the clearance between the upper edge of the choke and air horn wall is .120 inch for both manual and automatic transmission.

Solenoid adjustment:

Proceed exactly as for the MV type (see **Section 2:5**), but set the engine speed to 1200 rev/min for manual transmission and 700 rev/min for automatic.

Accelerator pump rod adjustment:

1 Refer to **FIG 2:24**. Unscrew the idle speed screw and fully close the throttle valves.
2 Measure the distance from the air horn ring to top of pump rod as shown. The dimension should be $1\frac{3}{8}$ inch.
3 Bend the pump rod where shown if necessary to obtain this dimension.
4 Reset the idle speed screw.

Choke coil rod adjustment (automatic choke):

1 Refer to **FIG 2:25**. Hold the choke valve wide open.
2 Disconnect the rod and push down as far as possible.
3 The top of the rod should cover half the diameter of the lever hole as shown. Bend rod to adjust if necessary.

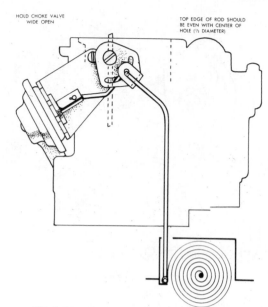

HOLD CHOKE VALVE WIDE OPEN

TOP EDGE OF ROD SHOULD BE EVEN WITH CENTER OF HOLE (½ DIAMETER)

FIG 2:25   Choke coil rod adjustment 2 GV

Slow idle adjustment:

Proceed exactly as described in **Section 2:5** for the MV Carburetter but turn both idle mixture screws together. The engine speed is also to be set to the same range as the MV carburetter.

Dismantling the carburetter:

1 Remove components in the following sequence: pump rod, fast idle cam, choke vacuum diaphragm hose, fuel inlet nut and filter assembly, automatic choke lever from choke shaft, vacuum break diaphragm screws, vacuum break diaphragm and the eight air horn to float bowl screws.

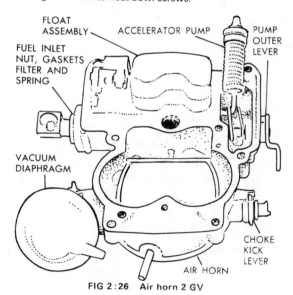

FLOAT ASSEMBLY   ACCELERATOR PUMP   PUMP OUTER LEVER

FUEL INLET NUT, GASKETS FILTER AND SPRING

VACUUM DIAPHRAGM

CHOKE KICK LEVER

AIR HORN

FIG 2:26   Air horn 2 GV

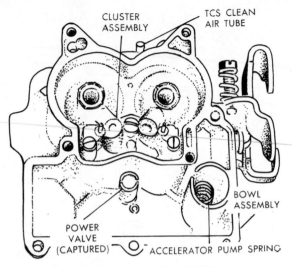

FIG 2:27 Float bowl 2 GV

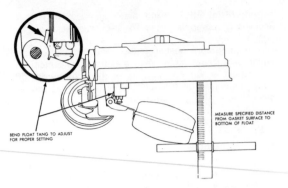

FIG 2:29 Float drop adjustment 2 GV

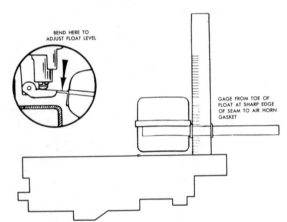

FIG 2:28 Float level adjustment 2 GV

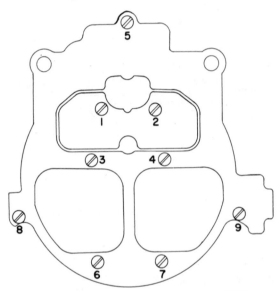

FIG 2:30 Screw tightening sequence 2 GV

2 Remove the air horn and invert on a clean bench (see **FIG 2:26**).

3 Remove the float hinge pin, float, float needle, seat and gasket.

4 Remove the pump assembly by loosening the set-screw and sliding the shaft outwards. Do not lose the plastic washer between the outer lever and air horn.

5 Remove the air horn to float bowl gasket.

6 Remove the pump plunger return spring, the two main jets and power valve from the float bowl (see **FIG 2:27**).

7 Remove the three screws on top of the venturi cluster noting that the centre screw has the fibre sealing gasket. Remove the cluster, gasket and main well inserts.

8 Remove the pump discharge spring retainer, invert the bowl and dislodge the spring and check valve.

9 If necessary, remove the two screws holding the throttle body to the bowl and part the body and bowl. If the throttle valves are damaged the throttle body and valves must be renewed as a unit. If the idle mixture screws are disturbed, the procedure for resetting their position by noting the turns necessary to seat them is identical with **Section 2:5**.

Cleaning and inspection:

The rules given in **Section 2:5** apply with the addition of the following:

1 See that the power enrichment valve is clean. Shake up and down to ensure that the valve inside is free.

2 Particularly inspect the fast idle cam and renew if any signs of wear are apparent.

3 See that the cluster assembly is undamaged.

Reassembling the carburetter:

Reverse the dismantling process noting the following points:

1 The pump discharge ball is $\frac{3}{16}$ inch diameter, fit the ball, spring and retainer then check to see that the retainer is level with the casting face.
2 See that the cluster centre screw has a fibre gasket.
3 Maintain .020 inch clearance between choke lever and collar assembly to ensure free movement.
4 Set the float lever by referring to **FIG 2:28**. The distance from the gasket to float seam must be $\frac{5}{8}$ inch with the air horn inverted.
5 Set the float drop as shown in **FIG 2:29**. With the air horn right way up the distance from the gasket to the float lower surface must be $1\frac{3}{4}$ inch.

Tighten the air horn to bowl screws in the sequence shown in **FIG 2:30**.

2:7 Fault diagnosis

(a) Fuel starvation

1 Pump failure caused by low oil pressure cutting electrical supply
2 Pump failure, internal
3 Punctured fuel line
4 Blocked fuel filter

(b) Flooding

1 Punctured float
2 Incorrect float level
3 Float valve not seating
4 Excessive pump pressure

(c) Excessive fuel consumption

1 Flooding
2 Automatic choke inoperative in closed position
3 Leaks at fuel lines and connections
4 Air cleaner choked

(d) Poor idling

1 Mixture control screws incorrectly set
2 Float level incorrect
3 Blocked jet
4 Fast idle cam damaged
5 Air leaks at manifold, etc.

(e) Hesitation on acceleration

1 Acceleration pump check ball not seating
2 Water in fuel bowl

(f) High speed 'miss'

1 Low fuel pump pressure
2 Water in fuel

(g) Lack of power

1 Partly blocked main jets
2 Blocked air filter
3 Throttle not opening fully

CHAPTER 3

THE IGNITION SYSTEM

3:1 Description

All models covered by this Autobook use basically similar distributors in which a mechanically-operated advance mechanism assisted by vacuum control adjusts the actual firing point according to the load on the engine. In addition, a system known as Transmission Controlled Spark (TCS) overrides the vacuum control in low forward gears. This is described in detail in this Chapter. Manual transmission vehicles are fitted with distributor type No. 1110492 and automatics with type 1110435. The difference lies in the centrifugal mechanical advance mechanism characteristics. See **Technical Data** for details.

The centrifugal advance mechanism consists of two weights which are pivoted on a plate attached to the distributor drive shaft. Above the weights and concentric with the shaft is the four lobed cam which operates the contact set. This cam is attached to the drive shaft by the outer ends of the weights. As the engine speed rises, the weights move outwards and advance the cam in relation to the drive shaft, thereby causing the spark plugs to fire earlier relative to the piston position. At low speeds and light loads the vacuum in the engine manifold is applied to a diaphragm mounted at the side of the distributor.

This diaphragm is connected by a link to the movable base plate which·carries the contact set; movement of the diaphragm causes the contact set to move against the direction of rotation of the cam thereby giving advanced ignition at speeds below those at which the mechanical device will operate. In addition to these timing devices the Transmission Controlled Spark system cuts the vacuum to the distributor when low gears are selected. This occurs only when the engine is at operating temperature; until then a coolant temperature sensitive switch prevents the vacuum being cut off.

3:2 Routine maintenance

Undo the two screws and lift off the distributor cap. Lift the rotor arm from the shaft; the distributor will now appear as shown in **FIG 3:1**. Wipe the inside of the distributor cap with a clean dry rag and inspect the cap and rotor arm for the faults illustrated in **FIG 3:2**. Renew the cap and rotor arm if any faults are found which cannot be rectified by cleaning. Note that carbon path 'tracking' always means renewal of the cap. Clean the cam surface and rotate the lubricator (see Item 6, **FIG 3:1**), through 180 deg. If the lubricator has seen much service it should be renewed.

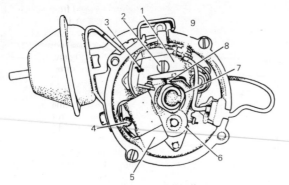

FIG 3:1   Top view of distributor

Key to Fig 3:1 1 Point set   2 Point set screw
3 Point gap adjusting notch   4 Condenser retaining
screw   5 Condenser   6 Distributor cam lubricator
7 Distributor cam   8 Rubbing block   9 Primary and
condenser lead clip

Cleaning the contact points:

Examine the contact points for signs of excessive burning or discoloration. A grey, rough surface is normal and is a good conductor. If burning of the points is evident, check that the condenser is properly connected and if the equipment is available, have it tested for breakdown. Otherwise substitute with a new one. High voltage across the points is another possibility. This can occur if the Delcotron regulator is out of adjustment or

if the point gap is too small thus allowing current flow for too long. Oil is also a likely cause of burnt points. See that oil mist is not being forced up into the distributor due to a blocked Positive Crankcase Ventilation (PCV) system. Never use emerycloth or sandpaper to clean points since particles can be left behind to cause severe arcing. Use a proper contact file and never let it come into contact with oil or grease. Rotate the engine until the points are closed, slip the file between the points and move the file a few strokes to remove scale or dirt only. Remove the file, put a piece of strong clean paper between the points and withdraw slowly to remove any swarf. Be very careful that no foreign matter or scrap of paper remains between the points. Clean the surrounding area.

Renewing contact points and setting gap:

Refer to **FIG 3:1**. Remove the two leads at clip 9. Undo screw 2, and remove the point set 1. Before fitting the new contact point set, carefully clean off any oil or preservative particularly between the point faces. Place the new set in position and tighten screw 1 just enough to hold in place. Rotate the engine by using a spanner on the crankshaft pulley until the rubbing block 8 on the moving contact is on one of the high points of the cam. Insert a screwdriver in slot 3 and move the point set until there is a gap of .019 inch between the points. If refitting a used point set adjust the gap to .016 inch. **FIG 3:3** shows the method of applying the screwdriver. Tighten screw 2 (see **FIG 3:1**). Replace the two leads at clip 9 (see **FIG 3:1**).

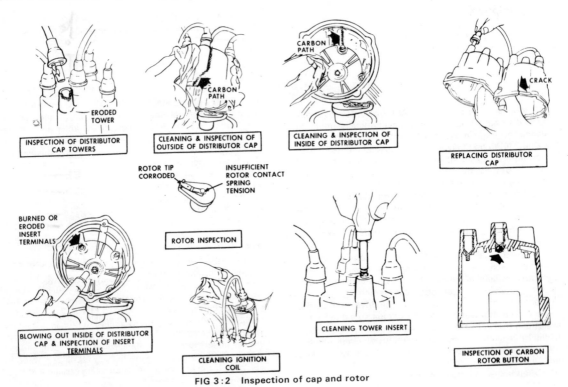

FIG 3:2   Inspection of cap and rotor

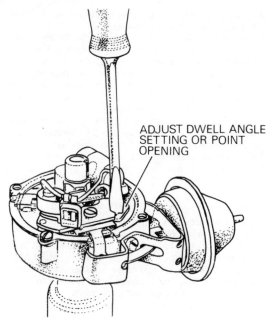

ADJUST DWELL ANGLE
SETTING OR POINT
OPENING

FIG 3:3   Adjusting point gap

the rotor arm rotates clockwise when viewed from above.
The plug lead tower in the distributor cap immediately
before the vacuum advance unit connects to No. 1 plug.
Refer to **FIG 3:1**. The tower in question should be
immediately above the condenser retaining screw item 4.
The connections following in a clockwise direction are
then 3-4-2.

Scribe a line on the distributor housing and engine in
line with the rotor arm. Do not rotate the engine further
until the distributor is refitted. Remove the rotor arm,
disconnect the vacuum advance unit pipe and the low
tension lead.

Note the position of the vacuum advance unit
relative to the engine. It is usual for it to be parallel to the
centre line of the engine with the vacuum pipe connection facing forwards.

Undo the clamp bolt, release the clamp and pull the
distributor upwards out of the cylinder head.

Timing mechanism inspection:

With the cap removed, turn the rotor arm clockwise and
see that it springs back against the centrifugal advance
weight springs. If not, dismantle the distributor and
correct the fault. Turn the movable plate anticlockwise
and see that the diaphragm spring returns it to the
retarded position. Any tightness or binding must be
found and corrected. This can be easily checked with the
engine running by allowing it to idle then opening the
throttle steadily. The link from the diaphragm should
move immediately in response.

Plug leads:

These are of the carbon core type and can be easily
damaged. When removing a lead from a plug always pull
on the rubber boot, never on the lead. Pulling on the lead
can break the core and this damage is undetectable
externally but will give rise to a mysterious and hard to
trace 'miss'. Examine plug leads for cracks or perished
rubber by bending gently. Do not double in half. Any
sign of deterioration means renewal since the high-
tension current will leak away at the slightest oppor-
tunity.

3:3 Servicing the distributor
Removal:

Release the two screws holding the distributor cap to
the body and lift the cap off. Disconnect the plug leads
by pulling on the rubber boots covering the spark plugs.
If in doubt, mark the leads with a dye marking pen or
spots of paint so that each lead is refitted to the correct
plug. Should this precaution be omitted remember that

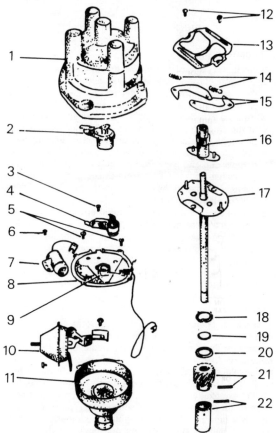

FIG 3:4   Dismantled view of distributor

Key to Fig 3:4   1 Distributor cap   2 Rotor   3 Contact
point attaching screw   4 Contact point assembly   5 Breaker
Plate attaching screws   6 Condenser attaching screw
7 Condenser   8 Breaker plate assembly   9 Cam lubricator
10 Vacuum advance control assembly   11 Distributor
housing   12 Weight cover attaching screws   13 Weight
cover   14 Weight springs   15 Advance weights   16 Cam
assembly   17 Distributor main shaft   18 Tanged washer
19 Wave washer   20 Flat washer   21 Drive gear and
roll-pin   22 Damper and roll-pin

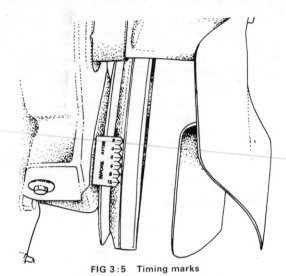

FIG 3:5 Timing marks

Dismantling:

1 Undo the vacuum unit screws and detach the unit.
2 Disconnect the low-tension lead and condenser lead then unscrew the contact set and condenser screws. Remove the contact set and condenser.
3 Refer to **FIG 3:1** and remove the two screws shown at the circumference of the body. Lift out the breaker plate. Do not dismantle the breaker plate any further.
4 Refer to **FIG 3:4**. Drive pins 21 and 22 from the damper cup and gear. Pull the cup and gear from the shaft after noting the position of the punch mark on the gear relative to the rotor slot in the cam boss.
5 Pull the shaft from the body.
6 Before dismantling the centrifugal advance mechanism mark every component, otherwise it is possible to refit the cam 180 deg. out of position with the shaft. Be careful not to stretch the springs; damaged springs will alter the distributor characteristics. Release screws 12 (see **FIG 3:4**) and then dismantle items 13 to 17.

Inspection:

Wash all parts except the cap, rotor, condenser, breaker plate and vacuum unit in clean fuel or solvent. Inspect the breaker plate for wear or damage. Renew if necessary. Check the fit of the shaft in the body. Any noticeable sideways play means renewal of either the shaft or bushes. Should this condition exist it is better to obtain an exchange distributor complete rather than attempt to fit new bearings, since other parts will be equally worn. See that the weights move freely on their pins and that the cam also moves easily on the shaft with no sign of binding or roughness. Inspect the contact points and renew if burnt or pitted.

Reassembly:

Refer to **FIG 3:4**.
1 Coat the top end of shaft 17 with a light grease. Refit cam 16.
2 Replace weights 15 and springs 14. Fit the cover 13 and secure with the two screws 12.

3 Smear engine oil on the bearing surfaces of the shaft and slide back into the housing 11.
4 Fit washers 18, 19 and 20 followed by the drive gear and roll-pin 21. Check that the shaft rotates freely.
5 Fit the damper cup and roll-pin 22. This cup is important since it has full engine oil pressure applied to its lower face in order that any shaft torsional vibration shall be damped out. If it is omitted or damaged the engine will lose all oil pressure.
6 Refit the breaker plate assembly, contact set and condenser. Set contact point gap (see **Section 3:2**). Connect the low-tension and condenser leads.
7 Attach the vacuum unit and tighten the screws.
8 Refit the rotor arm.

Installation. Engine crankshaft not moved:

1 Turn the rotor arm about $\frac{1}{8}$ turn clockwise beyond the mark made on the housing when dismantling.
2 Push the distributor home in the cylinder head with the scribed marks on the housing and cylinder head in line. The rotor should move into line as the gears engage. It may be necessary to move the rotor slightly to start engagement of the gears.
3 Fit the clamp and tighten the clamp bolt.
4 Reconnect the vacuum pipe, refit the cap and re-connect the low-tension lead and plug leads.
5 Refer to **Section 3:4** for final timing instructions.

Installation. Engine crankshaft moved:

1 Remove No. 1 spark plug and rotate the engine by using a wrench on the crankshaft pulley bolt until No. 1 piston is coming up the compression stroke. A finger placed over the plug hole will enable this to be felt.
2 Refer to **FIG 3:5**. Continue to rotate the engine until the mark on the pulley aligns with the 8 deg. mark after the 0 deg. mark on the timing scale fixed to the lower cover.
3 Position the distributor so that the vacuum unit points towards the front of the engine.
4 Turn the rotor arm until it is in line with the cap tower for No. 1 cylinder. The method of locating this tower was described in the first paragraph of this Section. In addition, the punch mark on the drive gear is in alignment with the rotor arm and the position of the rotor can therefore be set with the cap in place.
5 Turn the distributor anticlockwise $\frac{1}{8}$ turn and then push home in the cylinder head.
6 Fit the clamp and bolt. Rotate the distributor slightly until the points are just breaking.
7 Refit No. 1 spark plug and connect all distributor leads.

3:4 Timing the ignition

Accurate timing demands a stroboscopic light source. Two types are available, one requires external 12-volt power while the other is fired by the ignition spark alone. The first type gives the brightest light. Instructions for use are supplied with these devices but in general the one which uses external power has red and black leads which must be connected to the positive and negative battery posts. The remaining single lead is then attached to the No. 1 plug lead. The plug lead is connected to the plug by an adaptor. The second type of light source is simply connected by attaching one lead to No. 1 plug lead and the other lead to the plug. The circuit is then from the distributor, through the light and thence to the plug.

The timing is carried out with the engine running, therefore, **be extremely careful of the fan blades, driving belts and pulleys. Keep the hands and all equipment well clear and under no circumstances bend over the engine with a necktie hanging loosely from the collar.** Proceed to time the engine as follows:

1 Rub a little white chalk on the timing plate and the pulley notch (see **FIG 3 : 5**).
2 Start the engine and run up to operating temperature then switch off.
3 Disconnect and plug the distributor vacuum unit pipe.
4 Connect the timing light and secure it so that it shines on the timing plate marks. Do not hold it by hand.
5 Start the engine, allow to idle below 900 rev/min and watch the timing plate and pulley notch. The light should make it appear that the pulley notch is stationary.
6 Loosen the distributor clamp bolt and move the distributor body slightly to advance or retard the ignition until the pulley notch remains opposite the correct timing mark. Tighten the clamp bolt.
7 The timing marks are as follows:
Synchromesh transmission .. .. 6 deg. BTDC
Automatic transmission, base engine 6 deg. BTDC
Automatic transmission, RPO L-11
    engine .. .. .. 10 deg. BTDC
    TDC is signified by the 0 deg. mark on the scale. Note that these timing marks may be modified for a particular vehicle. If so, the relevant information will appear on the decal affixed to the underside of the hood.
8 Stop the engine, reconnect the distributor vacuum pipe and remove the timing light.

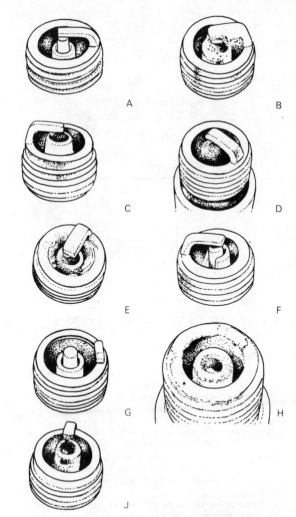

FIG 3 : 6   Spark plug condition

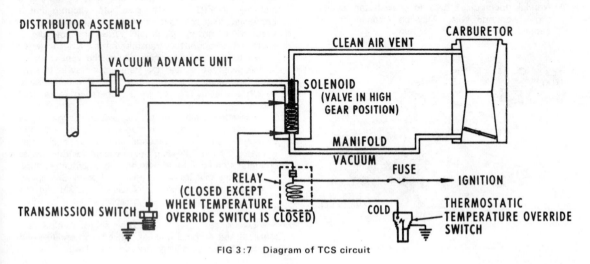

FIG 3 : 7   Diagram of TCS circuit

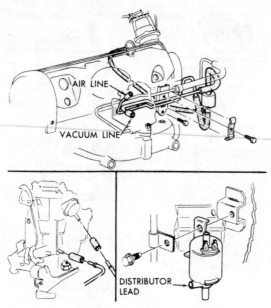

FIG 3:8 Vacuum system for TCS

3:5 The spark plugs

Plugs should be cleaned, inspected and regapped at regular intervals and renewed every 12,000 miles.

The Vega engine is designed to use the AC type R42TS as standard but the AC R41TS may be installed if a cold plug is favoured. Both types have the tapered seat and must be tightened to 15 lb ft in the cylinder head.

To remove a plug release the plug lead by pulling on the boot then, using compressed air or a tyre pump, blow away all dirt from the seat recess. Unscrew the plug using a deep socket spanner taking care not to damage the insulator.

Inspection of the firing end of the plug will give a very good indication of conditions inside the engine. Refer to **FIG 3:6 A to J.**

'A' Normal operation, brown to greyish tan deposit, slight electrode wear. May be cleaned and re-gapped.

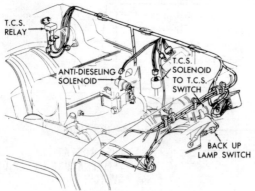

FIG 3:9 Electrical components of TCS system

'B' Red, brown, yellow and white powdery deposit caused by using fuel containing heavy additives. Can usually be cleaned and re-gapped.

'C' Deposits coloured as 'B' but having a hard glazed appearance. Caused by sudden burst of wide open throttle operation. Plug must be renewed.

'D' Carbon deposit, black and fluffy in texture. Caused by rich mixture, excessive idling or low spark voltage. Locate the cause, rectify, then clean and re-gap the plug.

'E' Wet oily deposit. Mechanical failure such as worn inlet valve guide, worn cylinder, piston or rings. Locate and rectify then degrease, clean and re-gap the plug.

'F' Heat shock. Ignition too far advanced or low grade fuel. Sometimes caused by attempting to bend the centre electrode.

'G' Detonation. Ignition too far advanced or low grade fuel causing severe shock in the combustion chamber.

'H' Loose plug. Plug not installed with sufficient torque, thereby resulting in poor heat path from body to cylinder head.

'J' Pre-ignition. Burned insulator and eroded electrodes. Caused by weak mixture, over-heated engine or sticking valves.

If the plugs prove fit for further service they should be cleaned by sand blasting and then re-gapped to .035 inch. Always bend the side electrode never the centre one to adjust the gap. When refitting plugs, check that they will screw in easily. If not, obtain a 14 mm tap, coat the flutes with heavy grease and run gently into the cylinder head threads. Do not run far enough in to foul the piston crown. The grease will retain pieces of carbon dislodged by the tap but the engine should be cranked several times after removing the tap and before installing the plug so that any remaining dirt is blown out.

3:6 Transmission controlled spark

This system (TCS) disconnects the vacuum advance unit when low forward gears are engaged, except when the engine is cold. A diagrammatic view of the circuit is shown in **FIG 3:7.** The distributor vacuum unit is connected to a solenoid valve which can either admit vacuum or vent to clean air. When the solenoid is energized through the transmission switch the valve moves to the position which allows the vent to open; as the gears are shifted the transmission switch opens and the vacuum line is connected. The temperature switch and relay are shown as operating for a cold engine.

To test the system connect a vacuum gauge to the vacuum pipe leading from the solenoid valve to the distributor unit. Full vacuum should be shown as indicated by the following table, except for the special conditions noted. Engine running at normal temperature.

3-speed transmission ..	Gear shift in 3rd speed
4-speed transmission ..	Gear shift in 3rd and 4th speeds
Torque drive	Drive shifted to high
Power glide	Drive shifted to high

Note: 3 and 4-speed manual transmission engines will not show full vacuum when the engine is idling.

Automatic transmission engines will not show vacuum until the gear shifts upwards.

It is necessary for the rear wheels to rotate when conducting these tests. **If roller equipment is not available and the rear wheels are supported clear of the ground, take every possible precaution to prevent the vehicle slipping off the supports or any person making contact with the wheels.**

If full vacuum is found in all gears, check as follows:

(a) Blown fuse.
(b) Disconnected electrical leads at solenoid or transmission switch.
(c) Faulty transmission switch.
(d) Faulty temperature switch.
(e) Solenoid failure.

If no vacuum is shown in the high gears, check the following:

(a) Air vent and distributor vacuum pipe reversed.
(b) Foreign matter in solenoid valve.
(c) Broken solenoid valve spring.
(d) Vacuum pipe broken or disconnected.
(e) Transmission switch or lead shorted to ground.

When the faulty component has been located it must be renewed, repair is not advisable.

FIG 3:8 shows the correct layout of the vacuum system and **FIG 3:9** identifies the main electrical components.

3:7 Fault diagnosis

(a) Engine will not fire

1 Battery discharged
2 Distributor cap interior damp, oily or tracking between contacts.
3 Contact points dirty or out of adjustment
4 No current reaching distributor
5 Rotor cracked or tracking
6 Coil failed
7 Automatic transmission lever not in Neutral or Park position

(b) Engine misfires

1 Check all plug and coil leads for cracks
2 Check contact set and points gap
3 Check all plugs (see **Section 3:5** for details)
4 Timing too far advanced

CHAPTER 4

THE COOLING SYSTEM

4 : 1 Description

All engines described in this manual incorporate an impeller assisted, pressurized, thermosyphonic cooling system. The coolant is drawn from the lower connection at the radiator by the impeller (water pump) and circulated through the engine waterways. At a predetermined temperature, the thermostatic valve mounted in the cylinder head opens and allows the coolant to pass to the top of the radiator. The cooling effect of the air passing through the radiator as the vehicle moves is supplemented by a four-bladed fan mounted on the forward end of the impeller shaft. Fan and impeller are driven by the outer, grooved face of the timing belt.

The radiator is of cross flow design and due to the deliberately low heat rejection of the engine is only 12 inch by 12 inch when fitted to a vehicle without air conditioning. When air conditioning is installed a radiator 18 inch wide is standard. For certain areas of operation the wider, heavy duty, radiator is fitted as an option in any case.

The system is intended to operate with anti-freeze and inhibitor in solution in the water at all times. It should never be operated with plain water only due to the lower boiling point and risk of corrosion. Note that these engines are intended to run at high temperature as an aid to emission control. The radiator cap pressure release valve is set to 15 p.s.i. and is a critical part of the cooling system by ensuring that coolant temperatures up to 247°F are safely maintained.

4 : 2 Maintenance

No mechanical maintenance or lubrication is required. Occasionally check all hoses for condition and clips for tightness. Should persistent coolant loss occur without visible leaks, have the radiator cap tested by a Chevrolet Agent. If found to be releasing pressure below 15 p.s.i. it must be renewed. Never remove a radiator cap from a hot engine due to the high pressure generated which will blow boiling water and steam out and cause serious scalds.

Testing the cooling system:

1 Run the engine up to operating temperature then switch off.
2 Feel the radiator surface. It should be hot along the left side viewed from the rear and less hot along the right side. There should be an even rise in temperature from bottom to top, right to left. Areas much cooler than others indicate an obstruction in the waterways.

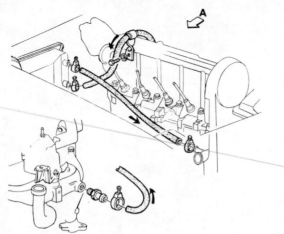

FIG 4:1 Heater hose connections

Flushing:

1 Close both drain taps and reconnect or renew the heater hose.
2 Fill the system with plain clean water and run the engine up to operating temperature.
3 Stop the engine and allow to cool down. Open the drain taps and disconnect the heater hose.
4 Repeat operations 1 to 3 until the water drains away as clean as it went in.

Reverse flusing:

This should be undertaken if evidence of blockage, corrosion or scale formation is found. It must also be carried out on an engine after rectifying a blown head gasket which has allowed exhaust gas or oil to enter the cooling system. A compressed air and water gun is necessary.

1 Drain the system and remove the radiator hoses and pressure cap.
2 Attach a temporary hose to the top radiator connection to lead water away from the engine. Fit a hose to the bottom connection and connect the flushing gun.
3 Refit the radiator pressure cap.
4 Turn on the water supply to the gun and run until water issues from the top hose. Turn on the air supply in short blasts allowing the radiator to fill between each blast. Remember that a blocked radiator will only stand 20 p.s.i. so apply the air with caution. Continue until the water runs clear.
5 Disconnect the gun and hoses from the radiator.
6 Remove the thermostat and fit a piece of hose to the water pump inlet to lead away expelled water.
7 Connect the flushing gun to a piece of hose thence to the water outlet on the cylinder head.
8 Disconnect the heater hoses at the engine and plug the holes.
9 Turn on the water, fill the engine waterways, then apply air in a similar way to that adopted for the radiator. Cease when the water runs clear.
10 Remove the gun and hoses.
11 Adopt the same method to flush the heater core but be even more careful when operating the air supply.
12 Renew and refit hoses as necessary. The correct layout of the heater hoses is shown in **FIG 4:1.**

3 Start the engine and run until certain that the thermostat is open. Keeping the hands clear of the fan, squeeze the top water outlet to radiator hose while gently speeding the engine up. A distinct surge of pressure should be felt immediately if the impeller is operating properly.
4 Switch off and allow the engine to cool down. Remove the radiator cap and dip a piece of clean wood in the coolant. Withdraw and inspect for any sign of an oily ring left at the point where the coolant level reached. If any evidence of oil is shown, the cylinder head gasket has probably blown.

Draining:

For normal operation the system should be drained every two years, flushed through and refilled with fresh coolant.
1 Remove the radiator cap.
2 Open the drain tap at the base of the radiator and also the tap at the side of the engine block.
3 Remove the lower hose from the heater core. Be very careful not to apply force to the heater core tubes while carrying out this operation. These are comparatively fragile and it is easy to start a leak. If the hose is stick to the tube, cut and discard the hose.

Cleaning the system:

Should the system not respond to flushing, a good quality chemical cleaner such as GM Cooling System Cleaner must be used. The following directions apply to this preparation.

1 Drain the entire cooling system and leave the radiator cap off.
2 Remove the thermostat and refit the housing.
3 Pour the liquid part of the cleaner into the radiator and then add plain water to a level 3 inches below the overflow pipe.
4 Cover the outer face of the radiator and run the engine until the solution reaches 195°F. Remove the cover and run for a further 20 minutes. Do not allow to boil.
5 Keep the engine running and add the powder part of the cleaner. Run for a further 10 minutes.

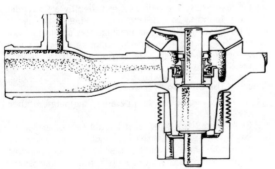

FIG 4:2 The water pump

6 Stop the engine, allow to cool enough to avoid any risk of scalding then drain the solution off. Remove the lower hose to ensure complete removal of sludge.

7 When the engine is cold pour clean water through the system to remove all traces of the chemical. The heater hoses must be released and reconnected after flushing through.

8 Refit the thermostat and refill the system with coolant.

Radiator:

Clean the external surface of the core by blowing out dead flies and leaves with compressed air applied from the engine side of the radiator. Do not poke wire through the fins since these are easily damaged.

4:3 Frost precautions

The system is designed to operate all the year round with antifreeze solution, inhibitor and sealing liquid as the coolant due to the higher boiling point and corrosion prevention of this mixture.

Every two years, drain and flush the system and add sufficient antifreeze to provide protection down to an ambient temperature of at least 0°F. The antifreeze must meet GM specification 1899-M for ethylene glycol based mixtures. Alcohol or methonal based types must not be used. Add the specified quantity of GM Cooling System Inhibitor and Sealer then fill with clean water to a level 3 inches below the filler neck, engine cold. Check this level again when the engine is again cold after the first run. The antifreeze and inhibitor sealer cans quote the correct proportions to use. The cooling system capacity is 13 US pints.

4:4 The water pump

This is illustrated in section in **FIG 4:2.** Should the seal or bearings fail the pump must be renewed as a unit. Components are not supplied separately.

To remove the pump proceed as follows:

1 Drain the coolant into a clean container ready for re-use.

2 Remove the fan and timing belt cover.

3 Undo the water pump to engine bolts and lift the pump from the cylinder block. Be careful not to disturb the timing belt.

4 Clean the cylinder block face to remove all trace of the gasket.

To install the water pump carry out the following operations:

1 Apply anti-seize compound to the bolt threads then fit the new gasket and pump with the bolts just hand tight.

2 Refer to **Chapter 1, FIG 1:20,** apply the torque wrench and adaptor J-23654 as shown. See that the grooves in the pump boss match the drive faces on the back of the timing belt then apply 15 lb ft to the wrench to force the pump against the belt at the correct pressure. Tighten the water pump bolts to 15 lb ft and then remove the torque wrench and adaptor from the side of the cylinder block. If a strand gauge, Part No. J-23600 is available the belt tension can be checked. It should read between 100 to 140 lb.

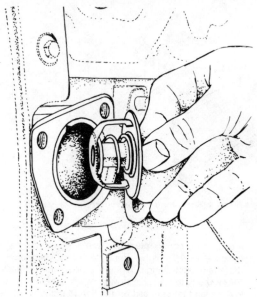

FIG 4:3   Removing the thermostat

3 Check the fan blades and if any signs of bending or damage are apparent, renew the fan.

4 Refit the timing belt cover and fan, tightening the fan bolts to 20 lb ft.

5 Refill the cooling system.

4:5 The thermostat

This should open between 192 deg. to 198 deg. If failure is suspected remove and test as follows:

1 Drain the cooling system and remove the water outlet to radiator hose. This is the one connected to the top of the radiator.

2 Remove the thermostat housing bolts and lift the housing away. Remove and scrap the gasket then lift the thermostat from the cylinder head as shown in **FIG 4:3.**

3 Inspect the thermostat for any sign of damage.

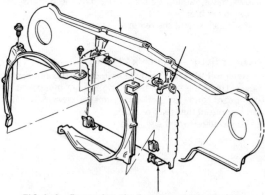

FIG 4:4   Removing the fan shroud, heavy duty

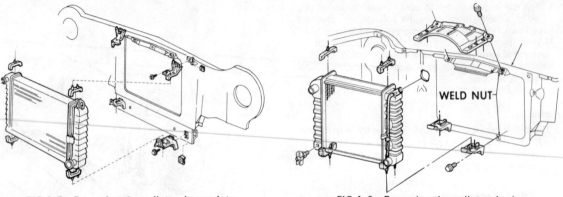

FIG 4:5　Removing the radiator, heavy duty

FIG 4:6　Removing the radiator, basic

4 If apparently sound, place in a container of water at a temperature 10° higher than the figure stamped on the thermostat flange. It should open immediately. Allow the water to cool down. At a temperature 10° lower than that stamped on the flange it should close completely. If these conditions are not met it must be renewed.

To replace the thermostat reverse the removal procedure using a new gasket and installing the thermostat with the spring towards the cylinder head. Tighten the bolts to 30 lb ft.

4:6 The radiator

To remove and refit either the basic or heavy duty radiator proceed as follows:

Heavy duty radiator—12 inch x 18 inch:

Refer to **FIG 4:4** and remove the two screws holding the shroud to the radiator upper brackets and then remove the screw holding the halves of the shroud together at the lower lefthand corner. Lift the lefthand section away followed by the righthand section.

Drain the cooling system, disconnect the hoses and then remove the nuts holding the top brackets. **FIG 4:5** shows the mounting points clearly. Lift the radiator out of the lower brackets.

To install reverse the removal procedure.

Basic radiator—12 inch x 12 inch:

Refer to **FIG 4:6.** Drain the system and disconnect the hoses. Undo the two bolts holding the fan guard and lift the guard and radiator top brackets away. Lift the radiator out of the lower brackets.

To install reverse the removal procedure.

4:7 Fault diagnosis

(a) Coolant loss

1 Blown head gasket
2 Cracked cylinder or head
3 Defective hose
4 Loose hose clip
5 Radiator cap releasing pressure below 15 p.s.i.
6 Heater core leaks

(b) Poor circulation

1 Blocked radiator
2 Collapsed hose
3 Water pump defective
4 Timing belt slipping due to slackness or oil contamination
5 Low coolant level
6 Thermostat failed shut

(c) Corrosion

1 Impurities in water
2 Use of plain water without anti-freeze, inhibitor and sealer
3 Infrequent changing of coolant and flushing through
4 Entry of air into system due to low coolant level, leaky water pump or defective hoses.
5 Cracked cylinder or head, blown gasket, etc; allowing exhaust gas to enter system

(d) Overheating

1 Mechanical condition of engine, e.g. new and tight
2 Incorrect ignition or valve timing, low oil level
3 Blocked radiator
4 Low coolant level
5 Slipping drive belt to pump
6 Damaged fan
7 Thermostat failed shut
8 Slipping clutch, automatic transmission will not shift upwards, binding brakes

CHAPTER 5

THE CLUTCH

5:1 Description

The clutch used with all manual transmission models is of conventional single dry plate, diaphragm spring design. Control of the clutch is by foot pedal connected to the throwout fork by a cable.

The friction (driven) plate has a spring damper hub to reduce the transmission of torsional vibration. Slots in the friction lining faces break any vacuum on disengagement thus preventing the plate from sticking to the flywheel or pressure plate.

FIG 5:1 shows the assembled clutch and throwout mechanism. From this will be seen the simple cable and fork design which moves the throwout bearing against the diaphragm spring thus releasing the pressure on the pressure plate and driven plate.

FIG 5:2 gives an exploded view of the clutch and flywheel. The 90 h.p. engine has an 8 inch driven plate but this is increased to 9.1 inch diameter for the 110 h.p. RPO-L11 engine.

5:2 Clutch mechanism adjustment

The clutch requires no maintenance apart from adjustment of the cable length to give the correct pedal free travel of .90 inch $\pm$ .25 inch.

Initial adjustment:

This must be carried out whenever a new cable is fitted or the clutch components are disturbed for any reason.
1 Remove the clutch fork cover from the side of the bellhousing.
2 Install gauge J-23644 as shown in **FIG 5:3** with its hooked end over the fork and the flat end against the front face of the clutch housing.
3 Refer to **FIG 5:1**, slacken the ball stud locknut and screw the ball stud in or out until the throwout bearing can be felt to just contact the diaphragm spring. Tighten the locknut to 25 lb ft.
4 Remove the gauge by pulling on the end hooked against the clutch housing.

Fitting and adjusting the clutch cable:

From the engine compartment push the cable through the bulkhead and route the inner cable round the pulley and down to the clutch pedal. Lubricate all bearing surfaces with graphite grease then attach the cable to the pedal with the pin, washer and clip.

Direct the cable through the engine compartment, over the fender skirt reinforcement and down to the clutch housing.

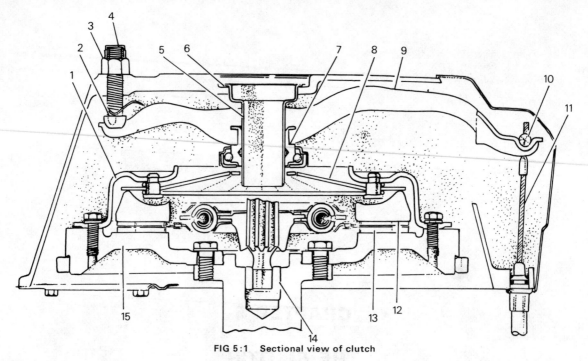

FIG 5:1 Sectional view of clutch

Key to Fig 5:1 1 Clutch cover 2 Fork ball stud 3 Locknut 4 Ball stud cap 5 Throwout bearing support 6 Support gasket 7 Throwout bearing 8 Diaphragm spring 9 Clutch fork 10 Clutch cable lockpin 11 Clutch cable 12 Pressure plate 13 Driven disc 14 Pilot bearing 15 Flywheel

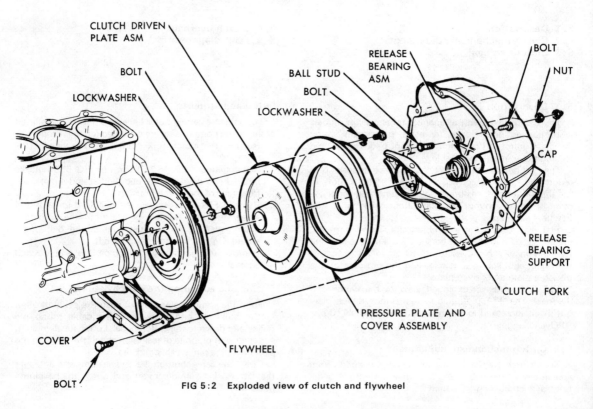

FIG 5:2 Exploded view of clutch and flywheel

Refer to **FIG 5:1** and install the cable through the clutch housing up to the stop on the outer conduit. Pass the inner cable through the clutch fork and pull on the cable so that the pedal is hard up against the return stop. Push the fork forward until it contacts the diaphragm spring. Screw up the pin on the cable until it just touches the fork. Turn a further $\frac{1}{4}$ turn clock wise then fit the pin into the groove in the fork. Attach the return spring and check to see that the pedal has the .90 inch $\pm$ .25 inch of free travel. Replace the fork cover and tighten the screws to 80 lb inch.

Adjusting the pedal free travel when necessary due to normal wear.

It is only necessary to slacken the ball stud locknut and screw the ball stud in or out to compensate for normal wear. Remember that the free travel will increase with linkage wear and decrease with driven plate wear. Always maintain the specified amount of free travel. After adjustment tighten the locknut to 25 lb ft.

5:3 Clutch removal

This can be achieved without disturbing the engine but a hoist to raise the car or a pit to work in below it are essential.

1 Disconnect the battery.
2 Place the shift lever in neutral. Removal of either the 3 or 4-speed shift levers is similar in method. Refer to **FIG 5:4**. From inside the car, remove the bezel retaining screws, lift off the bezel and gasket then pull the rubber boot upwards.
3 Unhook the anti-rattle spring, remove the lever pin retainer, spring washer and lever pin. Lift the shift lever up from the intermediate shift lever into the car.
4 Raise the car on the hoist if this is available.
5 Mark the relationship of the propeller shaft rear universal joint to the axle drive flange then remove the trunnion bearing U-bolts. Use adhesive tape to hold the bearing cups to the trunnions so that these do not fall off and spill the roller bearings.
6 Lower the rear of the shaft then withdraw from the gearbox and pass rearwards below the axle. Plug the aperture in the gearbox extension to prevent oil loss.
7 From the gearbox disconnect the speedometer cable, TCS switch and back up lamp switch.
8 Remove the bolts which hold the gearbox mounting to the transmission crossmember. This is shown in **FIG 1:22, Chapter 1**.
9 Support the engine with a suitable jack stand and remove the crossmember to frame bolts. Remove the crossmember.
10 Remove the top bolts from the gearbox to the clutch housing and replace with guide pins. These are threaded studs approximately 4 inch long with a screwdriver slot in the plain end. They can be easily made up by sawing the heads from suitable spare bolts. Their purpose is to guide the gearbox squarely away from the clutch so that the main drive gearshaft does not distort the driven plate due to the gearbox moving out of alignment. The same essential duty is performed on reassembly.
11 Remove the lower gearbox to clutch housing bolts and slide the gearbox rearwards from the car.
12 Remove the clutch fork cover and release the return spring and cable.

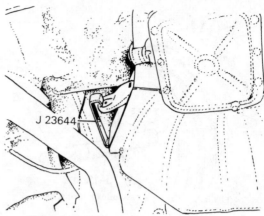

FIG 5:3   Adjusting the clutch fork position

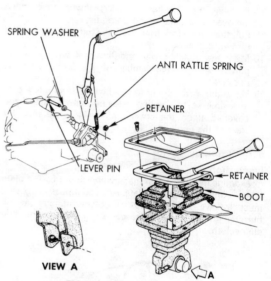

FIG 5:4   Shift lever removal

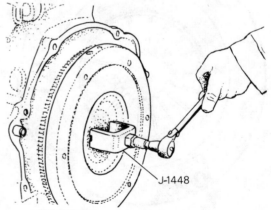

FIG 5:5   Removing the pilot bearing hub

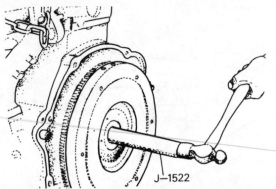

FIG 5:6 Fitting a new pilot bearing bush

13 Remove the main drive gear oil seal from the throwout bearing sleeve.
14 Remove the flywheel housing lower cover then remove the housing from the engine.
15 Pull the clutch fork from the ball stud and remove the throwout bearing.
16 Mark the clutch cover and flywheel with a centre punch in case reassembly of the same parts is possible.
17 Undo the clutch cover to flywheel bolts evenly a turn at a time so that spring pressure cannot distort the cover. Support the cover and driven plate then lift clear of the engine.

5:4 Clutch overhaul

Inspection:

Examine the surfaces of the flywheel and pressure plate which contact the driven plate. Any roughness or scoring must involve renewal, but discoloration due to oil burning off the driven plate can be removed with fine emerycloth.

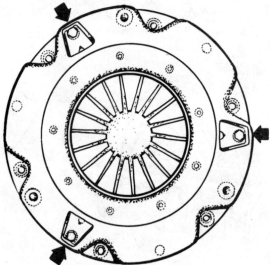

FIG 5:7 Drive strap bolts

The driven plate should not be highly glazed nor show signs of oil contamination. This will be recognisable as areas of a much deeper colour. Look for broken rivets, loose or broken damper springs and see that the plate is an easy sliding fit on the gearbox input shaft splines. If the linings are worn down to within $\frac{1}{16}$ inch of the rivets the plate must be renewed.

If the gearbox input shaft splines are worn with a noticeable ridge where the driven plate bears then this shaft must be renewed. Refer to **Chapter 6**.

Should oil have found its way to the driven plate it is most likely to have come from the gearbox. Examine the oil drain back hole in the gearbox face, the oil seal between the clutch housing and gearbox and the throwout bearing sleeve support gasket. Check the engine rear main bearing and if necessary renew the oil seal as described in **Chapter 1**. See that the throwout bearing is a free fit on the sleeve and rotate it to check for roughness. Any scoring on the contact face means that the bearing has partly seized at some time and must be suspect. Examine the throwout fork for wear and damage and see that the spring which clips to the ball stud has not lost tension. It may be bent in towards the fork if necessary.

The pilot bush in the crankshaft must be examined for wear or damage. If necessary pull the old bush out with tool J-1448 as shown in **FIG 5:5** and fit the new one with tool J-1522 (see **FIG 5:6**). Lubricate the bush with a few drops of engine oil before refitting the clutch. Do not over-oil.

It is permissible to remove the pressure plate from the clutch cover but further dismantling is not possible since the spring and pivot rings are riveted to the cover. Before dismantling the pressure plate mark it and the cover in case it is possible to refit these. The three drive strap to pressure plate bolts which must be released to dismantle the assembly are shown in **FIG 5:7**.

Cleaning:

Wash all parts, except the driven plate and throwout bearing in clean fuel or cleaning solvent. The throwout bearing is permanently packed with lubricant and cleaning will dissolve the lubricant.

Reassembly:

Refit the pressure plate to the cover making sure that the marks made when dismantling are re-aligned if the same components are re-used. Tighten the bolts to 18 lb ft.

Obtain a dummy gearbox input shaft or if a lathe is available turn up a mandrel from any scrap steel or brass bar stock. The small diameter should be a good fit in the crankshaft pilot bearing bush and the larger diameter a good sliding fit through the driven plate splines.

Position the mandrel or dummy shaft through the driven plate then fit plate and mandrel (or shaft) to the flywheel. **The longer end of the driven plate hub must go towards the flywheel.** Attach the pressure plate and cover assembly to the flywheel making sure the centre punch marks made when dismantling are in alignment. Tighten the cover bolts evenly, a turn at a time so that the cover is not distorted. Torque finally to 20 lb ft. Remove the mandrel.

Lubricate the clutch fork ball socket and the area which contacts the throwout bearing with high melting point grease.

Apply grease to the recess on the inside of the throw-out bearing collar and the groove in the clutch fork.

Install the fork in the clutch housing but do not push over the ball stud at this stage. Fit the bearing on the sleeve, position the fork over the bearing and now push home against the spring until it clips over the ball stud.

Fit the clutch housing to the engine and tighten the bolts to 25 lb ft. Replace the clutch housing dust cover and tighten the bolts to 80 lb inch.

Refit the gearbox by reversing the removal process. Use a new gasket between the gearbox and clutch housing. Make certain that the input shaft splines are clean and dry. Do not lubricate these before assembly.

Tighten the gearbox to clutch housing bolts to 24 lb ft, crossmember to frame bolts to 82 lb ft and the gearbox mounting bolts to 26 lb ft. Install the gearshift lever by reversing the removal process. Refit the propeller shaft and tighten the trunnion bolts. Check the gearbox oil level, fit and adjust the clutch cable and refit the fork cover.

5:5 Fault diagnosis

(a) Clutch drag

1 Excessive pedal free travel
2 Driven plate binding on input shaft splines
3 Oil or grease on driven plate
4 Bent driven plate

(b) Fierce clutch

1 Oil or grease on driven plate
2 Worn driven plate linings
3 Clutch cable binding in conduit

(c) Slip

1 Oil or grease on driven plate
2 Diaphragm spring weak
3 Seized clutch cable
4 No pedal free travel

(d) Judder

1 Worn driven plate linings
2 Oil or grease on driven plate
3 Damaged or loose engine mountings
4 Clutch cable binding
5 Driven plate distorted

CHAPTER 6

THE GEARBOX

6:1 Description—3 and 4-speed

The basic gearbox is a 3-speed, all synchromesh unit but an optional 4-speed type is available. Both are of similar design in which the clutch gear is in constant mesh with the countershaft. This drives the appropriate constant mesh main shaft gear, locked as required to the main shaft through sliding synchromesh units. These synchronizers are of the blocker ring type.

Both gearboxes are controlled by a floor mounted gearshift. The 3-speed shift lever moves through the normal four position pattern for selecting the three forward gears and reverse.

The 4-speed shift lever has a reverse lockout ring below the shift knob which has to be raised to allow the shift lever to move into reverse.

Note that all the nuts, bolts, screws and spiral pins are in metric sizes and cannot be interchanged with others from the car.

The gearbox lubricant has an orange dye incorporated so that any leak from the bellhousing can be identified as either engine or transmission seal failure.

6:2 Servicing the gearshift lever

The method of removing and refitting the shift lever was described in **Chapter 5**. This applies to both 3 and 4-speed transmissions.

3-speed

Refer to **FIG 6:1**. The only renewal likely to be needed after very long service is of the two grommets. Prise the retaining ring from the lower end of the shifter tube and pull the tube from the shift finger. The assembly of the components will be obvious. Renew the grommets, and slide the shifter tube back over the shift finger. Refit the washer and retaining ring. The action of the shift lever in selecting the gears is identical to the 4-speed except for the extra movement to select reverse in the latter box. See the next paragraph.

4-speed

Refer to **FIG 6:2**. Increasing the forward speeds to 4 makes an extra movement of the shift lever necessary to obtain reverse. To avoid accidental engagement, a reverse locknut is fitted and this mechanism is included in the shift lever.

In both 3 and 4-speed boxes, fore and aft movement of the shift lever moves the appropriate synchronizer into engagement with a gear. Side to side movement selects which one of the shifter shafts the shift lever will move. The fore and aft movement of the shift lever is transmitted to the selector shaft by the shift control rod on the righthand side of the gearbox looking towards the engine. Sideways movement actuates the selector rod

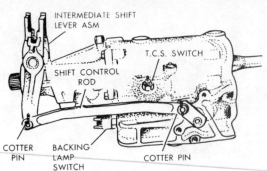

FIG 6:3   4-speed shift control rod linkage

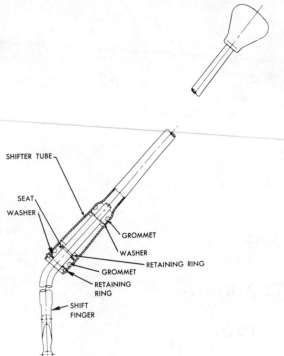

FIG 6:1   3-speed shift lever

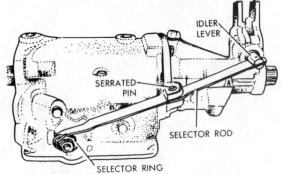

FIG 6:4   4-speed shift selector rod linkage

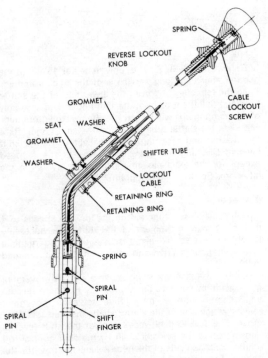

FIG 6:2   4-speed shift lever

which moves the selector shaft across the gearbox, thereby allowing the selector shaft levers to engage with the required shifter shaft ready to move the shifter shaft, forks and synchronizers as necessary. An extra sideways movement is needed to engage the reverse shifter shaft, thus the stop ring is raised to allow the shift lever to make this extra amount of movement. The external linkage is shown in **FIGS 6:3** and **6:4**.

Renewing the reverse locknut control wire:

Remove the shift lever from the car. Pull on the gearshift knob to free it from the shifter tube. Be prepared to have to break the knob up as in some cases it can be so tight that attempts to free it would distort the tube at the weak section where the top cable clamp is situated. Perform this part of the operation with great care. A new knob is fitted by immersing it in very hot water for a few moments then pressing onto the tube. With the knob removed, slacken the Allen screw holding the Bowden cable at the top of the tube. This is clearly shown in **FIG 6:5**. Refer to **FIG 6:6** and carefully drive the two spiral pins out. This will release the shift finger and the stop ring. The cable and lower spring will now be free to slide from the tube.

Lubricate the new cable and the stop ring with thin oil and smear some oil on the sliding surface of the tube. Insert the cable and spring into the tube and position the stop ring over the tube. Drive the long upper spiral pin (see **FIG 6:6**), right home so that both ends are below the stop ring surface.

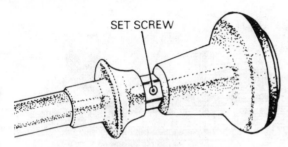

FIG 6:5 Gearshift cable retaining screw

SET SCREW

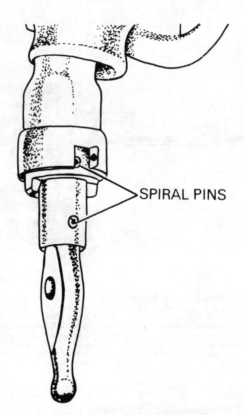

SPIRAL PINS

FIG 6:6 Spiral pins installed in shift lever

Fit the pull ring to the top of the shifter tube then position the clamp block over the cable and tighten the Allen screw (see **FIG 6:5**), so that the pull ring has $\frac{1}{8}$ inch free travel. Check that movement of the pull ring moves the stop ring easily and that when released, the stop ring returns immediately to its lowest position. If not, find the cause and rectify it at this stage. Fit the shift finger to the shifter tube and drive the lower spiral pin home (see **FIG 6:6**). Place the spring in the top of the shifter tube and press the knob on until .30 inch of space exists between the knob and pull ring as shown in **FIG 6:7**.

The two grommets between the shifter tube, upper and lower, are renewed as described earlier for the 3-speed shift lever.

Adjusting the stop ring:

Engage 2nd speed. Refer to **FIG 6:4**. Slacken the locknut on the selector ring and adjust the selector ring so that the ball form at the bottom of the shift finger is equidistant from both sides of the intermediate shift lever hole. Unscrew the selector ring a further $\frac{1}{4}$ turn then tighten the locknut. Check all gears for correct engagement.

6:3 Fitting a new extension oil seal—3 or 4-speed:

This operation can be performed without removing the gearbox from the car. Jack up and support on stands at the rear axle only so that the gearbox oil level is kept low at the extension housing.

Remove the propeller shaft as described in **Chapter 5.** Carefully prise the seal from the housing then wipe the seating surface clean and dry. Coat the outside diameter of the new seal with jointing cement and the inner lips with gear oil. Start the seal truly into the bore and drive home. Use a piece of tube and a hammer so that the force is applied to the circumference of the seal. Refit the propeller shaft and lower the car to the ground.

6:4 Overhauling the 3-speed gearbox

Throughout this Section, refer to **FIG 6:8** unless specifically directed to detail illustrations.

Remove the gearbox as described in **Chapter 5.**

Dismantling:

1 Disconnect the shift lever linkage by releasing the cotterpins and driving out the serrated pins. It will be found most convenient to slide the selector rod and

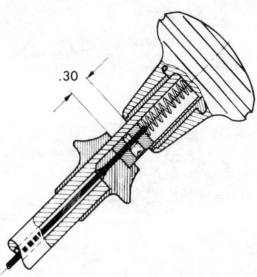

.30

FIG 6:7 Clearance between pull ring and shift knob

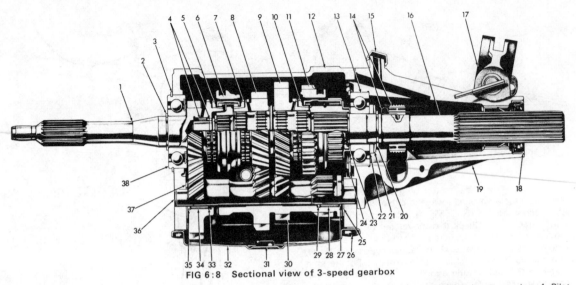

FIG 6:8 Sectional view of 3-speed gearbox

Key to Fig 6:8   1 Clutch drive gear   2 Retaining ring (bearing-to-drive gear)   3 Retaining ring (bearing-to-case)   4 Pilot bearing and spacer ring   5 3rd gear synchronizer ring   6 2-3 sliding sleeve and synchronizer assembly   7 2nd gear synchronizer ring   8 2nd speed gear   9 1st speed gear   10 1st gear synchronizer ring   11 1st-rev. sliding sleeve and synchronizer ring   12 Transmission case   13 Rear bearing   14 Speedometer gear and retaining clip   15 Vent cap   16 Mainshaft   17 Intermediate shift lever assembly   18 Extension seal   19 Rear extension   20 Retaining ring (bearing-to-shaft)   21 Belleville washer   22 Spacer   23 Synchronizer key stop ring   24 Retaining ring (bearing-to-extension)   25 Thrust washer   26 Cover screw   27 Spacer   28 Roller bearing   29 Spacer   30 Countergear   31 Magnet   32 Transmission cover   33 Spacer   34 Roller bearing   35 Spacer   36 Countergear shaft   37 Thrust washer   38 Clutch gear bearing

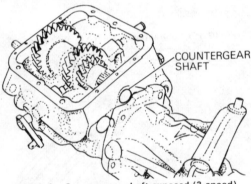

FIG 6:9 Countergear shaft exposed (3-speed)

shift idler lever from the intermediate shift lever if the selector ring is unscrewed simultaneously. **FIG 6:4,** although illustrating the 4-speed box, shows the components clearly.

2 Turn the gearbox over with the sump uppermost. Release the sump screws evenly, remove the sump and discard the gasket. Invert the gearbox to drain the oil then turn over again.

3 Remove the bolts holding the rear extension to the main case and turn the extension enough to expose the end of the counter gearshaft (see **FIG 6:9**). The extension cannot be drawn away from the main case at this stage (see operation 9).

4 Obtain tool J.23562 or make up a drift very slightly smaller than the counter gearshaft and a little shorter

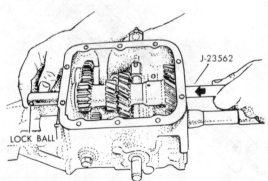

FIG 6:10 Removing countergear shaft

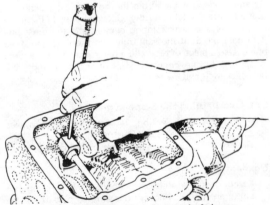

FIG 6:11 Removing selector shaft lever

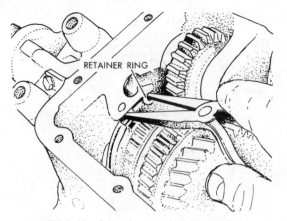

FIG 6:12 Releasing rear bearing retainer

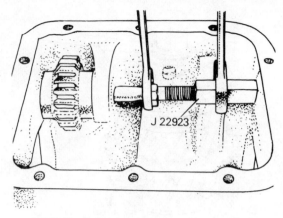

FIG 6:13 Removing the reverse idler gearshaft

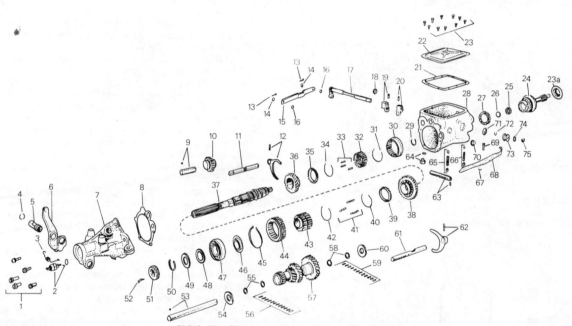

FIG 6:14 Exploded view of 3-speed gearbox

Key to Fig 6:14 1 Rear extension to case bolts 2 Back-up lamp switch and seal ring 3 Shift idler lever spring 4 Intermediate lever bushing snap ring 5 Intermediate lever bushing 6 Shift idler lever 7 Rear extension 8 Rear extension gasket 9 Reverse idler gearshaft and lock ball 10 Reverse idler gear and bushing assembly 11 2-3 speed shifter shaft 12 2-3 speed shift fork and spiral pin 13 Cotterpin 14 Waved washer 15 Shift selector rod 16 Washer 17 Selector shaft 18 Selector shaft seal 19 2-3 intermediate shift lever and spiral pin 20 1st-reverse intermediate shift lever and spiral pin 21 Cover gasket 22 Cover assembly 23 Cover-to-case screws 23a Clutch drive gear seal 24 Clutch drive gear assembly 25 Mainshaft pilot bearing assembly 26 Pilot bearing spacer ring 27 3rd gear synchronizer ring 28 Transmission case 29 2-3 speed synchronizer assembly retaining ring 30 2-3 speed synchronizer sleeve 31 Synchronizer spring 32 2-3 Synchronizer hub 33 2-3 synchronizer keys 34 Synchronizer spring 35 2nd gear synchronizer ring 36 2nd speed gear 37 Mainshaft 38 1st speed gear 39 1st speed gear synchronizer ring 40 Synchronizer spring 41 1st-reverse synchronizer keys 42 Synchronizer spring 43 1st-reverse synchronizer hub 44 1st-reverse synchronizer sleeve 45 Rear bearing to extension locking ring 46 1st-reverse key stop ring 47 Mainshaft rear bearing 48 Rear bearing spacer 49 Belleville washer 50 Rear bearing retaining ring 51 Speedo drive gear 52 Speedo drive clip 53 Countergear shaft and lock ball 54 Countergear thrust washer 55 Countergear bearing washer 56 Countergear roller bearings (24) 57 Countergear 58 Countergear bearing washer 59 Countergear roller bearings (24) 60 Countergear thrust washers 61 1st-reverse shift shaft 62 1st-reverse shift fork and spiral pin 63 Intermediate lever shaft and pin 64 TCS switch and gasket 65 2-3 shift detent ball, spring and hole plug 66 1-reverse shift detent ball, spring and hole plug 67 Pivot pin lock ring 68 Shift selector rod 69 Selector lever pivot pin 70 Oil filler plug 71 Selector shaft oil seal 72 Selector shaft lock ring 73 Selector shaft ring 74 Belleville washer 75 Selector shaft lock ring

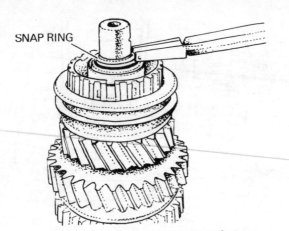

FIG 6:15 Removing forward snap ring

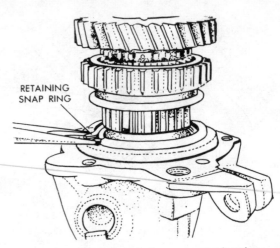

FIG 6:18 Fitting mainshaft to extension housing

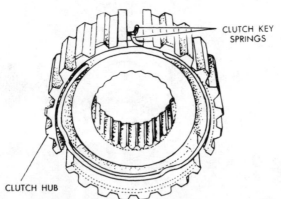

FIG 6:16 Installing synchronizer key springs

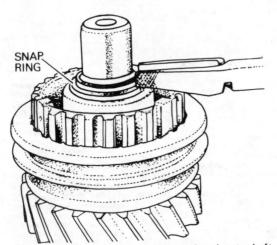

FIG 6:17 Securing 2nd-3rd speed synchronizer to shaft

than the counter gear itself. Refer to **FIG 6:10**. Tap the drift into the case from the front and drive out the counter gearshaft. Do not lose the lock ball in the shaft. With the drift right home in the counter gear, lift the complete gear (see 30, **FIG 6:8**), the two thrust washers 25 and 37 and the roller races, 27, 28, 29, 33, 34 and 35 from the case. While the drift is left in the counter gear the roller races will stay in place.

5 With a $\frac{1}{8}$ inch pin punch drive out the lockpins from the shifter forks. It will be necessary to engage 3rd gear, making sure that the 2nd-3rd intermediate lever engages the shifter shaft. This allows the selector shaft and intermediate levers to pivot as the shifter shaft is driven out.

6 Insert a long thin drift through the bolt hole at the rear of the case and drive out the 2nd-3rd shifter shaft. Lift the fork from the case. This shaft and fork operate the synchronizer nearest the front of the case (see Item 6, **FIG 6:8**).

7 Repeat operation 6 on the 1st-Reverse shifter shaft and fork. These operate item 11, **FIG 6:8.**

8 Remove the selector shaft intermediate lever lock pins and remove the shaft and levers from the case. **FIG 6:11** shows this operation in detail.

9 With a pair of round nose pliers remove retainer ring (see item 24, **FIG 6:8**). Refer to **FIG 6:12**) for an enlarged view. The rear extension can now be pulled carefully away from the case leaving the main shaft in position.

10 Gently pull the clutch drive gear (see item 1, **FIG 6:8**) from the case. The bearings, item 4, may fall into the case. Bearing item 38 can remain on the shaft unless slackness or damage to the shaft demands further dismantling.

11 Move item 11, synchronizer, as far to the rear as possible then manoeuvre the mainshaft, item 16 and all its gears out through the rear of the case.

12 Pick out the lock pins, detent balls, etc., which have fallen into the case.

13 With a long punch, drive the shifter shaft detent ball spring plugs out of the case. Do this by inserting the punch through the shaft housings from inside the case.

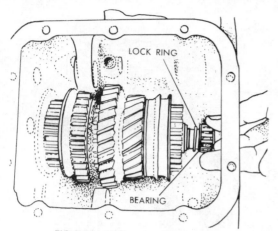

FIG 6:19   Fitting the pilot bearing

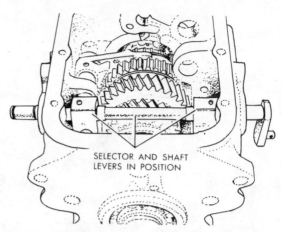

FIG 6:20   Fitting the selector shaft

14 Press out the reverse idler shaft as shown in **FIG 6:13.** The tool can be improvized from a nut, bolt and piece of tube if necessary.

Most of the dismantling is now confined to the mainshaft. Remember that the synchronizers are a selected assembly and must be kept as originally fitted. Do not mix components but lay every part out in order as it is removed. **FIG 6:14** gives a good exploded view of the gearbox.

15 Support the mainshaft vertically with the forward end uppermost. Remove the snap ring (see **FIG 6:15**).

16 Reverse the shaft, making sure that the 2nd-3rd synchronizer ring cannot fall off and then release the speedometer drive gear (see item 14, **FIG 6:8**), by depressing the clamp.

17 With the shaft still in position as for operation 16, remove snap ring 20, Belleville washer 21 and spacer 22 (see **FIG 6:8**). Use a pair of split collars under an arbor press and support the shaft on the 1st gear item 9. Press on the end of the shaft and force the shaft free of all components (including 1st gear, item 9), at the rear of the flange on the shaft. This

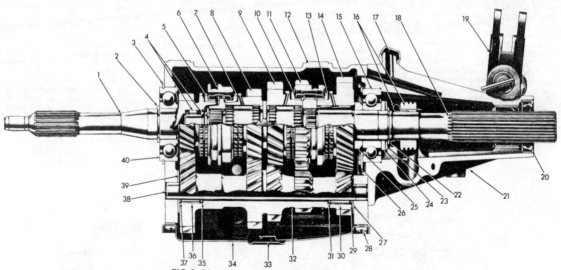

FIG 6:21   Sectional view of 4-speed gearbox

Key to Fig 6:21   1 Clutch drive gear   2 Retaining ring (bearing-to-shaft)   3 Retaining ring (bearing-to-case)   4 Pilot bearing and spacer   5 4th speed synchronizer ring   6 3-4 synchronizer assembly   7 3rd speed synchronizer ring   8 3rd speed gear   9 2nd speed gear   10 2nd speed synchronizer ring   11 1-2 synchronizer assembly   12 Transmission case   13 1st speed synchronizer ring   14 1st speed gear   15 Rear bearing   16 Speedometer gear and clip   17 Vent cap   18 Mainshaft   19 Intermediate shifter lever   20 Rear seal   21 Rear extension   22 Retaining ring (bearing-to-shaft)   23 Belleville washer   24 Spacer   25 Spacer   26 Retaining ring (bearing-to-extension)   27 Thrust washer   28 Cover screw   29 Spacer   30 Roller bearing   31 Spacer   32 Countergear   33 Magnet   34 Cover   35 Spacer   36 Roller bearing   37 Spacer   38 Countergear shaft   39 Thrust washer   40 Clutch gear bearing

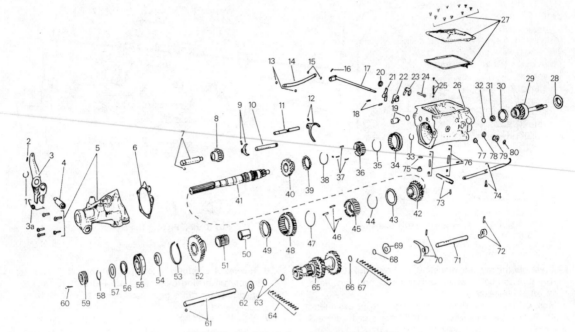

FIG 6:22 Exploded view of 4-speed gearbox

Key to Fig 6:22 1 Intermediate lever bushing snap ring 2 Cotterpin 3 Shift idler lever and spring 4 Intermediate lever bushing 5 Rear extension and retaining bolts 6 Rear extension gasket 7 Reverse idler gearshaft and lock ball 8 Reverse idler gear and bushing assembly 9 Reverse idler gearshift fork and spiral pin 10 Reverse idler gear shifter shaft 11 2-4 speed shifter shaft 12 3-4 speed shift fork and spiral pin 13 Washers 14 Shift control rod 15 Washers 16 Cotterpin 17 Selector shaft 18 Spiral pins 19 Back-up lamp switch and seal ring 20 Selector shaft oil seal 21 3rd-4th speed intermediate shifter lever 22 1st-2nd intermediate shift lever 23 Reverse intermediate lever 24 Reverse intermediate lever pin 25 Reverse shifter shaft detent ball, spring and cap 26 Transmission case 27 Cover gasket, cover and screws 28 Clutch drive gear to housing seal 29 Clutch drive gear assembly 30 4th gear synchronizer ring 31 Mainshaft pilot bearing assembly 32 Pilot bearing spacer ring 33 3-4 speed synchronizer assembly retaining ring 34 3-4 speed synchronizer sleeve 35 Synchronizer spring 36 3-4 synchronizer hub 37 3-4 synchronizer keys 38 Synchronizer spring 39 3rd speed gear synchronizer ring 40 3rd speed gear 41 Mainshaft 42 2nd speed gear 43 2nd speed synchronizer ring 44 Synchronizer spring 45 1st-2nd synchronizer hub 46 1st-2nd synchronizer keys 47 Synchronizer spring 48 1st-2nd synchronizer sleeve 49 1st speed synchronizer ring 50 1st speed gear bushing 51 1st gear needle bearing assembly 52 1st speed gear 53 Rear bearing to extension locking ring 54 Rear bearing spacer ring (front) 55 Mainshaft rear bearing 56 Rear bearing spacer (rear) 57 Belleville washer 58 Rear bearing retaining ring (bearing-to-mainshaft) 59 Speedo drive gear 60 Speedo drive clip 61 Countergear shaft and lock ball 62 Countergear thrust washer 63 Countergear bearing washers 64 Countergear roller bearings (24) 65 Countergear 66 Countergear bearing washer 67 Countergear roller bearings (24) 68 Countergear bearing washer 69 Countergear thrust washer 70 1st-2nd shift fork and spiral pin 71 1st-2nd shift shaft 72 1st-2nd selector lever cam and spiral pin 73 Intermediate lever shaft and pin 74 Shift selector rod, pivot pin and lock ring 75 TCS switch and gasket 76 Shifter shaft detent balls, springs and hole plugs 77 Oil filler plug 78 Selector shaft oil seal 79 Selector shaft adjusting ring 80 Selector shaft locknut

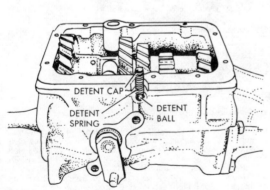

FIG 6:23 Reverse shifter shaft detent components

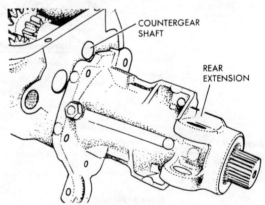

FIG 6:24 Countergear shaft exposed (4-speed)

flange shows up as the largest diameter on item 37, **FIG 6:14**. Store the components carefully as they are released.

18 Reverse the shaft and support under the press on the 2nd gear (see item 8, **FIG 6:8**). Press the shaft from the gears. The mainshaft is now completely dismantled.

19 If the clutch gear bearing must be renewed, remove the snap ring item 2 and press the bearing from the shaft. Refit by reversing this procedure but be sure to apply pressure to the bearing inner race. Use a piece of tube over the shaft to apply the thrust.

Inspection:

Wash all parts in clean fuel or solvent. Examine all gears for chipping, discoloration and damage. Renew as necessary. Repeat for the shafts. Renew the synchronizer rings, keys and springs if any sign of weak synchronizing has been noticed. Examine the bearings for roughness, slack or binding. Renew at the slightest hint of any of these defects.

Reassembly:

Coat all components with SAE 30 gear oil as assembly proceeds.

1 Support the mainshaft with the forward end uppermost. Refer to **FIG 6:8**. Slide the 2nd speed gear, item 8, on the shaft, the cone must face forward and the gear must rotate freely.

2 Slide the synchronizer ring, item 7, onto the gear.

3 Assemble the 2nd-3rd synchronizer, item 6, as follows:
Fit the key springs to the hub as shown in **FIG 6:16** with both spring ends in the same slot and the raised portion of the springs towards the synchronizer (blocker) rings.
Fit the three keys in the hub slots with the arrow on each key facing the front of the shaft.
Slide the sleeve over the hub while holding the keys in position. The shifter fork groove in the sleeve must be nearest the front of the shaft.

4 Press item 6 onto the shaft. Secure with snap ring (see **FIG 6:17**).

5 Assemble the 1st-reverse synchronizer as described for the 2nd-3rd synchronizer, operation 3. The longer key flat and the shifter fork groove must face towards the rear of the shaft.

6 Support the shaft horizontally and slide the 1st speed gear (see item 9, **FIG 6:8**) onto the shaft. The cone must face to the rear and the gear must rotate freely.

7 Slide item 10, 1st speed synchronizer ring, over the 1st speed gear cone.

8 Now assemble item 11, synchronizer, item 23 stop ring, item 24 bearing retainer and item 13, rear bearing to the shaft by pressing the parts together. The bearing retainer must, of course, be free. Make sure the slots in the synchronizer ring align with the keys. If a new rear bearing is fitted, the shielded side faces the rear of the shaft.

9 Fit item 22, spacer, item 21 Belleville washer and secure with snap ring, item 20.

10 Install the speedometer drive gear and clamp, item 14.

11 Slide the assembled shaft into the gearbox extension and secure with the bearing retainer (see **FIG 6:18**).

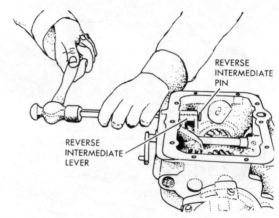

FIG 6:25   Removing reverse intermediate lever pin

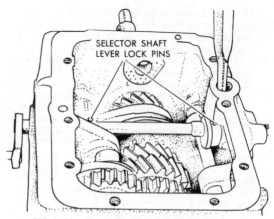

FIG 6:26   Removing selector shaft lock pins

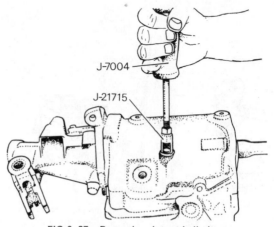

FIG 6:27   Removing detent ball plugs

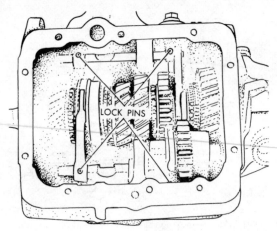

FIG 6:28 Position of shafts preparatory to removing lock pin

12 Fit a new gasket to the extension housing and slide the mainshaft into the gearbox case. Temporarily fit one or two bolts to hold the extension and case together to prevent damage to the gasket.

13 From the front of the case, slide the pilot bearing and lock ring onto the mainshaft (see **FIG 6:19**). Coat the bearing with grease.

14 Fit item 5 (see **FIG 6:8**), 3rd speed synchronizer ring to item 1, clutch drive gear and then insert item 1 into the case, over the pilot bearing and up to the retaining ring item 3, on the bearing, item 38. The mainshaft is now assembled.

Try all the shifter forks on their shafts to see that they slide on freely. If not, remove any burrs or damage until they do assemble easily.

15 Insert the 1st-reverse shifter shaft at the front of the case, notches downwards. Push it through the fork making sure that the shoulder on the fork faces the front of the case. Drive the lock pin home to within $\frac{1}{16}$ inch of the surface.

16 Repeat for the 2nd-3rd speed shifter shaft.

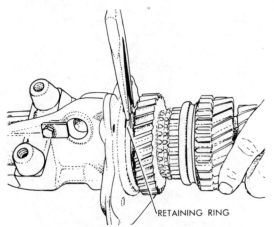

FIG 6:29 Removing rear bearing retainer

17 Install the selector shaft and levers as shown in **FIG 6:20**.

18 Insert the detent balls and springs in their bores and then drive the end plugs home.

19 Remove the bolts fitted temporarily to the extension housing and carefully rotate the housing until the reverse idler gearshaft bore is exposed. Hold the gear in place then drive the shaft through case and gear. Do not omit the lock ball from the shaft.

20 If the dummy shaft was removed from the counter gear it must be re-installed after the roller bearing assemblies are replaced. Thick grease will hold the rollers in place during this operation.

21 Apply grease to the thrust washers (see items 25 and 37, **FIG 6:8**) and stick in position in the case with the lugs in the case slots.

22 Rotate the extension until the counter gearshaft bore is exposed. Lower the counter gear into the case. Fit the lock ball to the shaft then push the shaft through the case, thrust washer, counter · gear, opposite thrust washer and home into the forward face of the case. This will automatically push the dummy shaft out while retaining the roller bearings in place.

23 Align the extension housing in its correct position, fit all the bolts and tighten to 31 lb ft.

24 Refit the external selector linkages and adjust the selector ring until equal movement of the shaft is obtained. Tighten the locknut.

25 Fit the sump with a new gasket and tighten the screws evenly to 48 lb inch.

6:5 Overhauling the 4-speed gearbox

Removal of the shift lever and then the gearbox requires similar methods to those adopted for the 3-speed gearbox (see **Section 6:4**).

Work on the 4-speed gearbox demands a special tool for releasing the shifter shaft detent balls. This is illustrated and described in this Section. Refer to **FIGS 6:21** and **6:22** for assembled and exploded views of the components.

Dismantling:

1 Remove the switches and external selector linkages as described for the 3-speed gearbox.

2 Turn the gearbox until the sump is uppermost. Unscrew the cover screws evenly, so that the cover is not distorted. **Note that the reverse shifter shaft detent ball, spring and cap are held in place by the cover** (see **FIG 6:23**). Discard the gasket and invert the gearbox to drain the oil. Store the detent ball, spring and cap.

3 Remove the rear extension housing bolts and rotate the housing relative to the main case so that the counter gearshaft is exposed (see **FIG 6:24**). Do not pull the housing and case apart at this stage.

4 Make up a dummy counter gearshaft slightly smaller in diameter than the real shaft and shorter in length than the counter gear itself. Drive the dummy shaft through the counter gear from the front of the box thereby driving the counter gearshaft out. Do not lose the lock ball fitted to the shaft. This will emerge

from the end of the shaft nearest the extension housing. Leave the dummy shaft in place to retain the counter gear roller races then lift the counter gear out followed by the thrust washers.

5 Refer to **FIG 6 : 25.** Slide the reverse shifter shaft to the rear then drive out the reverse intermediate pin and remove the reverse intermediate lever.

6 Return the transmission to neutral then position the selector shaft so that the lock pins are vertical. **FIG 6 : 26** shows the method of driving the lock pins out. Drive the pin out of the 3rd-4th speed lever cam first followed by the 1st-2nd speed lever cam. Remove the shaft.

7 The special tool referred to in the first paragraph is now needed to remove the plugs holding the 1st-2nd and 3rd-4th speed detent balls and springs. **FIG 6 : 27** shows the tool in use.

8 Move the shifter shafts to the position shown in **FIG 6 : 28** then drive out the lock pins beginning with the 1st-2nd lever pin.

9 From the rear of the box drive out the 1st-2nd shaft and remove the shifter fork. Push the 3rd-4th shaft rearwards until the shifter fork can be lifted clear.

10 Remove the clutch drive gear (see item 1, **FIG 6 : 21**), then carefully pull the extension housing and mainshaft assembly from the rear of the box. Discard the gasket.

11 The 3rd-4th shifter shaft can now be driven out by using a punch through the clutch drive gear bearing aperture in the front of the box.

12 Press the reverse idler shaft out from front to rear using a nut, bolt and piece of suitable tube. **FIG 6 : 13** shows the method being applied to the 3rd speed box.

13 Use a brass drift and drive the reverse shifter shaft out. The shaft must be driven out towards the rear of the box.

14 Carefully collect all lock pins, bearing rollers, etc. which may have fallen into the box during dismantling.

15 Remove the snap ring from the rear bearing as shown in **FIG 6 : 29** and slide the extension housing from the main shaft. Depress the clamp and slide the speedometer drive gear from the mainshaft.

16 The 3rd-4th speed synchronizer sleeve, ring, springs and keys can now be removed. Note that these are a selected assembly and must be kept with the 3rd-4th speed synchronizer hub.

17 Remove the snap ring from the front of the shaft then reverse the shaft and remove the rear snap ring, Belleville washer and spacer (see items 22, 23 and 24, **FIG 6 : 21**).

18 Support the shaft on the 2nd speed gear (see item 9, **FIG 6 : 21**), and press on the rear of the shaft. Remove the rear bearing, 1st speed gear, 1st-2nd synchronizer and 2nd speed gear. Keep the synchronizer components together and separate from the 3rd-4th synchronizer.

19 Reverse the shaft and support it on the 3rd speed gear. Press on the front of the shaft and remove the 3rd-4th synchronizer hub and 3rd speed gear. This completes the dismantling of the mainshaft.

20 If the clutch drive gear assembly is damaged, the snap ring (see item 2, **FIG 6 : 21**), must be removed and the bearing pressed off.

21 Removal of the dummy shaft from the counter gear will release the roller bearings for inspection.

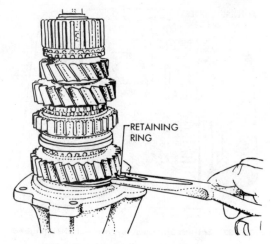

FIG 6 : 30   Fitting rear bearing retainer

Inspection:

Wash all parts in clean fuel or solvent. Examine the gears for chipping, discoloration and damage. Renew where necessary. Repeat for the shafts. Renew any worn or damaged synchronizer parts, particularly the blocker rings (see items 30, 39, 43 and 49, **FIG 6 : 22**). The hubs and sliding sleeves must be renewed as a pair. Pay attention to the bearings, looking closely for roughness, slack or binding. Renew if any of these defects are apparent.

Reassembly:

Coat all components with SAE.90 gear oil as assembly proceeds.

1 Refer to **FIG 6 : 21.** Slide the 3rd speed gear, item 8, onto the mainshaft from the front. The coned seating for the blocker ring must face forward and the gear must spin freely pn the shaft.

2 Fit the blocker (synchronizer) ring, item 7, to the 3rd speed gear.

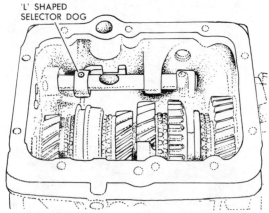

FIG 6 : 31   Fitting the 1st-2nd speed shifter shaft

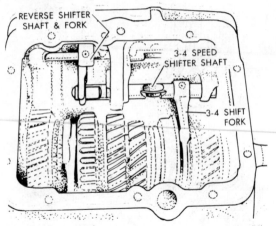

FIG 6:32   3rd-4th and reverse shifter shafts installed

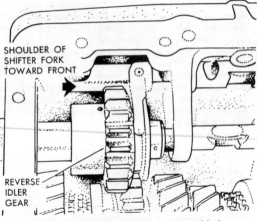

FIG 6:34   Reverse idler gear assembled

3 Fit the springs to the 3rd-4th synchronizer hub. Reference to **FIG 6:16** will show how to position the springs. The method is the same for both 3 and 4-speed transmissions.

4 Press the 3rd-4th speed synchronizer hub (see item 36, **FIG 6:22**) onto the front of the mainshaft and secure with the snap ring, item 33.

5 Reverse the mainshaft and slide the 2nd speed gear into place (see item 42, **FIG 6:22**). This gear must turn freely onto the mainshaft. Fit the blocker ring, item 43, to the 2nd speed gear.

6 Fit the springs to the 1st-2nd speed synchronizer hub, item 45, in exactly the same way that the springs were fitted to the 3rd-4th speed hub (see Operation 3).

7 Fit the keys (see item 46, **FIG 6:22**), to the hub, item 45 then slide the sleeve, item 48, over the hub.

8 Fit the 1st-2nd speed synchronizer assembly to the mainshaft then slide items 49 to 54 into place. Align the slots in the blocker rings with the keys.

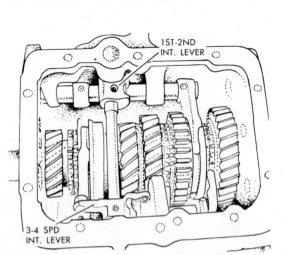

FIG 6:33   Installing selector shaft

9 Press the bearing, item 55, onto the shaft by applying pressure to the inner race element. Fit items 56 to 60. Note that the concave side of item 57, Belleville washer, must face the bearing.

10 Position the mainshaft assembly in the rear extension housing and secure with the snap ring (see **FIG 6:30**).

11 At the front of the mainshaft assemble the 3rd-4th speed synchronizer keys and sleeve to the hub. The springs were assembled at operation 3. The arrows on the keys point towards the front of the shaft.

12 Coat a new gasket with jointing cement and fit to the rear extension then slide the assembled mainshaft and rear extension into the main case.
   Do not bolt together at this stage.

13 From the front of the main case fit the spacer and needle bearing (see item 4, **FIG 6:21**) to the nose of the mainshaft then fit items 1, 2, 3, 40 and 5 in place. These are, of course, pre-assembled. Coat the needle bearing with grease before assembly.

14 Check that all the selector and shifter shaft components assemble easily then coat with oil.

15 Assemble the 1st-2nd speed shifter shaft, detent notches downwards (towards detent ball bores) from the front towards the rear of the main case. Pass it first through the 'L' shaped selector dog then through the shifter fork. **FIG 6:31** shows how the dog and shifter fork must be positioned. Drive the lock pins in to within $\frac{1}{16}$ inch of the surface of the dog and shifter fork.

16 Fit the 3rd-4th shifter shaft in the same way as the 1st-2nd shifter shaft then install the reverse shifter shaft from the rear of the case. **In this instance the detent notches face upwards. FIG 6:32** clearly shows the arrangement of these two shafts.

17 Fit the transverse selector shaft, passing it through the 3rd-4th speed intermediate lever first then through the 1st-2nd speed lever. Refer to **FIG 6:33**. Fit the lock pins.

18 Engage the reverse intermediate lever with the 3rd-4th speed intermediate lever and fit the pivot pin. The end play between lever and pin should be .004 inch to .012 inch. **FIG 6:25** shows this pin and lever.

19 Invert the case and fit the 1st-2nd and 3rd-4th speed shifter shaft detent balls and springs then drive the end plugs home. **FIG 6:27** shows the location of these. Turn the case over again.

20 Rotate the rear extension housing until the reverse idler gearshaft bore is exposed. Fit the lock ball to the shaft, position the gear in the case and push the shaft home. **FIG 6:34** shows how the components should assemble.

21 If the dummy shaft was left in position in the counter gear it will assemble without further work. If however the shaft was removed the needle rollers will have fallen out. In this case, smear some grease in the roller race bores at each end of the counter gear and then insert a washer, 24 rollers and another washer at each end. Insert the dummy shaft.

22 Coat the thrust washers with grease and stick these at each end of the counter gear position in the main case. The lugs must fit into the slots in casting. Turn the rear extension housing until the counter gearshaft bore is exposed. Fit the lock ball to the counter gearshaft.

23 Position the counter gear in the case being careful not to dislodge the thrust washers. Push the shaft home, pushing the dummy shaft out through the front of the case in the process.

24 Align the rear extension housing and fit the bolts. Tighten these evenly to 31 lb ft.

25 Refit the external gearshift links by reversing the dismantling process.

26 Engage 2nd speed and turn the gearbox on its side. Fit the shift lever temporarily then adjust the selector ring (see **FIG 6:4**), so that the ball form at the end of the shift finger has equal clearance at each side of the intermediate shift lever. This lever is identified in **FIG 6:3**. Turn the selector ring back a $\frac{1}{4}$ turn then tighten the locknut. Check the shift operation and if correct remove the shift lever. Turn the gearbox with the sump uppermost.

27 Fit the reverse shifter shaft detent ball, spring and cap (see **FIG 6:23**).

28 Fit a new gasket, install the sump and tighten the screws to 48 lb inch.

6:6 Lubrication

Use SAE.80 or 90 gear oil to specification AP1-GL-5. Refill the gearbox after installation using a syringe or special plastic bottle oil pack. With the transmission cold the oil level should be $\frac{1}{2}$ inch below the filler plug hole.

6:7 Fault diagnosis

(a) Inadvertent gear disengagement

1 Broken or collapsed shifter detent ball spring
2 Worn shifter fork
3 Worn synchronizer or gear dogs

(b) Noisy transmission

1 Low oil level
2 Worn counter gear bearings (noise on all gears)
3 Worn pilot bearing (noise on 1st, 2nd and 3rd)
4 Worn roller race on mainshaft (noise in 1st gear)
5 Worn or damaged mainshaft bearings (noise on all gears)
6 Damaged gear teeth

(c) Difficulty in gear engagement

1 Sticking clutch
2 Worn synchronizer blocker rings
3 Weak synchronizer key springs
4 Incorrect selector ring adjustment

CHAPTER 7

AUTOMATIC TRANSMISSION

7:1 Description
7:2 Maintenance and adjustment

7:3 Removing and refitting transmission

7:1 Description

The automatic transmission may be specified as either the Powerglide or Torque Drive unit. The former is completely automatic in operation, whereas the latter has the automatic shift mechanism removed. In this case the change of gear ratio is made manually by the driver. The units are basically similar and the description which follows applies to both except for the valve mechanism which is much simplified for the Torque Drive Transmission.

Refer to **FIG 7:1.** This shows the Powerglide transmission in sectional form. A three element hydraulic torque converter is bolted to the engine drive plate and is coupled to a two-speed and reverse epicyclic gear train. At the front of the transmission case a gear type oil pump is attached to the torque converter and provides hydraulic pressure for gear operation and lubrication as soon as the engine starts. Behind the oil pump and inside the main case is the high forward gear clutch. This locks the planet carrier to the output shaft at the appropriate conditions of road speed and load. To the rear of this clutch is the epicyclic gear train which provides low forward gear and reverse. Release of the high forward gear clutch automatically directs the drive through the gear train for low forward gear. The reverse clutch which

locks the gear case to the transmission case is located outside the gear case to the rear of the grear train. The governor is mounted on the output shaft inside the extension housing. Below the gear assembly is the valve block and below that, the oil sump. The Powerglide transmission has a connection from the throttle so that a kickdown facility is provided for overtaking. Fully depressing the throttle causes the transmission to change from high to low gear.

The Torque Drive valve block is distinguished by case letters 'TD'. All valves except the pressure regulator, hydraulic modulator and manual shift have been eliminated. There is no connection to the throttle, therefore the rod locating hole is missing from the range selector lever.

It must be noted that the Powerglide and Torque Drive transmissions have only one oil pump and that this is engine driven. There is no secondary pump driven from the road wheels. For this reason the car cannot be tow started and must not be towed on its rear wheels for more than 50 miles or at speeds higher than 35 mile/hr. For distances or speeds in excess of these figures either raise the rear wheels and tow on the front wheels with the steering secured in the straight-ahead position or disconnect the propeller shaft. The latter is the best

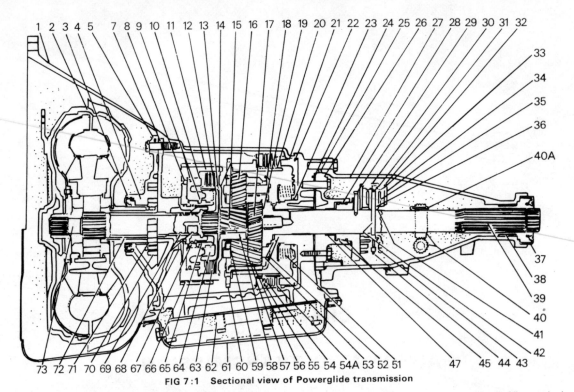

FIG 7:1 Sectional view of Powerglide transmission

Key to Fig 7:1 1 Transmission case 2 Welded converter 3 Oil pump seal assembly 4 Oil pump body 5 Oil pump body square ring seal 7 Oil pump cover 8 Clutch relief valve ball 9 Clutch piston inner and outer seal 10 Clutch piston 11 Clutch drum 12 Clutch hub 13 Clutch hub thrust washer 14 Clutch flange retainer ring 15 Low sun gear and clutch flange assembly 16 Planet short pinion 17 Planet input sun gear 18 Plant carrier 19 Planet input sun gear thrust washer 20 Ring gear 21 Reverse piston 22 Reverse piston outer seal 23 Reverse piston inner seal 24 Governor support gasket 25 Extension seat ring 26 Governor support 27 Extension 28 Governor hub 29 Governor hub drive screw 30 Governor body 31 Governor shaft retainer clip 32 Governor outer weight retainer ring 33 Governor inner weight retainer ring 34 Governor outer weight 35 Governor spring 36 Governor inner weight 37 Extension rear oil seal 38 Extension rear bushing 39 Output shaft 40 Speedometer drive and driven gear 40a Speedometer driven gear retaining clip 41 Governor shaft urethane washer 42 Governor shaft 43 Governor valve 44 Governor valve retaining clip 45 Governor hub seal rings 47 Governor support thrust bearing 51 Reverse piston return springs, retainer and retainer ring 52 Transmission rear case bushing 53 Output shaft pinion 54 Reverse clutch pack 54a Reverse clutch cushion spring (waved) 55 Pinion thrust washer 56 Planet long pinion 57 Low sun gear needle thrust bearing 58 Low sun gear bushing (splined) 59 Pinion thrust washer 60 Parking lock gear 61 Transmission oil pan 62 Valve body 63 High clutch pack 64 Clutch piston return spring, retainer and retainer ring 65 Clutch drum bushing 66 Low brake band 67 High clutch seal rings 68 Clutch drum thrust washer (selective) 69 Turbine shaft seal rings 70 Oil pump driven gear 71 Oil pump drive gear 72 Stator shaft 73 Input shaft

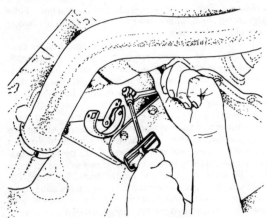

FIG 7:2 Adjusting the low band

method if there is any doubt about the proper operation of the transmission. Whenever the car is towed on its rear wheels without disconnecting the propeller shaft, ensure that the selector is at the 'N' (neutral) position.

7:2 Maintenance and adjustment

(a) Oil lever check, draining and refilling transmission:

The oil level should be checked every 6000 miles or 4 months whichever is the earlier. Only General Motors 'DEXRON' Automatic Transmission Fluid is to be used. The correct grade for the Powerglide or Torque Drive transmissions is available against Part Nos. 1050568, 69 or 70.

Transmission hot 180°F:

The car should be driven for several miles at varying speeds with frequent stops and starts. This will ensure

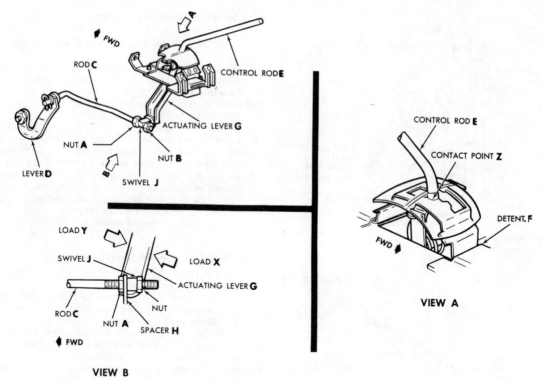

FIG 7:3 Selector linkage adjustment

that the oil is at the proper temperature. Place the car on a level surface with the engine idling, the selector lever in 'park' and the parking brake fully on. Remove and inspect the dipstick. If necessary add oil to bring the level to the full mark on the dipstick. Note that 1 pint of oil raises the level from the 'ADD' to the 'FULL' mark.

Transmission cold 60° to 80°F:

Place the car on a level surface and fully apply the parking brake. Start, but do not race the engine, allow to idle and move the selector lever through all positions and return to 'park'. Immediately check the fluid level with the engine idling. If necessary add fluid to bring the level $\frac{1}{4}$ inch below the full mark on the dipstick. This will allow for expansion as the transmission warms up.

Never overfill the transmission. It is intended that the planetary unit shall not run in oil; if the oil level is too high, the planetary unit will cause foaming and aeration and this aerated oil passed into the valve chambers will give rise to malfunctioning and overheating.

Every 24,000 miles normal use, or 12,000 miles if the transmission is used daily in very hot weather in city traffic, the oil must be changed.

Position the vehicle on a level surface, run the engine for one minute at a low speed in neutral, stop the engine and remove the drain plug. Do not change the oil immediately after a run when the transmission is at operating temperature since the oil will be hot enough to cause serious scalding. With a clean cloth, wipe the

drain plug and its seating then replace and tighten fully. Remove the dipstick and add 3 US pints (2½ Imperial pints) of 'Dexron' transmission fluid. Start the engine and move the selector through all the ranges. With the engine idling check the oil level, it should be as specified for the 'oil level check, transmission cold'.

(b) Low band adjustment:

This must be carried out at the time of the first oil change or sooner if slip in low is noticed. Special torque tool J.21848 is essential and if not available the adjustment must be made by a Chevrolet Service Agent. If the tool is available proceed as follows:

1 Place the selector in neutral and raise the car enough to obtain access to the underside.
2 Refer to **FIG 7:2.** Remove the protective cap from the adjusting screw and slacken the locknut a $\frac{1}{4}$ turn. Hold in this position with a wrench. **This is important.**
3 Apply special tool J.21848 and tighten the adjusting screw to 70 lb inch. If the transmission has covered less than 6000 miles, back off the screw exactly four turns. If the transmission has covered more than 6000 miles, back the screw off three turns. These back off figures are critical and not approximate. Tighten the locknut to 15 lb ft without distrubing the setting.
4 Replace the protective cap and lower the car to the ground.

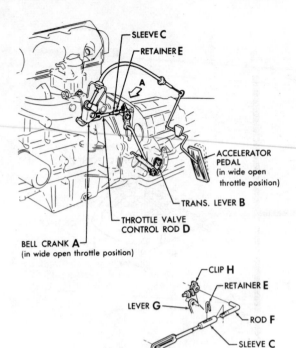

SLEEVE **C**

RETAINER **E**

A

ACCELERATOR
PEDAL
(in wide open
throttle position)

TRANS. LEVER **B**

THROTTLE VALVE
CONTROL ROD **D**

BELL CRANK **A**
(in wide open throttle position)

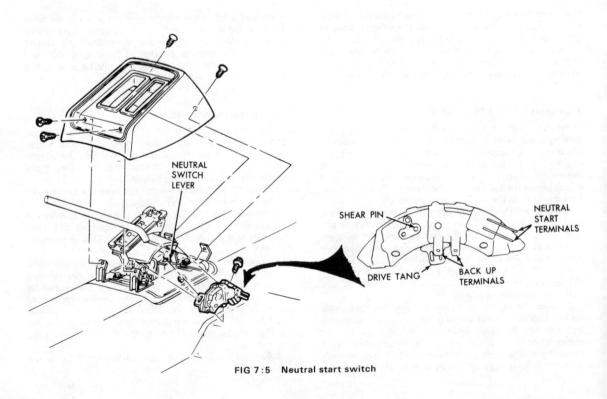

CLIP **H**

RETAINER **E**

LEVER **G**

ROD **F**

SLEEVE **C**

THROTTLE VALVE
CONTROL ROD **D**

BELL CRANK
LEVER STUD **A**

FIG 7:4   Throttle valve linkage adjustment

(c) Selector linkage adjustment

Refer to **FIG 7:3**.

1 Temporarily assemble nuts A and B with swivel J to rod C.
2 Move the transmission lever D clockwise to the 'PARK' detent then anticlockwise two detent positions to 'NEUTRAL'.
3 Refer to view 'A' and set the control rod E in the 'NEUTRAL' notch.
4 Press on the actuating lever 'G' in the direction of arrow 'Y' until the rod 'E' makes contact at point 'Z'.
5 Holding the actuating lever and rod in position obtain .073 inch gap between nut 'A' and swivel 'J'. This is shown in view 'B' as a spacer 'H'. A set of feeler gauges will serve as the spacer. Tighten nut 'A' until the gauge or spacer is just gripped between the nut and swivel. Remove the gauge or spacer.
6 Tighten nut B against the swivel J.

(d) Throttle valve link adjustment:

Refer to **FIG 7:4**.

1 Depress the accelerator fully.
2 The bell crank 'A' must now be in the wide open throttle position and the transmission lever 'B' against the internal stop.
3 Fit the rod 'D' to lever 'A' and adjust the sleeve 'C' to align rod 'F' with the hole in lever 'G'. A tolerance of plus or minus one turn is allowed.
4 Insert the retainer 'E' through the sleeve 'C' and rod 'F'. Attach the clip 'H' to lever 'G' and rod 'F'.

NEUTRAL
SWITCH
LEVER

SHEAR PIN

NEUTRAL
START
TERMINALS

DRIVE TANG

BACK UP
TERMINALS

FIG 7:5   Neutral start switch

(e) Neutral safety switch renewal:

Refer to **FIG 7:5**.

This switch cannot be repaired; renew as described in this paragraph.

1 Remove the four screws holding the floor console and lift clear.
2 Note the position of the electrical connections and the cable colour code. Identify the cables and remove from the neutral start terminals and the back-up light switch.
3 Place the shift lever in neutral, remove the two screws holding the indicator plate then the two holding the curved cover and finally the two holding the switch assembly.
4 Tilt switch to the right and lift out.
5 See that the shift lever is in neutral then assemble the new switch to the bracket by inserting the drive tang into the hole in the neutral switch lever and fitting the two screws.
6 Replace the curved cover and indicator plate. Move the shift lever from neutral to shear the plastic locating pin in the switch.
7 Remake the electrical connections and check that the engine will start in 'Neutral' or 'Park' positions only. Check that the back-up light is illuminated in 'Reverse'.
8 Refit the console.

7:3 Removing and refitting transmission

It is not possible for the transmission to be overhauled by the average private owner due to the quantity of special tools which are required. In addition, the need for clean room conditions and expert diagnostic skill make this essentially an operation for the Chevrolet Service Station. There is no reason, however, why the transmission should not be removed and refitted by the owner if necessary. Proceed as follows:

1 Disconnect the battery.
2 Raise the vehicle and drain the transmission oil.
3 Disconnect the vacuum modulator line, throttle valve rod (Powerglide), manual control lever and speedometer cable.
4 Disconnect the propeller shaft as described in **Chapter 5.**
5 Place a jack with its head protected by a piece of soft wood under the transmission and just take the weight. Disconnect the transmission from the frame crossmember then disconnect and remove the crossmember.
6 Remove the convertor underpan, and mark the convertor and drive plate for correct reassembly. Remove the drive plate to convertor bolts.
7 Place a jack under the engine sump then remove the convertor housing to engine bolts.
8 Carefully remove the transmission rearwards watching the convertor to see that it comes away from the drive plate and moves with the transmission. Take the greatest care to see that it does not fall out as the transmission is lowered. A piece of strong wire across the convertor housing will hold the convertor in place. The transmission can now be removed from below the car.

Refitting the transmission is a reversal of the removal procedure. The convertor housing to engine and convertor to drive plate bolts must be tightened to 30-35 lb ft. Refill the transmission with oil as described in **Section 7:2**. Road test the car and see that the shift points (Powerglide) are in agreement with the chart in **Technical Data.**

CHAPTER 8

THE PROPELLER SHAFT, REAR AXLE AND REAR SUSPENSION

8:1 Description

The rear suspension components and the axle are shown in **FIG 8:1**. A tubular propeller shaft with a sliding splined sleeve at the forward end takes the drive from the transmission to a rigid rear axle. The universal joints are packed with lubricant and need no periodic maintenance or grease gun application. Coil springs and four links provide the suspension and axle location. Telescopic shock absorbers are mounted between the axle and frame and a stabilizer bar can be fitted between the lower control arms as an optional extra. The differential unit is a hypoid gear and pinion design in which all gear adjustments are made by shim washers.

8:2 Servicing the universal joints

Remove the propeller shaft as described in **Chapter 5, Section 5:3**. Refer to **FIG 8:2**. Dismantle the joints as follows:

1 Scribe a line on the sliding sleeve yoke and a corresponding line on the shaft. This will indicate the front of the shaft and its relationship to the sleeve. Refitting the shaft 180 deg. out could lead to shaft vibrations.

2 Prise the snap rings from the bearings then support the shaft on the bench with the yoke in a vice (see **FIG 8:3**). A solid spacer slightly smaller than the bearing is placed at one side and a piece of tube $1\frac{1}{4}$ inch inside diameter is held at the other side for the bearing cup to pass into as the vice is tightened. Press the cup out as far as possible; it may be necessary to grip the cup in the vice and work the shaft about to release the cup finally. Reverse the yoke and press the trunnion in the opposite direction to release the other bearing.

3 The shaft and sleeve can now be disconnected. Repeat the operation to release the other two bearings at the sleeve end of the shaft and also those at the axle end.

Wash all components in clean fuel and inspect for damage. If renewal is indicated, a repair kit consisting of a trunnion, bearings, cups, seals and snap rings is available (see **FIG 8:4**).

Assemble the joint as follows:

1 Press a seal onto each arm of the trunnion with the cavity in the seal facing outwards. A suitably sized piece of pipe is needed for this operation.

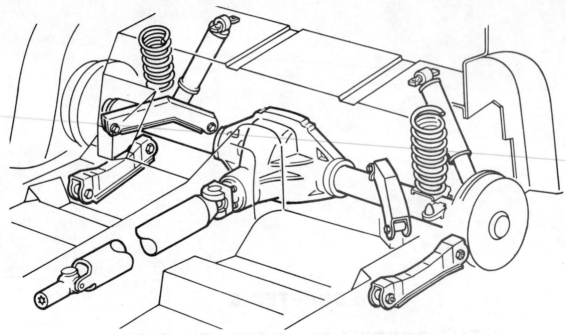

FIG 8:1   Major component layout, rear suspension and drive

2 Insert a quantity of good quality, water repellent chassis grease into each bearing cup and then load with the roller bearings. Make sure that the bottom of the cup is well filled with grease to provide a lubricant reservoir.

3 Fit the trunnion in position in the sleeve yoke then press one bearing into the yoke just far enough to hold it in place. Enter the trunnion into this bearing, support it and press the other bearing in. See that the trunnion is guided into this bearing and continue pressing in until the snap ring can be fitted. Reverse

the sleeve, press the first bearing home and fit the snap ring. Make sure that the trunnion can move freely.

4 Align the sleeve and trunnion with the scribed mark on the shaft and fit the trunnion into place in the shaft yoke. Press the bearing cups in from each side as described at operation 3. Fit the snap rings and check for freedom of movement.

5 Repeat operation 4 for the trunnion at the axle end of the shaft. Tape the two bearing cups which are to be held by the drive flange 11 bolts so that they cannot fall off when the shaft is being re-installed.

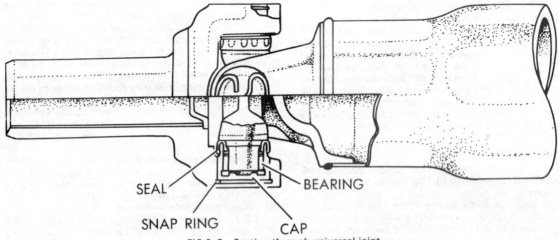

FIG 8:2   Section through universal joint

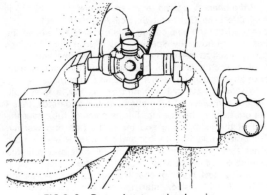

FIG 8:3   Removing trunnion bearings

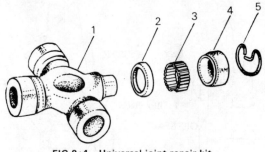

FIG 8:4   Universal joint repair kit

Key to Fig 8:4   1 Trunnion   2 Seal   3 Bearings   4 Cap
5 Snap ring

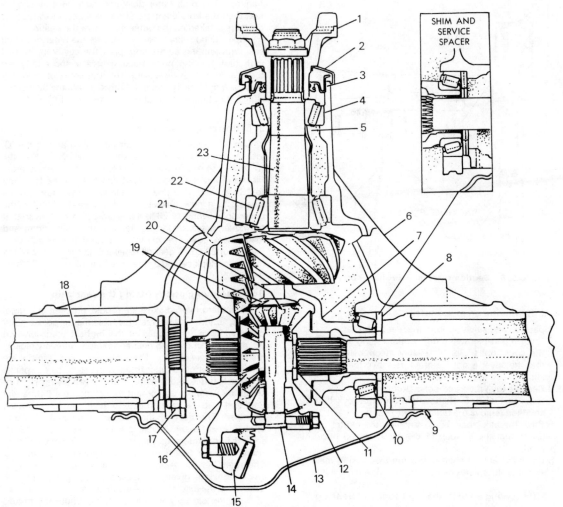

FIG 8:5   Section through differential assembly

Key to Fig 8:5   1 Companion flange   2 Deflector   3 Pinion oil seal   4 Pinion front bearing   5 Pinion bearing spacer
6 Differential carrier   7 Differential case   8 Shim   9 Gasket   10 Differential bearing   11 'C' lock   12 Pinion shaft lock bolt
13 Cover   14 Pinion shaft   15 Ring gear   16 Side gear   17 Bearing cap   18 Axle shaft   19 Thrust washer   20 Differential
pinion   21 Shim   22 Pinion rear bearing   23 Drive pinion

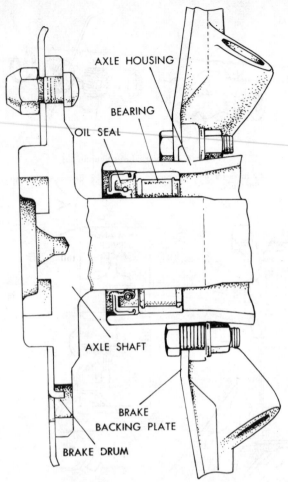

AXLE HOUSING

BEARING

OIL SEAL

AXLE SHAFT

BRAKE
BACKING PLATE

BRAKE DRUM

FIG 8:6   Section through axle shaft bearing

8:3 Removing an axle shaft

1 Jack up and safely support the rear of the car.
2 Place a pan below the differential casing and remove the cover bolts. Do this evenly at opposite bolts so that the cover is not distorted. Remove the cover and allow the oil to drain into the pan.
3 Remove the wheel and brake drum.
4 Refer to **FIG 8:5**. Remove pinion shaft lock bolt 12 and then remove the pinion shaft 14.
5 Push the axle shaft 18, in towards the centre of the car so that the 'C' lock 11 can be extracted from the shaft.
6 Carefully pull the shaft out of the axle casing making sure that the splines do not cut the oil seal.

8:4 Renewing an axle shaft oil seal and bearing

Refer to **FIG 8:6**.

To remove the oil seal, insert the axle shaft so that the groove for the 'C' lock catches behind the steel case of the oil seal. Press on the shaft and prise the seal from the axle taking care not to damage the bore of the axle casing.

If the bearing is to be renewed, special tool J.22813 is available from Chevrolet Service Agents for pulling the bearing from the axle casing. It is possible to remove the bearing without the special tool if workshop facilities can be used to make up a thick steel bar long enough to contact each side of the bearing outer track and narrow enough to push through the bearing into place. A half inch tapped hole in the centre of the bar, a long bolt, washer and piece of tube complete the apparatus. Insert the bar behind the bearing. Fit the piece of tube over the end of the axle casing and insert the bolt and washer. The bolt screws into the bar and the washer seats on the outer face of the tube. Tighten the bolt and pull the bearing out of the axle into the piece of tube.

To fit a new bearing, coat the bore of the axle casing with a thin film of oil, start the bearing squarely in the bore then drive hard home with a length of pipe and hammer. The pipe outer diameter must be only slightly less than the bore diameter of the axle casing so that the pressure is taken on the outer element of the bearing. Wipe the bore dry, coat the outside diameter of the oil seal with jointing compound, pack the cavity in the seal with high melting point bearing grease and gently tap the seal into the axle casing. Use the piece of pipe that was used to fit the bearing and drive in until the face of the seal is just below the end of the axle (see **FIG 8:6**).

8:5 Refitting an axle shaft

Carefully slide the axle shaft into place and fit the 'C' lock in the groove. Pull the shaft outwards so that the 'C' lock is seated in the counter bore in the bevel pinion. Fit the differential pinion shaft and tighten the lock bolt to 125 lb inch. See that the axle and cover surfaces are clean, use a new gasket and fit the cover. Tighten the cover bolts evenly to 20 lb ft in a crosswise pattern so that the cover is not distorted. Replace the brake drum and road wheel. Lower the car to the ground. Fill the axle with SAE.80 or 90 GL-S gear oil to level with the bottom of the filler hole. Replace and tighten the filler plug.

8:6 Removing and refitting the rear axle

All modern hypoid axles are robust, efficient and quiet running units. These features are made possible by manufacturing techniques of the highest precision and the assembly of the ring gear and pinion with very closely maintained clearances. The ring gear and pinion are accurately matched and fitted only as a pair. Special purpose gauges and a large quantity of varying sizes of shims are essential equipment for setting up a differential unit that can be guaranteed to give the long service expected. The cost of the gauges alone make it quite uneconomic for the private owner (even if he is skilled enough) to undertake the repair of a defective differential unit. For this reason the axle must be given to a Chevrolet Service Agent in exchange for a new unit. Instructions are given in succeeding paragraphs for the removal of the axle and its re-installation.

1 Jack the car up and support safely under the frame. Place a jack at each side under the axle and raise the axle slightly.
2 Remove both road wheels and brake drums. Be careful that the footbrake pedal is not depressed until the brake drums are refitted.

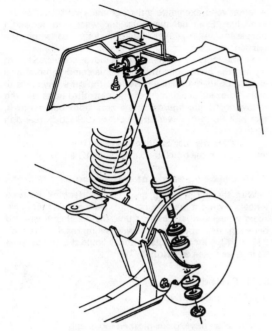

FIG 8:7   Shock absorber mounting

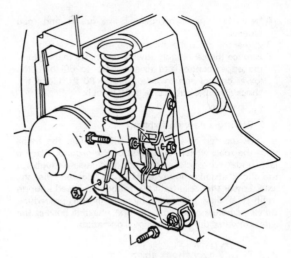

FIG 8:8   Lower control arm detail

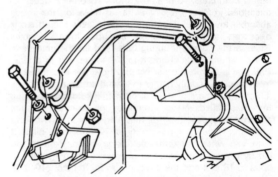

FIG 8:9   Upper control arm detail

3 Remove the propeller shaft (see **Chapter 5, Section 5:3**).

4 Remove both axle shafts (see **Section 8:3**).

5 Disconnect the shock absorbers at their lower ends.

6 Release the upper control arms from the axle.

7 Release the brake pipe line from the clips on the axle casing then undo the bolts holding the brake back plates to the axle flanges. Leave the brakes assembled to the back plates, manoeuvre the brakes from the axle and tie up to the frame. Exercise the greatest care not to bend or damage the brake lines. This procedure obviates the need to bleed the brake hydraulic system.

8 Release the lower control arms at the axle pivots.

9 Lower the jacks under the axle until the pressure on the coil springs is relieved then lift the springs complete with the top and bottom insulators away from their seats. The axle can now be removed from below the car.

Refitting the axle:

1 Position the axle below the car and raise until the coil springs are held in their seatings. Check that the springs are in place then continue lifting until the axle is in approximately the correct relationship to the frame.

2 Fit the upper and lower control arms but do not fully tighten the bolts at this stage.

3 Refit the brake assemblies and replace the hydraulic pipe line in the clips on the axle casing.

4 Refit the axle shafts (see **Section 8:5**).

5 Connect the propeller shaft. Tighten the trunnion U-bolts to 14 lb ft.

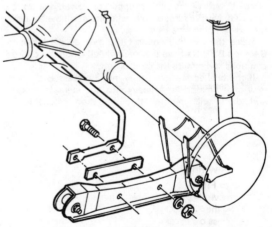

FIG 8:10   Stabilizer bar installation

6 Refit the shock absorbers, brake drums and road wheels.

7 Lower the car to the ground and refill the axle with oil.

8 Bounce the car up and down a few times then tighten the upper control arm to axle bolts to 60 lb ft, the lower control arm to axle bolts to 80 lb ft and the shock absorber nut to axle to 80 lb inch.

8:7 Fitting a new coil spring

Jack the car up and support safely under the frame with the road wheels well clear of the ground. Place a jack under each side of the axle and raise enough for the shock absorber lower ends to be released from the axle. Lower the jacks until the spring is relieved enough to lift clear. Fit a new spring by reversing this procedure. Be very careful not to strain the brake flexible hose as the axle is lowered during the removal operation.

8:8 Fitting new shock absorbers

Shock absorbers cannot be repaired and after an extended mileage must be renewed. Unless the car has covered a very low mileage and a shock absorber has failed prematurely or been accidentally damaged, always renew both units. To fit a new shock absorber proceed as described in **Section 8:7** as far as releasing the shock absorber lower end. Do not lower the jacks more than is necessary to free the shock absorber from the axle. Release the upper mounting bolts and lift the unit clear. Keep the unit vertical and grip the lower end in a vice. Pull and push on the casing and note the resistance. It must be considerably harder to extend it than to compress it. Easy movement or signs of oil seepage confirm that the unit has failed. Never compress or extend a shock absorber except when it is held vertically in its working position. There is a possibility of aerating the oil if it is moved when horizontal or upside down. Refit to the car by reversing the removal process, tightening the top bolts to 18 lb ft and the lower nut to 80 lb inch. **FIG 8:7** shows the mounting details.

8:9 Fitting new control arms

FIGS 8:8 and **8:9** show the installation of the control arms. If both arms, either upper or lower, are to be renewed, always remove and refit one at a time to avoid the axle slipping sideways.

Raise the car and support the axle as described in **Section 8:7**. Remove the road wheel. Undo the control arm bolts and release the control arm.

If the bushes are worn they may be pressed out and new ones pressed in. A heavy vice and suitable spacers and drifts will perform this operation satisfactorily.

Alternatively, exchange arms complete with bushes are available. Examine the bolts for wear and renew if necessary. Always use genuine Vega parts on the suspension.

Fit the arms by reversing the removal process. Do not tighten the pivot bolts until the car is standing on a level surface on its road wheels. Bounce the car a few times to settle the suspension then tighten the bolts to the following torque figures: upper arm, front bolt 60 lb ft, rear bolt 60 lb ft, lower arm, front bolt, 80 lb ft, rear bolt 80 lb ft.

If a stabilizer bar is fitted between the lower control arms, tighten the bolts to 36 lb ft (see **FIG 8:10**).

8:10 Checking height of suspension

With the car standing on a level surface on its road wheels, without passengers but with a full fuel tank, spare wheel and jack in the trunk, the distance measured between the upper and lower spring seats must be $9\frac{11}{16}$ inch $\pm\frac{3}{8}$ inch. If outside these limits the spring must be renewed (see **Section 8:7**).

8:11 Fault diagnosis

(a) Rear axle noise

1 Lack of lubricant
2 Whine on drive, gears meshed too deeply
3 Whine on overrun, gears have too much backlash
4 Knocking from differential, broken gear teeth
5 General noise on drive and overrun, worn bearings

(b) Oil leaks

1 Damaged cover gasket or loose bolts
2 Worn pinion shaft oil seal

(c) Drive not transmitted

1 Broken axle shaft
2 Damaged gear teeth
3 Differential broken at carrier

(d) Propeller shaft vibration

1 Large piece of foreign matter (underbody compound) stuck to one side of shaft
2 Worn universal joints
3 Loose U-bolts at pinion drive flange
4 Worn sliding sleeve splines

(e) Suspension knock

1 Worn bushes in control arms
2 Loose control arm bolts
3 Damaged shock absorber
4 Wrongly positioned exhaust pipe fouling suspension

CHAPTER 9

FRONT SUSPENSION AND HUBS

9:1 Description

A general layout illustration of the front suspension is given by **FIG 9:1**. It will be noted that the steering knuckles, coil springs and shock absorbers have been omitted for the sake of clarity. The suspension consists of unequal length control arms bolted to the frame and carrying the steering knuckle between upper and lower ends. Coil springs fit between the lower arms and the frame sheet metal with telescopic shock absorbers mounted concentrically in the springs.

The ball joints at top and bottom steering knuckle eyes require periodic greasing. Wheel hubs and brake discs are cast in one piece and run on tapered roller bearings. Camber and castor angle adjustment is made by rotating the cam bolts which attach the lower control arm to the frame.

9:2 Routine maintenance

At 6000 miles or 4 month intervals the ball joints at top and bottom of the steering knuckle must be lubricated with water resistant EP (extreme pressure) grease to specification GM 6031 M or equivalent. Use a grease gun and force lubricant through the nipples until clean grease can be seen exuding round the rubber seals. Wipe off excess grease.

Jack the car up at the front and support on stands or wooden blocks. Inspect the tyres for wear, damage or eccentric running. Grasp the road wheel and attempt to rock it on the spindle. Very slight movement is correct. Spin the wheel and listen for clicks or scraping noise from the hubs. Some noise will be heard if a brake pad is just touching the disc but this can be ignored. If the wheel seems slack on the spindle or untoward noises are evident, strip the hub as described in the next paragraph which details a 24,000 mile hub service.

Every 24,000 miles, or earlier if the slightest doubt exists concerning the bearing condition, the hubs must be dismantled, cleaned and repacked with grease. It is essential that bearing grease specially formulated for disc brake hubs is used; long fibre, viscous lubricants are not permissible. GM Lubricant, Part No. 1051195 is recommended for this critical service.

Proceed as follows:
1 See that the road wheel is clear of the ground and that the car is safely supported. Remove the road wheel.
2 Remove the brake caliper as described in **Chapter 11** and hang on a piece of strong wire attached to the frame. Never allow the weight to be taken on the hydraulic hose. Place a wooden block of approximately the same thickness as the brake disc between the caliper friction pads (see **FIG 9:2**).

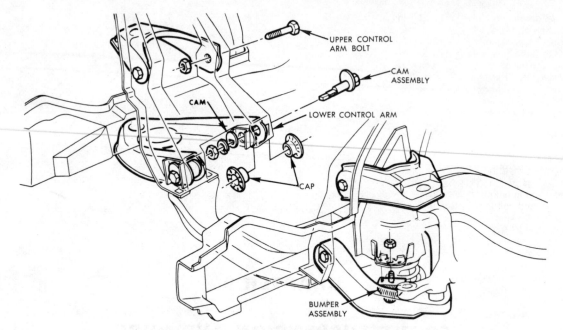

FIG 9:1   Front suspension, general arrangement

3 With a pair of pipe grips or adjustable pliers remove the hub dust cap. Extract and discard the cotterpin which locks the spindle nut to the spindle. In no circumstances may a cotterpin be re-used.

4 Unscrew the spindle nut then grip the edges of the brake disc and rock the hub to loosen the outer bearing. Pull the hub from the spindle carefully so that the outer bearing does not fall out.

5 With a hammer handle, release the inner bearing and dust seal (see FIG 9:3).

6 Wash all components in clean fuel and inspect the rollers and tracks for any sign of discolouration, flaking or pitting. Reject any bearing which has the slightest sign of these faults. Drive the bearing outer track from the hub with a brass drift if renewal is necessary (see FIG 9:4), and fit new tracks by the same method.

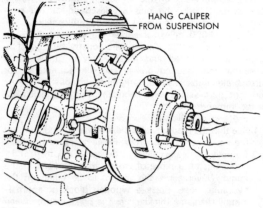

FIG 9:2   Removing a front hub

Make sure that the tracks are started squarely and are driven right home.

7 Fill the roller cages with grease and smear a small quantity on the tracks in the hub. Do not try to fill the hub cavity; as the grease heats up it can expand and force its way past the seal if the hub has no air space.

8 Place the inner bearing in the hub and insert a new dust seal. Tap it home level with the hub face. Fit the hub to the spindle, install the outer bearing, washer and nut.

9 Tighten the nut, hand tight only, while rotating the hub using the finger tips. Continue to tighten the nut until the hub becomes slightly more difficult to turn. If a torque wrench is used it should register 12 lb ft. Back the nut off to the nearest vertical or horizontal hole in the spindle and insert a new cotterpin. Bend the ends of the cotterpin round the nut. The hub should now have between .001 inch and .008 inch end movement. This is important.

10 Half fill the hub cap with grease and refit to the hub.

11 Make sure that the brake disc is clean and free of grease then refit the brake caliper (see Chapter 11).

12 Refit the road wheel and lower the car to the ground.

9:3 Shock absorber renewal

The hydraulic shock absorbers are not adjustable or capable of repair. After an extended mileage or in cases of damage they must be renewed. Unless the car has covered a very low mileage always renew both units, otherwise the safety and correct handling of the car may be affected.

Refer to FIG 9:5. The road wheels are not removed but sufficient clearance must be obtained below the shock absorber to allow it to pass down through the lower control arm for removal. Raising the car on a hoist, running it up a ramp or over an inspection pit will provide this clearance.

Open the hood and grip the shock absorber centre stud with a wrench. Hold the stud stationary while the nut is unscrewed. Remove the nut, retainer and grommet. Unscrew the bolts from the lower end of the shock absorber and release it from the car. Fit the new shock absorber by reversing the removal process. Tighten the two lower bolts to 20 lb ft and the upper nut to 120 lb inch.

9:4 Renewing front springs

Springs may need renewal due to fracture or gradual reduction in length under load. To check for evidence of the second condition, place the car on a level surface in normal working weight but without load or occupants. Refer to **FIG 9:6**. If dimension 'Z' is outside 1.69 inch ± .38 inch the spring must be renewed. It is wise to renew springs as a pair using only genuine Chevrolet parts.

Proceed as follows:
1 Remove the shock absorber (see **Section 9:3**).
2 Unbolt the stabilizer bar (if fitted) from the lower control arm.
3 Jack the front of the car up and support it under the frame.
4 Remove the road wheel.
5 Place a jack with small closed height and large lift such as a hydraulic trolley jack under the lower control arm. Protect the arm by interposing a piece of wood between the jack head and the underside of the arm. Raise the jack to take the weight of the suspension and loop a safety chain through the spring in case of accident. Remember that a compressed spring of this size stores a great deal of energy. **FIG 9:7** shows the arrangement when the arm is lowered.
6 Remove the ball stud which connects the lower control arm to the steering knuckle. **FIG 9:8** shows the method being applied to the removal of the upper ball stud; the removal of the lower one is similar. Remove the cotterpin and loosen the nut three or four turns. Place a wheel stud nut over the ball stud and press out with tool J-8806-1. The tool will be reversed to the position shown in **FIG 9:8**. If the tool is not available, a short piece of pipe, a washer, nut and bolt can be arranged as a practical substitute. (Note that this operation and the next one, operation 7, can be interchanged at the operator's discretion).
7 Remove the tie rod ball stud from the steering knuckle. Pull out the cotterpin and unscrew the nut. Hold a heavy weight behind the steering arm and tap on the opposite side of the arm with a light hammer to free the tapered stud. **FIG 9:9** shows the use of two hammers for this operation.
8 Lower the jack to the position shown in **FIG 9:7** while supporting the hub assembly and steering knuckle. Do not allow the hydraulic hose to take the weight of the assembly. The spring can now be lifted clear when the safety chain is released.
9 Wipe the spring seats in the control arm and frame clean then install the new spring making sure that it is fitted properly against the stop in each seat. Raise the jack enough to just hold the spring in place. Fit the safety chain.

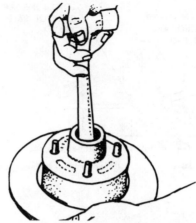

FIG 9:3   Removing a hub bearing

BRASS DRIFT

FIG 9:4   Removing a bearing outer race

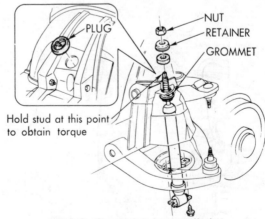

PLUG

NUT
RETAINER
GROMMET

Hold stud at this point to obtain torque

FIG 9:5   Shock absorber installation

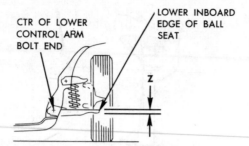

CTR OF LOWER CONTROL ARM BOLT END

LOWER INBOARD EDGE OF BALL SEAT

FIG 9:6   Front suspension height check

Key to Fig 9:6   Dimension Z=1.69 inch±.38 inch

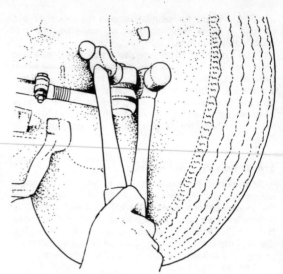

FIG 9:9   Freeing a tie rod ball stud

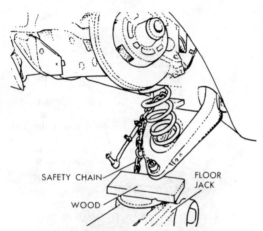

SAFETY CHAIN

FLOOR JACK

WOOD

FIG 9:7   Removing a front spring

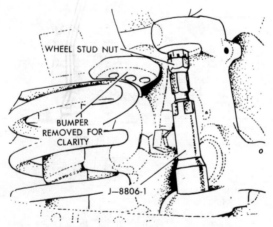

WHEEL STUD NUT

BUMPER REMOVED FOR CLARITY

J—8806-1

FIG 9:8   Releasing a ball stud from the steering knuckle

10 See that the taper on the lower control arm ball stud and the taper in the steering knuckle are clean and dry. Raise the jack until the ball stud can be guided home in the steering knuckle. Fit the ball stud nut and tighten to 60 lb ft plus a maximum of $\frac{1}{6}$ turn to enable a new cotterpin to be fitted. Never back off a ball stud nut to align a cotterpin hole. This applies everywhere throughout this Chapter. Fit the cotterpin and open the ends.

11 Fit the tie rod ball stud and tighten the nut to 35 lb ft. The same general instructions apply to this operation as for operation 10 but in this case do not exceed 50 lb ft torque when aligning the nut castellations for fitting the new cotterpin. Remove the jack.

12 Refit the road wheel and lower the car to the ground.

13 Refit the shock absorber (see **Section 9:3**).

14 Refit the stabilizer bar and tighten the bar to control arm nut to 120 inch lb.

9:5 Renewing a steering knuckle

If damage has occurred to the front suspension due to accidental collision it is a wise precaution to renew the steering knuckle even if this component appears to be unaffected. It should only be used again if proper checking gauges and crack detection equipment show that it is safe to do so.

1 Raise the front of the car and support on blocks under the frame.

2 Remove the road wheel.

3 Remove the caliper and hub (see **Section 9:2**).

4 Remove the splash shield which is bolted to the steering knuckle behind the hub.

5 Place a jack under the lower control arm as described in **Section 9:4** and raise the arm so that the coil spring is compressed. Be very careful to see that the jack cannot slip as damage to the shock absorber could result if the spring is inadvertently released with the steering knuckle disconnected.

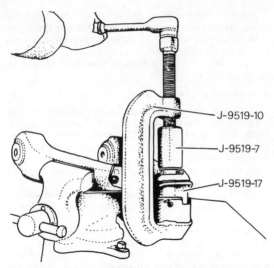

FIG 9:10   Removing the lower control arm ball joint

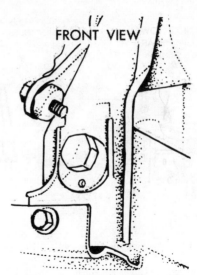

FIG 9:11   Front view of cam bolt

6 Remove the tie rod ball stud from the steering knuckle (see **Section 9:4**).

7 Remove both the upper and lower control arm ball studs from the steering knuckle using the method described in **Section 9:4**. The knuckle is now free.

Fit the new steering knuckle by reversing the removal process taking note of the instructions given in **Section 9:4** regarding the fitting of ball stud tapers. Tighten the upper control arm to knuckle ball stud nut to 30 lb ft the lower one to 60 lb ft and the tie rod to 35 lb ft.

9:6 Renewing steering knuckle ball joints

The steering ball joints are not adjustable and in the event of wear must be renewed. Check for the presence of wear by jacking the car up and safely supporting it under the frame. Enlist the aid of an assistant to grip the circumference of the tyre and try to rock the suspension in the vertical plane while the ball joints are closely watched. Any movement between the ball and seating means that wear has taken place sufficient to warrant renewal. A new ball joint should require between 2 and 4 lb ft of torque applied to the stud before it will move in the seating. It is possible to renew ball joints without removing the control arms from the car although the illustrations show work being performed at the bench. The tools used are the same whichever method is adopted.

Proceed as follows:

1 Remove the steering knuckle (see **Section 9:5**), if both ball joints are to be renewed or if only one needs attention release the appropriate control arm from the knuckle.

2 To renew the upper ball joint, cut off the rivets holding the seating to the control arm and push the joint from the arm.

3 Fit the new ball joint and secure to the arm with the bolts and nuts supplied in the kit.

4 The lower ball joint is removed as shown in **FIG 9:10**. If the correct tool is not available it is possible to

improvise a satisfactory substitute with the aid of a heavy clamp and pieces of pipe.

5 Fit the new ball joint by pressing home in the arm using the extractor tool in the reverse direction. Position the grease bleed hole in the rubber boot so that it faces in towards the centre of the car.

6 Refit the ball studs to the knuckle and tighten the nuts to the torque figures given in **Section 9:5**.

9:7 Renewing control arm bushes

Before dismantling the control arms refer to **FIG 9:1** and note the cam bolts which serve as pivots for the lower control arm. These adjust the camber and castor angles of the suspension and these angles are set or

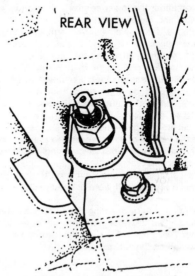

FIG 9:12   Rear view of cam bolt

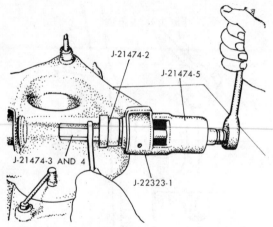

FIG 9:13   Removing the lower control arm bushes

checked with high precision gauges. Mark the position of each cam in relation to the control arm by scribing a line across the cam and arm. After any extensive work on the suspension it is advisable to have the angles checked by a Chevrolet Service Agent with the manufacturers gauges. The method of altering the angles of the suspension is given in **Section 9:8** and close up views of the cam bolt are shown in **FIGS 9:11** and **9:12**.

To remove both control arms, release the shock absorber (see **Section 9:3**), steering knuckle (see **Section 9:5**) and the coil spring (see **Section 9:4**).

Undo the upper control arm pivot bolts and remove the arm.

Mark the cam position at the lower control arm to aid refitting then undo the nuts and extract the front and rear cam bolts, thus releasing the arm. If only one control arm is to be removed it is not necessary to dismantle the hub or steering knuckle. To remove the upper arm, support the suspension under the lower control arm and just remove the ball stud and the pivot bolts.

To remove the lower control arm, carry out the operations necessary to release the coil spring (see **Section 9:4**), and then release the cam bolts.

The bushes are a press fit in the arms and can be removed with the service tools as shown in **FIG 9:13**. Suitable tools can be improvised from pieces of pipe, a bolt, washers and a nut. Note the spacer shown in **FIG 9:13** as tool No. J-22323-1. This is a half circle of steel cut from pipe or bent from strip and is placed between the flanges of the lower arm to prevent collapse.

Pull the new bushes into place using the same tools with the directions reversed.

Before installing the control arms on the car, examine the pivot and cam bolts. If worn or damaged they must be renewed.

Fit the upper arm by inserting the pivot bolts from each outer side so that the nuts are inside the arm and facing each other (see **FIG 9:1**). Hold the arm in a horizontal plane and tighten the nuts to 60 lb ft.

Assemble the lower arm to the car with the cam bolts facing inwards as shown in **FIG 9:1**. Position the marks made on the cams with the marks on the arm and then tighten the nuts to 125 lb ft.

Continue to rebuild the suspension as described in earlier Sections.

9:8 Steering geometry

The castor and camber angles are adjusted by turning the cam bolts referred to in **Section 9:7** and illustrated in **FIGS 9:1, 9:11** and **9:12**. Measurement of these angles is critical and can only be undertaken if the manufacturers gauges or proprietary measuring equipment is available. Incorrect setting will seriously affect the safe handling of the car.

Whatever equipment is used for measurement, adhere to the manufacturers instructions for its use. The angles should be as follows:

Camber ..   ..   .. $+\frac{1}{4}$ deg. ± 1 deg.
Castor ..   ..   .. $-\frac{3}{4}$ deg. ± 1 deg.

These are taken with the vehicle level and without load or occupants. Before altering any adjustment see that the tyres are inflated to the correct pressures and that the coil spring height is as specified (see **FIG 9:6**).

Refer to **FIG 9:1**. The front cam adjusts the camber angle and must be moved first. The rear cam adjusts the castor angle. Loosen the nut and turn the bolt head until the desired angle is obtained. Hold the bolt head with the wrench while tightening the nut to 125 lb ft. Repeat for the other cam bolt. Movement of the front cam moves the lower control arm in or out and movement of the rear cam moves the control arm fore and aft.

Note that toe-in adjustment can only be made after the camber and castor angles are set.

9:9 Fault diagnosis

(a) Wheel wander

1 Slack hub bearings
2 Worn tyres
3 Incorrect toe-in
4 Worn steering linkage
5 Worn suspension bushes
6 Worn ball joints

(b) Wheel shimmy

1 Slack hub bearings
2 Unbalanced wheels
3 Unevenly worn tyres
4 Loose or worn suspension bushes
5 Worn ball joints

(c) Instability

1 Shock absorber failed
2 Slack hub bearings
3 Incorrect steering angles
4 Worn suspension bushes
5 Worn ball joints

(d) Suspension 'bottoms'

1 Weak coil springs
2 Shock absorber failed

CHAPTER 10

THE STEERING GEAR

10:1 Description

The manual steering gear is a recirculating ball type with a collapsible steering shaft and mast jacket. The steering shaft is designed to telescope under impact by the shearing of specially fitted plastic pins. At the same time the mast jacket collapses by moving a plastic sleeve in which ballbearings are embedded (see **FIG 10:1**). This arrangement is of considerable value in reducing injury to the driver in the event of a frontal collision. Not only does the design improve driver safety but the incorporation of the ignition lock and steering lock in the jacket reduces the risk of the car being stolen. The locking device is such that the key cannot be removed until it is turned to the 'Lock' position.

As an alternative option, power steering can be fitted. Hydraulic pressure is supplied by an engine driven vane type pump through hoses to the steering box rotary spool valve. This is held in the neutral position by a torsion bar. When force is applied to the steering shaft by the driver, the torsion bar allows the spool to move in relation to the valve body thus permitting oil to flow to the appropriate side of the piston nut.

The more the steering wheel is turned against a resistance the greater the oil pressure applied to the piston nut in the direction of movement thus providing the power assistance to the driver. This steering gear is controlled through a similar energy absorbing steering mast and jacket assembly to that fitted with the manual steering gear. A flexible joint and lower bearing are incorporated in the power steering mast which are not necessary with the manual steering. The main details of both systems are shown in **FIG 10:2**.

The linkage from the steering gear is by Pitman arm to relay rod and idler. From each end of the relay rod, tie rods are connected to steering arms on the steering knuckles. The ball joints require greasing at 6000 mile intervals but the manual steering box is filled with lubricant and sealed for life. **FIG 10:3** illustrates the linkage layout.

10:2 Maintenance and adjustment, manual steering

Lubrication:

Every 6000 miles or 4 months, whichever occurs first, lubricate the steering ball joints with EP grease to specification GM 6031 M or equivalent.

At 36,000 mile intervals inspect the steering box for leakage of lubricant past the seals. Ignore evidence of an

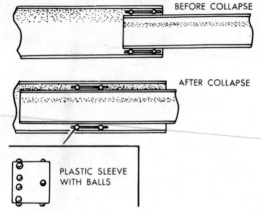

FIG 10:1 Mast jacket collapsible joint

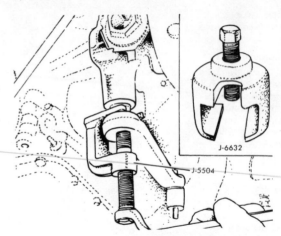

FIG 10:4 Removing the pitman arm

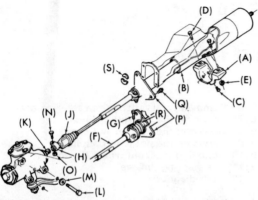

FIG 10:2 Steering column assembly, manual and power

Key to Fig 10:2   **A** Bracket   **B** Mast jacket
C Bracket to mast bolt   **D** Bracket bolt   **E** Bracket nut
F Intermediate shaft   **G** Flexible coupling bolt   **H** Pot joint
clamp   **J** Pot joint   **K** Wormshaft   **L** Mounting bolt
M Washer   **N** Clamp bolt   **O** Nut   **P** Toe plate   **Q** Toe
plate screw   **R** Alignment flange   **S** Alignment spacers

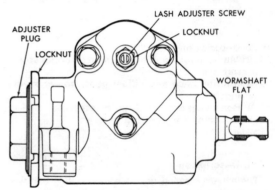

FIG 10:5 Steering gear adjusting details

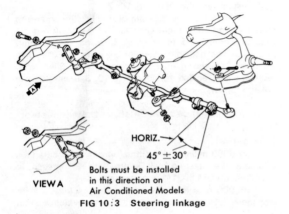

VIEW A

HORIZ.

45° ± 30°

Bolts must be installed
in this direction on
Air Conditioned Models

FIG 10:3 Steering linkage

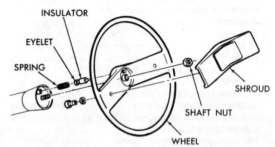

FIG 10:6 Removing steering wheel shroud

oily film but if actual grease is visible the seal must be renewed. Lubricant to specification GM 4673 M or equivalent is used for the steering box.

Adjustment:

Correct adjustment of the steering gear is vital to the safe handling of the car and must be carried out in the proper sequence with the greatest care. Before making any alterations or adjustments always check that the cause of the trouble is not to be found in worn tyres, incorrect wheel or suspension alignment or worn out shock absorbers. The following instructions, if followed step by step, will ensure that a mechanically sound steering gear is perfectly adjusted. Part of the sequence involves the removal of the Pitman arm. It is mandatory that the proper extractor is used, **never hammer the arm to release it from the shaft.** With the arm removed the steering box will be free from the restraint of the steering linkage. In this condition do not turn the steering hard against the end of travel in either direction. Doing this will cause expensive and final damage to the ball guides on the steering nut. Throughout the operations in this Chapter utter cleanliness and a delicate touch are essential for success.

Steering gear:

1 Disconnect the battery and raise the front of the car so that the Pitman arm can be reached.

2 Mark the relationship of the Pitman arm to the shaft then remove the nut. Pull the arm from the shaft with one of the extractors shown in **FIG 10:4.**

3 Refer to **FIG 10:5.** Loosen the large adjuster plug locknut at the side of the steering gearbox and unscrew the adjuster $\frac{1}{4}$ turn.

4 Refer to **FIG 10:6** or **10:7** and remove the steering wheel shroud or horn button so that the shaft nut in the centre of the wheel is exposed.

5 Very gently turn the steering wheel in one direction as far as it will go without force. The direction chosen does not matter. Turn back $\frac{1}{2}$ turn.

6 Fit a $\frac{3}{4}$ inch socket to a torque wrench and apply to the steering wheel nut as shown in **FIG 10:8.** The torque wrench used must not have a maximum reading of more than 50 lb inch. Move the wrench back and forth through 90 deg. and record the figure obtained. This is the 'free bearing drag'.

7 The thrust bearing preload must now be set. Tighten the adjuster plug (see **FIG 10:5**), until the torque wrench reading increases by 5 to 8 lb inch over the figure obtained at operation 6. Record this new figure (7 lb inch if the gear is being adjusted out of the car at the bench). Tighten the adjuster plug locknut to 75 lb ft making sure that the adjuster plug does not move. Recheck the thrust bearing preload figure. Remove the torque wrench and turn the steering wheel by the fingers lightly touching the rim. If any lumpiness at all can be felt, this indicates that the bearing tracks are indented. Dismantle the steering gear and renew the bearings.

8 If the adjustment of thrust bearing preload has been satisfactorily achieved at operation 7, then the over-centre preload must now be set. Turn the steering wheel gently from one full lock to the other counting the number of turns. Turn back exactly half the turns counted. This will give the centre position. Refer to

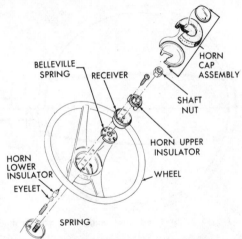

FIG 10:7   Removing horn button. GT model or ZK4

FIG 10:5. Loosen the lash adjuster screw locknut and gently tighten the lash adjuster screw until there is no lash between the ball nut and Pitman shaft sector teeth. Tighten the locknut to 15 lb ft. Fit the torque wrench to the steering wheel nut in the same manner that it was used for operations 6 and 7. Turn the steering with the torque wrench through the centre position and to each side. The torque reading should reach a maximum at the centre position and fall away at each side of centre. The correct maximum reading must lie between 4 and 10 lb inch above the figure obtained at operation 7 (thrust bearing pre-load). If the steering gear is being adjusted at the bench this figure must be 14 lb inch. If these figures are exceeded, readjust the lash adjuster screw. Finally take the total torque figure reading. This is the product of the readings obtained at operations 6, 7 and 8. The total must not exceed 16 lb inch if the gear is adjusted in the car or 21 lb inch at the bench.

9 Reassemble the Pitman arm to the shaft in alignment with the marks made when dismantling and tighten the nut to 93 lb ft. Reconnect the battery and lower the car to the floor. Refit the steering wheel shroud or horn button.

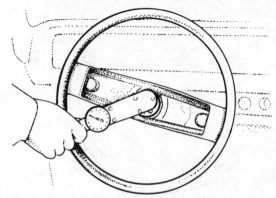

FIG 10:8   Checking bearing drag

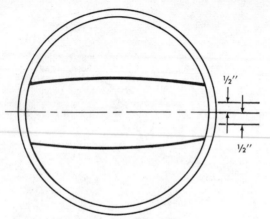

FIG 10:9   Steering wheel alignment, standard

Steering wheel centring:

When the car is driven in a straight line on a level surface the steering wheel spokes should appear within the limits illustrated in **FIG 10:9** or **10:10**. If they are displaced beyond the limits shown, carry out the following actions after checking to see that the steering gear is correctly adjusted as described in earlier paragraphs.

1 Drive the car on a flat surface until it is travelling in a straight path. Note that the average road with its camber towards the kerb is not suitable.
2 When the car is following a straight path, stop without disturbing the steering wheel and open the hood. Check the position of the wormshaft flat (see **FIG 10:5**). It should be at 12 o'clock on the top of the shaft as shown. If it is displaced to either side the steering is not on the high point and the relative lengths of the tie rods must be altered.
3 Refer to **FIG 10:3.** Loosen the two clamps on each tie rod sleeve and rotate each sleeve by an equal amount in the same direction until the worm shaft flat is correctly positioned and the car travels in a straight path. It is essential that the tie rod sleeves are

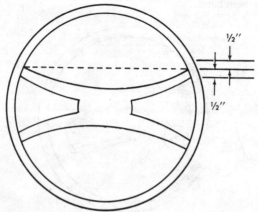

FIG 10:10   Steering wheel alignment. GT model or ZK4

each rotated by the same amount otherwise the front wheel alignment will be upset. Refer to **FIG 10:11** when tightening the clamps to ensure that the correct clamping effect is obtained. The nuts must be tightened to 132 lb inch. If the wormshaft flat is correctly positioned and the car runs in a straight path but the steering wheel spokes do not appear as illustrated in **FIGS 10:9** or **10:10** then the wheel must be moved on the shaft splines. Remove the shroud or horn button and unscrew the centre nut. Fit puller J-2927 as shown in **FIG 10:12** and remove the wheel. See that the position of the road wheels and wormshaft flat has not been altered then refit the steering wheel with the embossed part of the bottom surface of the hub at the 6 o'clock position. Refit and tighten the nut to 30 lb ft. Do not exceed this figure or steering wheel rub may result. Refit the shroud or horn button. Note that on the GT steering wheel the three screws holding the horn components must be removed before undoing the centre nut. **FIG 10:7** shows the correct assembly sequence.

10:3 Maintenance and adjustment, power steering

The general instructions regarding procedure given at the beginning of **Section 10:2** apply to this Section with equal emphasis. Maintenance of a power steering system is divided between the hydraulic and mechanical components in the steering gear. The steering linkage is similar to that used for the manual steering and requires greasing at the same intervals.

Hydraulic fluid level:

. . Check this with the dipstick when the fluid is at operating temperature 150° to 170°F. If necessary bring up to the proper level by the addition of GM Power Steering Fluid. Should this not be available it is possible to use Automatic Transmission Fluid, Type 'A', provided it carries the mark 'AQ-ATF' followed by a number and the suffix letter 'A'. Power steering fluid should be to GM Part No. 1050017.

Bleeding the hydraulic system:

The presence of air in the system will be indicated by noise from the pump. This defect can only occur if the fluid level is allowed to fall too low through leakage. Check for the cause and rectify.

Bleed the system as follows:
1 Fill the reservoir with the correct grade of fluid and allow to stand for two minutes then start the engine and almost immediately stop it again. It should not run for more than a second or two.
2 Add fluid if necessary and repeat operation 1 until the fluid level remains constant.
3 Raise the car so that both front wheels are off the ground.
4 Start the engine and run up to approximately 1500 rev/min. If the car is fitted with automatic transmission be extremely careful to see that the transmission is in 'park' and the parking brake is full on. In any case, whatever transmission is fitted do not allow anyone to stand in front of, or behind, the car while the engine is running.

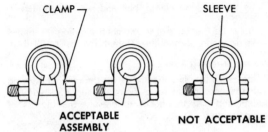

FIG 10:11 Tie rod clamp position

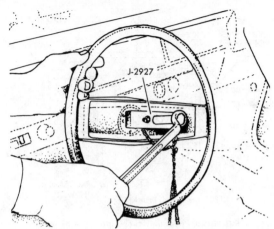

FIG 10:12 Removing the steering wheel

5 With the engine running, turn the wheels onto full lock, right and left, lightly touching the stops. Add more fluid if necessary at this stage.

6 Stop the engine, lower the car to the ground, restart and then turn the wheels from lock to lock once more. Again check the fluid level. If the oil is heavily foamed, allow the car to stand for a few minutes with the engine stopped then repeat operations 1 to 6. If noise and foaming persist then the pump should be checked by a Chevrolet Service Agent equipped with a pressure gauge and adaptor set. It would be uneconomic for the private owner to purchase this apparatus.

Steering gear over centre adjustment:

This is the only mechanical adjustment which the private owner can reasonably be expected to make. Refer to **FIG 10:13** which shows the position of the Pitman shaft adjusting screw. Continue as follows:

1 Disconnect the battery and remove the steering wheel shroud or horn button as described in **Section 10:2**.

2 Disconnect the Pitman arm from the relay rod at the relay rod ball joint.

3 Loosen the Pitman shaft adjusting screw locknut and unscrew the adjusting screw as far as it will go (see **FIG 10:13**).

4 Gently turn the steering wheel from lock to lock counting the number of turns. Rotate the wheel back half the turns counted. This will give the centre point.

5 Fit a torque wrench to the steering wheel nut as described in **Section 10:2**. Rotate the wheel through the centre and back again by approximately a $\frac{1}{8}$ turn each way. Record the highest reading. This is the preload figure for the thrust bearing.

6 Gradually tighten the Pitman shaft adjusting screw until the torque reading increases by between 3 and 6 lb inch over the reading obtained at operation 5. The reading given by the wrench must not exceed 14 lb inch in total. Tighten the locknut to 32 lb ft.

7 Reconnect the Pitman arm to relay rod and tighten the ball stud nut to 35 lb ft. Fit a new cotterpin. Refit the steering wheel shroud or horn button and reconnect the battery.

Adjusting pump belt tension:

The belt tension should be checked with tool No. J-23600. A new belt should read 125 lb and a used one, 75 lb. If the tool is not available inspect the belt for signs of slipping which will show as a highly glazed surface

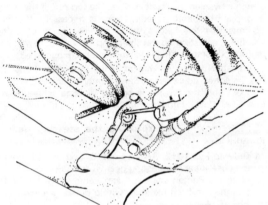

FIG 10:13 Power steering over centre adjustment

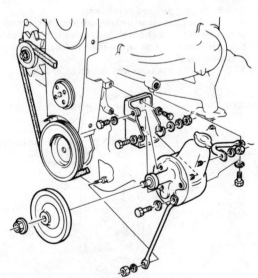

FIG 10:14 Power steering pump mounting details

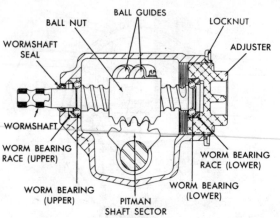

FIG 10:15   Manual steering gear, side view

Labels: BALL NUT, BALL GUIDES, LOCKNUT, WORMSHAFT SEAL, ADJUSTER, WORMSHAFT, WORM BEARING RACE (UPPER), WORM BEARING RACE (LOWER), WORM BEARING (UPPER), WORM BEARING (LOWER), PITMAN SHAFT SECTOR

on the belt 'Vee' faces. If the belt is not glazed and $\frac{1}{2}$ inch movement is possible when the top run of the belt is gripped by hand, no adjustment is necessary. If it is obvious that the belt is worn, release the pivot bolt and brace adjusting nuts at the pump mounting, fit a new belt and adjust so that the $\frac{1}{2}$ inch movement is maintained.

Adjustment is by movement of the Delcotron. Loosen the Delcotron adjusting nut and gently lever the Delcotron out until the tension is correct. A large screwdriver is ideal as a lever. Firmly tighten the adjusting nut.

10:4 Removing and refitting the steering gear, manual steering

1 Refer to **FIG 10:2**. Remove nut 'O' and bolt 'N' from the pot joint at the steering gear wormshaft.
2 Mark the Pitman shaft and arm, remove the nut and pull the arm from the shaft with a puller as shown in **FIG 10:4**.
3 Remove the bolts holding the gear and lift away from the car.
To refit the gear proceed as follows:
1 Position the gear on the frame, aligning the groove across the pot joint end with the wormshaft flat. Push the gear home until the wormshaft will go no further into the coupling.
2 Fit the gear to frame bolts and tighten to 70 lb ft.

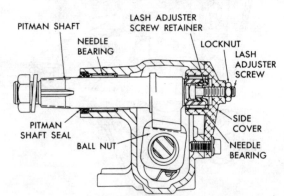

FIG 10:16   Manual steering gear, end view

Labels: PITMAN SHAFT, NEEDLE BEARING, LASH ADJUSTER SCREW RETAINER, LOCKNUT, LASH ADJUSTER SCREW, PITMAN SHAFT SEAL, BALL NUT, SIDE COVER, NEEDLE BEARING

3 Fit the pot joint clamp, bolt and nut and tighten to 55 lb ft.
4 Refit the Pitman arm to the shaft aligning the marks made when dismantling. Tighten the nut to 93 lb ft.

Power steering gear:

The procedure is the same as for the manual steering with the addition of hose removal. Plug the hydraulic outlets and cap the hoses to prevent the ingress of foreign matter.

Power steering pump:

Refer to **FIG 10:14**.
1 Disconnect the hoses at either the pump or the steering gear as convenient. Cap the ends of the hoses and plug the outlets.
2 Remove the driving belt by first moving the Delcotron to release the tension then ease the belt over the pulley.
3 Undo the mountings and lift the pump clear.
To refit the pump reverse the preceding sequence but fit the hoses and fill the reservoir with fluid before refitting the belt. Bleed the pump by turning the pulley anticlockwise when viewed from the front until no more air bubbles appear in the reservoir. Refit and tension the belt (see **Section 10:3**). Bleed the system.

10:5 Servicing the steering gear

Manual steering

Remove the gear as described in **Section 10:4**. Wipe the exterior clean then commence operations on a clean bench, preferably covered with newspaper which can be renewed as required. Refer to **FIGS 10:15** and **10:16** for general assembly details.

Dismantling:

1 Grip the gear in a vice by one of the mounting bosses with the wormshaft horizontal.
2 Rotate the wormshaft from stop to stop counting the turns then turn back halfway to the centre position.
3 Remove the side cover bolts and tap gently on the end of the Pitman shaft to free it and the cover from the gear housing.
4 Remove the wormshaft adjuster plug and wormshaft lower ball race.
5 Draw the wormshaft and ball nut from the gear housing by holding the nut. Never allow the nut to spin freely to the end of the worm as this will damage the ball guides when the nut stops suddenly.
6 Pry the ball race retainer from the adjuster plug and remove the ball race. Remove the ball race from the worm shaft.
7 Undo the locknut from the lash adjuster screw then thread the screw out of the side cover and remove the cover. The adjuster screw cannot be dismantled from the Pitman shaft and in the event of damage the whole shaft and screw must be renewed.
8 With a screwdriver pry out and scrap the worm shaft and Pitman shaft seals.
This is usually as far as dismantling need go but if the ball nut shows any sign of binding or tightness continue as follows:
Hold the nut and shaft over a clean tray and remove the screws and clamp that hold the ball guides in

position. Pull the guides from the nut. Invert the nut and rotate the shaft until all the balls have dropped out. Pull the nut from the worm noting which way round it is fitted.

Inspection:

Thoroughly wash all parts in clean fuel or solvent and dry off. Inspect the bearings, races, worm shaft and nut for the slightest sign of chipping, indenting, cracking, flaking or discolouration. Reject any part found affected. Check the ball guides for damage, particularly at the ends where they pick up the balls from the worm. Renew as necessary. If the side cover bearing is damaged the cover and bearing must be renewed. Check the wormshaft for straightness. **Never in any circumstances repair steering parts by straightening or welding.**

Repair:

The Pitman shaft and adjuster must be renewed as an assembly as must the side cover and bearing if damaged or worn. The adjuster plug and race are also in this category. New seals can be pressed in using a piece of tube or a socket as a drift but check the condition of the Pitman shaft needle bearing and the worm shaft upper race first. These can be pressed out and new pressed in if necessary. When pressing the Pitman shaft bearing in refer to **FIG 10:17** and avoid bottoming the race. Press against the bearing on the end which has the identity marking.

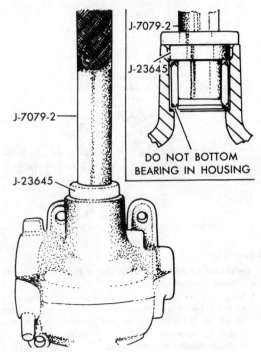

FIG 10:17   Fitting pitman shaft bearing

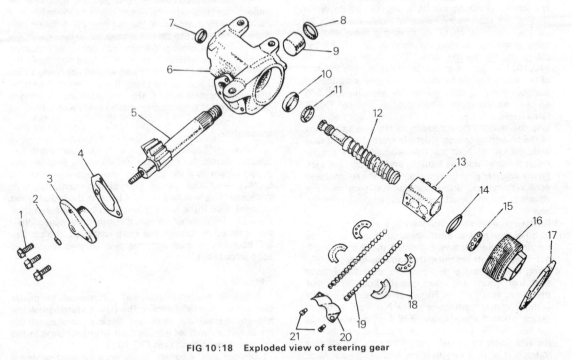

FIG 10:18   Exploded view of steering gear

Key to Fig 10:18   1 Side cover bolts   2 Lash adjuster locknut   3 Side cover and needle bearing   4 Side cover gasket 5 Pitman shaft and lash adjuster   6 Steering gear housing   7 Wormshaft seal   8 Pitman shaft seal   9 Pitman shaft needle bearing   10 Worm bearing race—upper   11 Worm bearing—upper   12 Wormshaft   13 Ball nut   14 Retainer—lower worm bearing   15 Worm bearing—lower   16 Adjuster plug and bearing   17 Adjuster plug locknut   18 Ball guides   19 Balls   20 Ball guide clamp   21 Clamp screw and washer assemblies

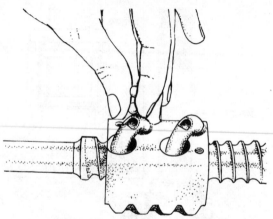

FIG 10:19   Assembling the ball nut

Assembly:

Reference to **FIG 10:18** will be of help in following the assembly sequence.

1 Assemble the ball nut and wormshaft first. Refer to **FIG 10:19.** Place the wormshaft and nut on the bench as shown. Line up the grooves in nut and worm by looking through the holes in the nut. Without moving the nut or shaft fit the ball guides to the nut. Assemble 24 balls to the circuit at the upper end of the worm, i.e. nearest the steering wheel. Do this by dropping the balls into the guide while turning the shaft away from that hole. Assemble 24 balls to the other circuit by dropping them into the other guide and turning the shaft as before. Fit the clamp and tighten the screws (see items 20 and 21, **FIG 10:18**). Do not allow the nut to spin to the end of the worm, handle carefully and keep in a horizontal position. Coat a little grease to specification GM 4673 M on the worm while rotating it to see that it turns freely.

2 Grip the steering gear housing in the vice using one of the mounting bosses. Coat the wormshaft ball race with grease and fit to the wormshaft. Carefully insert the shaft into the housing and through the seal. Fit the adjuster plug ball race, press in the retainer and coat with grease. Screw the adjuster plug into the housing until nearly all end play is removed from the worm.

3 Rotate the wormshaft until the nut is near one end of its travel then pack as much grease into the housing as possible without losing any from the Pitman shaft bore. Repeat with the nut at the opposite end.

4 Bring the nut to the mid position, coat the Pitman shaft with grease and insert into the housing so that the centre tooth of the Pitman shaft sector engages with the centre tooth space of the nut. Pack as much grease, up to the total capacity of 9 oz, as possible in the housing. Fit a new side cover gasket and then fit the side cover by screwing the Pitman shaft adjuster through it until it can turn no further. Screw back $\frac{1}{4}$ turn. Tighten the locknut temporarily. Fit and tighten the side cover bolts to 18 lb ft.

5 Tighten the adjuster plug until all end play is taken up then back off $\frac{1}{4}$ turn. Carefully turn the worm shaft as

far as it will go one way, back off $\frac{1}{2}$ turn. Apply a torque wrench to the worm shaft and tighten the adjuster plug until 7 lb inch are required to turn the shaft. Tighten the locknut to 73 lb ft.

6 Bring the nut to the centre point by turning the worm shaft from one stop to the other counting the turns needed then turning back half the number of turns. Loosen the lash adjuster locknut then screw in the Pitman shaft lash adjuster screw until all end play has been removed from the Pitman shaft. Fit the torque wrench to the wormshaft and move back and forth through the high point. The torque required to pass this point should be 21 lb inch. Do not exceed this figure. Tighten the locknut to 15 lb ft.

Power steering:

It is not advisable for the private owner to attempt to overhaul either pump or steering gear. Special tools and experience are required in addition to clean room conditions. If either of these units fails it is certain to be due to long service or major component breakdown. In each case it is more satisfactory to exchange the unit for a new or factory rebuilt one. **FIGS 10:20** and **10:21** are included in this Section to assist a professional auto engineer who possesses the necessary equipment and expertise but needs to know the assembly sequence.

10:6 Removing and refitting the steering column

The steering column is designed to telescope on impact, thus reducing the risk of injury to the driver in a collision. When servicing the column the greatest care must be taken not to drop, hammer, jar or lean upon any part as unintentional movement can occur necessitating renewal of the affected items. It is vital that only the specified nuts, bolts, screws and washers are used in the assembly and that all fastening devices are tightened to the quoted torque figures. **Do not attempt to service the column if a torque wrench is not available.**

Inspection:

After any frontal impact, no matter how slight, the column should be inspected for damage. Examine the support bracket, if the capsules have separated from the bracket then the jacket will almost certainly have collapsed. This will be seen as a bend in the jacket or felt as looseness. If the shaft plastic pins have sheared then the shaft will rattle when struck lightly on one side. Note that if no other damage has been sustained, the car can still be safely steered with the pins sheared. Renew as soon as possible.

Removal:

Although the columns used for manual or power steering are basically similar, the power steering column has an intermediate shaft and flexible coupling at the lower end as well as the pot joint coupling fitted to the manual steering shaft (see **FIG 10:2**).

1 Disconnect the battery and remove the steering wheel (see **FIG 10:12**).

2 Manual steering. Remove the pot joint clamp bolt. Power steering. Remove the flexible coupling clamp bolt at the upper steering shaft.

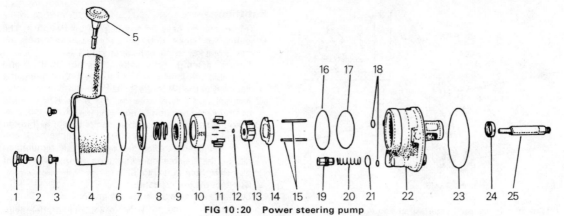

FIG 10:20   Power steering pump

Key to Fig 10:20   1 Union   2 Union O-ring seal   3 Mounting studs   4 Reservoir   5 Dip stick and cover   6 End plate retaining ring   7 End plate   8 Spring   9 Pressure plate   10 Pump ring   11 Vanes   12 Drive shaft retaining ring   13 Rotor   14 Thrust plate   15 Dowel pins   16 End plate O-ring   17 Pressure plate O-ring   18 Mounting stud square ring seals   19 Flow control valve   20 Flow control valve spring   21 Flow control valve square ring seal   22 Pump housing   23 Reservoir O-ring seal   24 Shaft seal   25 Shaft

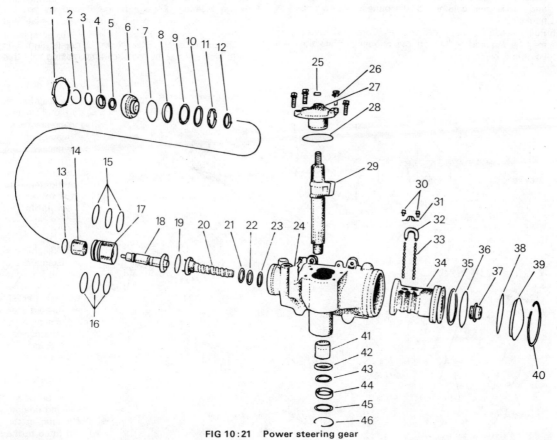

FIG 10:21   Power steering gear

Key to Fig 10:21   1 Locknut   2 Retaining ring   3 Dust seal   4 Oil seal   5 Bearing   6 Adjuster plug   7 O-ring   8 Thrust washer (large)   9 Thrust bearing   10 Thrust washer (small)   11 Spacer   12 Retainer   13 O-ring   14 Spool valve   15 Teflon oil rings   16 O-rings   17 Valve body   18 Stub shaft   19 O-ring   20 Wormshaft   21 Thrust washer   22 Thrust bearing   23 Thrust washer   24 Housing   25 Locknuts   26 Attaching bolts and washers   27 Side cover   28 O-ring   29 Pitman shaft   30 Screws and lockwashers   31 Clamp   32 Ball return guide   33 Balls   34 Rack-piston   35 Teflon oil seal   36 O-ring   37 Plug   38 O-ring   39 Housing end cover   40 Retainer ring   41 Needle bearing   42 Oil seal   43 Back-up washer   44 Oil seal   45 Back-up washer   46 Retaining ring

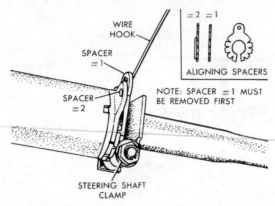

FIG 10:22 Manual steering, alignment spacers

3 Move the driving seat back and remove the three floor pan screws.

4 Remove the column bracket to instrument panel nuts and lower the column to disconnect the wiring harness.

5 Pull the column back into the car. Some assistance may be required to tap on the coupling while the column is being removed.

Refitting:

This operation calls for the help of an assistant. The sequence of steps detailed here must be followed exactly. For a key to the parts refer to **FIG 10:2**.

1 Power steering. Fit clamp H to pot joint J and assemble the joint and shaft to shaft K, aligning the flat on K to the flat in the joint.

2 Manual and power steering. Place steering column carefully into position through the toe pan.

3 Manual steering. Assemble clamp and pot joint to steering gear as described in step 1.

Power steering. Align the steering shaft flat with the flat in the flexible coupling then gently push right home. Tighten bolt G to 30 lb ft.

4 Connect the wiring harness.

5 Loosely assemble the bracket A and nuts E.

6 Fit the bolt N and nut O to the pot joint clamp, align the clamp with the groove in the joint and tighten nut O to 55 lb ft.

7 The car must now be standing on its road wheels. Tighten nuts E to 19 lb ft then slide the toe plate P down to the toe pan.

8 Power steering. Engage flange R and tighten the three screws Q to 40 lb inch through the toe plate and flange.

Manual steering. The screws Q are tightened to 40 lb inch to hold the toe plate after making sure that

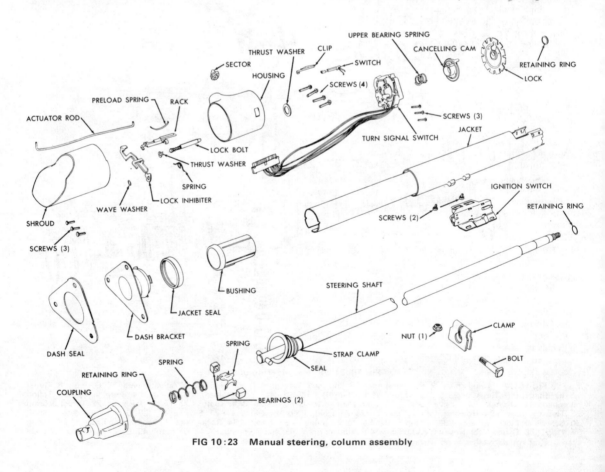

FIG 10:23 Manual steering, column assembly

the column lies easily in line and no strain or sideways movement is apparent.

9 Manual steering. Remove the alignment spacers S as shown in detail in **FIG 10:22.** Make sure that at least .18 inch clearance exists between the steering shaft and the column jacket lower plastic bush after the spacers are removed.

10 Refit the steering wheel, tightening the nut to 30 lb ft.

11 Reconnect the battery.

10:7 Servicing the steering column

Dismantling:

Throughout this Section refer to **FIG 10:23** except where specific detail illustrations are given.

1 Remove the dash panel mounting bracket and store in a place where the mounting capsules can not be damaged. This is important.

2 Grip the column in the vice by either pair 'A' or 'B' weld nuts shown in **FIG 10:24.** The jaws must clamp on the sides of the nuts in the direction of the arrows. Never grip the jacket, one weld nut only or one nut each from 'A' and 'B' since expensive damage could result.

3 Remove the directional signal switch, ignition key warning switch, ignition switch and lock cylinder as described in **Section 10:8.** The steering shaft will now come free from the lower end of the column. If a power steering column is being dismantled, remove the lower bearing from the plastic adaptor at this stage.

4 Refer to **FIG 10:25** and remove the set bolts arrowed then loosen the three screws (not shown) holding the shroud to the housing.

5 Refer to **FIG 10:26.** Remove the lock inhibitor lever and spring wire, being careful that the latter does not suddenly fly off.

6 Refer to **FIG 10:27** and remove the rod and rack assembly. Carefully lift the flat spring out from the rack housing. This spring preloads the rack towards the sector.

7 Push the ignition switch sector out through the lock cylinder hole as shown in **FIG 10:28.**

The column will now be completely dismantled and any worn or damaged components can be renewed.

Assembly:

Coat all friction surfaces with a lithium based grease as assembly proceeds.

1 Refit the sector as shown in **FIG 10:27,** insert the flat spring in the rack guide then the rack and lock bolt assembly. Line the first tooth on the rack up with the first tooth space on the sector and check that the sector block tooth meets the space on the rack.

2 Install the spring wire and lock inhibitor lever (see **FIG 10:26**). Fit the shroud and tighten the three screws then place the housing assembly over the end of the column, fit the four set bolts and tighten to 60 lb inch (see **FIG 10:25**).

3 Power steering column only. Fit the bearing at the lower end in the plastic adaptor.

4 Insert the steering shaft in the column from the lower end and guide carefully up through the top bearing.

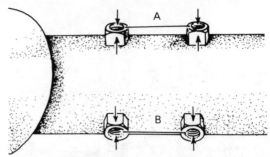

FIG 10:24   Vice mounting points

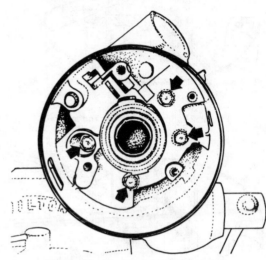

FIG 10:25   Directional signal housing

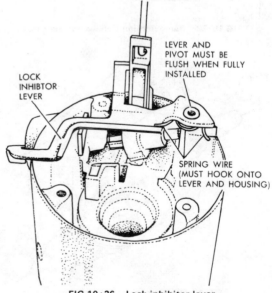

FIG 10:26   Lock inhibitor lever

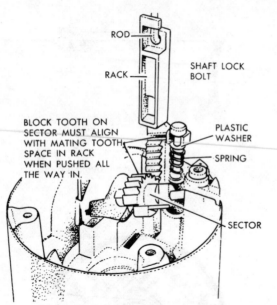

ROD

RACK

SHAFT LOCK
BOLT

BLOCK TOOTH ON
SECTOR MUST ALIGN
WITH MATING TOOTH
SPACE IN RACK
WHEN PUSHED ALL
THE WAY IN.

PLASTIC
WASHER

SPRING

SECTOR

FIG 10:27 Ignition switch, rod and rack

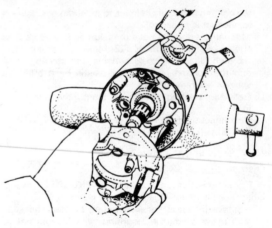

FIG 10:30 Releasing the directional signal switch

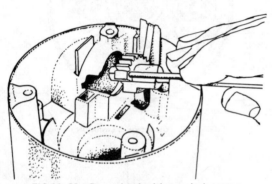

FIG 10:28 Removing ignition switch sector

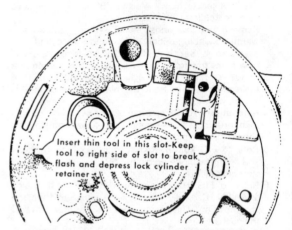

Insert thin tool in this slot-Keep
tool to right side of slot to break
flash and depress lock cylinder
retainer

FIG 10:31 Depressing the lock cylinder retainer

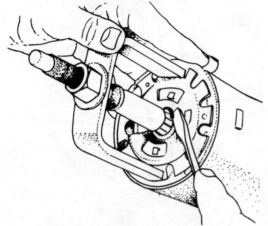

FIG 10:29 Removing the lock plate

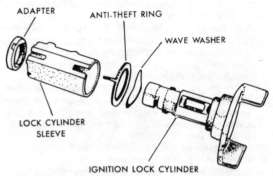

ADAPTER

ANTI-THEFT RING

WAVE WASHER

LOCK CYLINDER
SLEEVE

IGNITION LOCK CYLINDER

FIG 10:32 General assembly. Ignition lock

5 Refit the switches (see **Section 10:8**). Note that on manual steering columns there will be $\frac{3}{16}$ inch axial clearance between the shaft clamp and the lower jacket. Do not move the clamp.

6 Remove the column from the vice and refit the dash panel mounting bracket. Tighten the four bolts to 15 lb ft. Be absolutely certain that the slotted openings in the bracket face the steering wheel end of the column.

10:8 Servicing the column switches

Directional signal switch:

This can be removed and refitted without disturbing the column.

Removal:

1 Remove the steering wheel, loosen the three shroud screws and lift the shroud off.

2 Compress the lock plate with tool J-23653 and prise the snap ring from the shaft (see **FIG 10:29**). The tool can be improvised from a flat strip and packing pieces at each end, using the steering wheel nut to press on the strip. However the snap ring is removed, remember that the shaft is now free. If working at the bench, the shaft could fall out and be damaged.

3 Withdraw the cam, preload spring and thrust washer from the shaft. Undo the signal lever screw and remove the lever.

4 Push the hazard warning knob in and unscrew the knob.

5 Wrap the signal leads and connector with adhesive tape to prevent damage, remove the three switch mounting screws and pull the switch straight out (see **FIG 10:30**). The leads must be guided up through the housing.

Refitting:

Reverse the removal process noting the following points:

1 Before fitting the cam, spring and thrust washer make sure that the signal lever is in the mid position and the hazard warning knob is out.

2 Use a new snap ring, never refit a used one.

3 Use the correct length screws or bolts.

Lock cylinder:

The steering column need not be disturbed.

Removal:

1 Turn the key to lock if possible; if, due to damage this cannot be achieved, the cylinder can still be removed. Remove the steering wheel and directional signal.

2 Refer to **FIG 10:31**. Push a small screwdriver into the slot, break the flash and depress the cylinder spring latch. Pull the lock cylinder from the housing.

Assembly:

The lock cylinder cannot be repaired. To fit a new cylinder proceed as follows:

1 **FIG 10:32** shows the general assembly of components to be fitted to the new cylinder. Place the wave washer and anti-theft ring onto the cylinder as shown in **FIG 10:33**. Push the key in only part way.

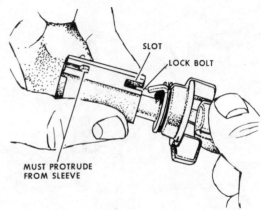

FIG 10:33   Fitting the cylinder to the sleeve

2 Align the lock bolt on the cylinder, the tab on the anti-theft ring and the slot in the sleeve (see **FIG 10:33**). Slide the sleeve up to the anti-theft ring, push the key right in and rotate the lock cylinder clockwise. Rotate the lock counter clockwise to the 'lock' position.

3 Place the assembly in a soft jaw vice, gripping the finger plates and holding the assembly vertical. Refer to **FIG 10:34**. Fit the adaptor in the position shown and stake in four places with an $\frac{1}{8}$ inch punch. Check the lock operation.

Refitting:

1 Hold the sleeve and rotate the knob against the stop in a clockwise direction.

2 Push the sleeve into the housing with the key on the sleeve in line with the keyway in the housing. Continue until the cylinder and sector touch. Place a .070 inch drill between the lock bezel and housing. Press gently against the sector, rotating the cylinder anticlockwise until the drive end of the cylinder mates with the sector. Press in until the snap ring locks the cylinder in the housing. Remove the drill and check the lock for freedom of rotation.

3 Refit the directional signal switch and steering wheel.

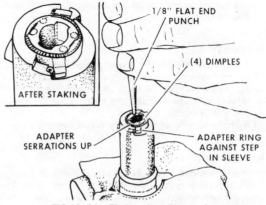

FIG 10:34   Fitting the adaptor ring

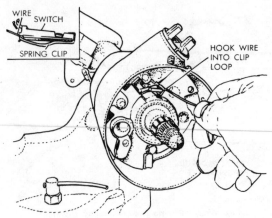

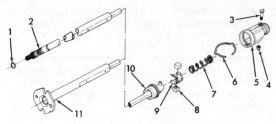

FIG 10:35 Removing the ignition key warning switch

FIG 10:37 Pot joint coupling

Key to Fig 10:37 1 Steering shaft stop ring 2 Manual steering shaft 3 Coupling bolt 4 Nut 5 Coupling 6 Snap ring 7 Spring 8 Bearings 9 Bearing clip 10 Seal 11 Intermediate steering shaft (power steering)

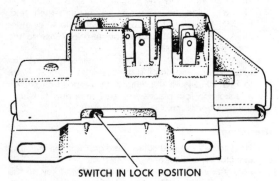

SWITCH IN LOCK POSITION

FIG 10:36 Ignition switch in 'lock' position

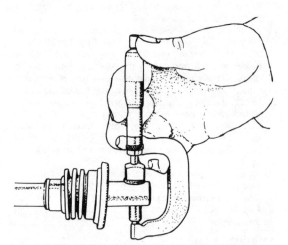

FIG 10:38 Centring the coupling pin

Ignition key warning switch (buzzer switch):

Removal:

1 Remove the steering wheel and directional signal switch.
2 Turn the lock cylinder to 'on'.
3 Hook a piece of wire through the loop of the clip and pull the switch and clip up and out of the housing (see **FIG 10:35**).

Refitting:

1 The buzzer switch actuating button on the lock cylinder must be depressed.
2 Fit the switch with the contacts towards the steering wheel and the formed end of the clip round the lower end of the switch.
3 Refit the directional signal switch and steering wheel.

Ignition switch:

This is mounted on top of the jacket inside the brake pedal support therefore the steering column must be removed or lowered (see **Section 10:6**). Move the switch to the 'lock' position. If the lock cylinder has been removed, pull the actuating rod up to the stop then down one detent to the 'lock. position. Undo the two screws and remove the switch.

To refit the switch, reverse the removal process but first make sure that the switch is in the 'lock' position as shown in **FIG 10:36**.

10:9 Servicing the pot joint coupling

This will require attention if the cover seal is damaged or if slackness shows between the shaft and coupling. **FIG 10:37** shows the coupling dismantled.

Dismantling:

1 Disconnect the battery. On manual steering models remove the steering column (see **Section 10:6**). Power steering, remove the intermediate shaft by removing the steering gear bolts and pushing the gear housing forward until the shaft will clear the flexible coupling pins. Do not detach the hydraulic hoses.
2 Pry the snap ring free and push the coupling (pot joint) from the shaft.
3 Remove the square bearings and tension spring from the cross pin. Do not lose any washers.

4 Scribe a location mark on the pin and press from the shaft. Never hammer the pin out.

5 Remove the seal.

6 Wash the components in clean fuel and renew where necessary.

Reassembly:

1 Refit the seal and clamp.

2 Press the pin in to the shaft up to the scribed mark. Centre the pin by placing just enough washers on the pin to prevent the bearing bottoming. Measure as shown in **FIG 10:38**. Reverse the washers and bearing and re-measure. The readings must be within .012 inch. If not, press the pin towards the low reading side.

3 Coat the inside of the coupling and the bearings liberally with wheel bearing grease. Refit the bearings, washers and tension spring. Slide the coupling over the bearings, fit the seal and snap ring.

4 Refit the steering column (Manual steering) or the intermediate shaft (Power steering).

10:10 Adjusting the front wheel alignment

The 'toe-in' must be adjusted within the limits of $\frac{3}{16}$ inch to $\frac{5}{16}$ inch measured at the road wheel circumference at hub height. It is necessary for this adjustment to be made by a Chevrolet Service Agent equipped with optical gauges but in emergency the following procedure may be adopted as a temporary measure only.

1 Set the camber and castor angles if the front suspension has been dismantled.

2 Refer to **Section 10:2** or **10:3** and check that the steering wheel is centred.

3 Move the vehicle on a level surface until it runs in a straight path.

4 Mark one of the front wheels with a piece of chalk. This should be on the tyre at hub height and must be towards the front of the vehicle.

5 Make up an extending gauge from two pieces of wood in such a way that it can be placed between the front wheels and touch the tyre of each side. The gauge must be held at hub height in front of the axle. Clamp the halves so that the gauge length is maintained then remove it from the wheels.

6 Push the car forwards a half turn of the wheels. The chalk mark will now be at hub height behind the axle. Measure between the tyres at the new position of the chalk mark. There must now be a gap between the gauge and tyres of $\frac{3}{16}$ to $\frac{5}{16}$ inch. If not, refer to **FIG 10:11** and slacken the tie rod clamp bolts. Turn each tie rod by the same amount in **opposite** directions until the clearance is achieved. It may be necessary to repeat operations 5 and 6 two or three times. Tighten the clamp bolts to 132 lb inch.

10:11 The steering linkage

Refer to **FIG 10:3**. Check the linkage for wear as follows:

1 Jack up and safely support the front of the car at one side so that one front wheel only is off the ground.

2 Have an assistant grip the raised wheel and attempt to turn the steering back and forth against the resistance of the wheel still on the ground. Closely inspect each ball joint while this rocking is proceeding. Any slackness will show up during this test.

3 Remove the worn ball joint as described in **Chapter 9** and illustrated in **FIG 9:9**. If the idler is worn this must be renewed as a unit. It is important to refit the special plain washers under the mounting bolt heads.

4 All ball joint tapers must be clean and dry. Tighten the nuts to 35 lb ft then tighten further to allow a new cotterpin to be fitted. Do not exceed 50 lb ft. The idler to frame nuts are tightened to 30 lb ft.

10:12 Fault diagnosis

(a) Wheel wobble

1 Unbalanced wheels
2 Worn steering connections
3 Incorrect steering geometry
4 Worn or out of adjustment steering gear
5 Worn suspension
6 Slack hub bearings

(b) Wander

1 Check 2, 3, 4 and 6 in (a)
2 Uneven tyre pressures
3 Weak shock absorbers

(c) Heavy steering

1 Check 3 in (a)
2 Very low tyre pressures
3 Toe-in incorrect
4 Tightness in steering gear or linkage
5 Hydraulic pump output low (power steering)
6 Power steering gear valve damaged

(d) Lost motion

1 Steering gear out of adjustment (manual steering)
2 Worn steering connections
3 Loose steering gear mounting
4 Worn steering gear or idler
5 Worn suspension

(e) Noise from steering

1 Pins sheared in steering shaft
2 Air in hydraulic system
3 Lack of lubrication

CHAPTER 11

THE BRAKING SYSTEM

11:1 Description

All models covered by this manual are fitted with hydraulically operated disc front and drum rear brakes. The parking brake is mechanical and acts through cables from a centre mounted lever to the rear drums. Application of the parking brake automatically adjusts the rear brake shoe to drum clearance through a swinging lever and strut mechanism and this is clearly described in the rear brake servicing Section. The front disc calipers are of the single piston design which necessitates endwise movement of the caliper relative to the mounting when the brakes are applied.

A particular safety aspect of the hydraulic system is the dual circuit design and brake failure warning light arrangement. The master cylinder has two independent reservoirs, one for the front brakes and the other for the rear brakes (see **FIG 11:1**). Two pistons are mounted in tandem in the cylinder and each is fed by its own reservoir and operates one brake circuit. In the event of a brake line failure or loss of fluid by any other accident only the damaged circuit will become inoperative. Although the brake pedal will travel further and require greater pressure the circuit not affected will remain in full operation. This is achieved by either the front piston

bottoming on the cylinder and providing a pressure seal for the rear piston or the rear piston moving against the front piston and the front piston then moving normally. Even a small leak affecting one circuit causing the pressures to become unbalanced between the two circuits will make the warning lamp light on the dashboard. This lamp also warns of air in the system.

It is a design characteristic of the Vega braking system that when the car is at rest the pedal will feel 'soft'. When the car is in motion, the pedal should feel solid.

11:2 Maintenance and adjustment

It cannot be too strongly emphasized that any operation carried out on the braking system must be characterised by a full understanding of the procedure, absolute cleanliness and the use of nothing but the manufacturers components and materials. Before dismantling or adjusting any part, wipe the exterior clean using only a dry cloth, denatured alcohol or brake fluid. Under no circumstances use gasoline, kerosine, carbon tetrachloride, acetone, paint thinner, or any mineral based solvent near the hydraulic seals. All these cleaners can contaminate the fluid and will rapidly spread throughout the system causing softening, swelling and collapse of

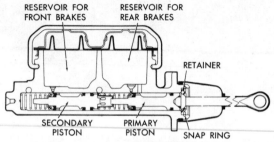

RESERVOIR FOR FRONT BRAKES RESERVOIR FOR REAR BRAKES

RETAINER

SECONDARY PISTON PRIMARY PISTON SNAP RING

FIG 11 : 1   Section through master cylinder

the rubber components. The results of a brake failure from this cause could be disastrous. Never touch the friction pads or linings with greasy, oily or dirty hands and keep all grease, oil, paint, varnish, etc. away from these surfaces. If an air-line is used, be sure the air is dry and filtered. The average service air-line may contain minute traces of mineral oil. New brake drums are stored with a light coating of rustproofing oil on the braking surfaces. Before fitting one of these, clean it with a non-toxic volatile, greaseless type solvent. Carry out this operation in the open air well away from the car. When working with hydraulic fluid remember that it is a very good paint stripper and keep it away from the car bodywork.

Maintenance:

Every 6000 miles or 4 months, remove the cover from the master cylinder reservoirs and top up the fluid to within $\frac{1}{4}$ inch of the lowest edge of each reservoir upper surface. Use GM Hydraulic Brake Fluid, Supreme No. 11 or equivalent. The level in the reservoir feeding the front disc brakes will gradually fall as the pads wear but the level of the reservoir feeding the rear drums should show very little change. Remember that when new pads are fitted to the disc brakes, the pistons will be positioned further back in the cylinders and the fluid level in the reservoir will rise considerably. Be prepared for over-flowing of the fluid from the reservoir.

Examine all brake pipes for leaks or corrosion and all hoses for leaks or signs of chaffing against any part of the suspension or frame. Look for any tell-tale discolouration of the drum brake backplates indicating fluid loss from the cylinders.

Apply water resistant grease GM 6031M to the parking brake cable, cable guides and all other bearing surfaces. Renew the front brake pads when the friction material has worn down to $\frac{1}{8}$ inch thickness and the rear shoes at $\frac{3}{32}$ inch. See following Sections for details.

The hydraulic system requires no adjustment, but the parking brake, although it corrects the shoe to drum clearance automatically, should be adjusted periodically as follows:

1 Raise the car until the rear wheels are clear of the ground. Put axle stands under the rear axle.
2 With the parking brake fully released check that both rear wheels rotate freely.
3 Pull the parking brake lever up one notch only.
4 Refer to **FIG 11 : 2** and release the locknut at the equalizer. Tighten the adjusting nut until slight resistance can be felt when the rear wheels are

rotated. Release the lever and check that both wheels again rotate freely. If correct, tighten the locknut to 85 inch lb.
5 If one wheel drags or correct adjustment cannot be reached, dismantle the rear brakes as described in this Chapter and rectify the fault.
6 Lower the car to the ground.

11 : 3 The master cylinder

Removal:

Refer to **FIG 11 : 3**. Disconnect the pushrod at the pedal, undo the two outlet pipe unions and plug the pipes, release the nuts holding the cylinder to the bulkhead and lift the cylinder from the car. Do not spill fluid on the bodywork.

Dismantling:

1 Wipe the exterior of the cylinder to remove all dirt.
2 Remove the reservoir cover, drain off and discard the fluid. Depress the pushrod a few times to expel fluid from the bore.
3 Pull the rubber boot back along the pushrod and release the snap ring which prevents the pushrod from moving out of the cylinder. Extract the pushrod and retainer.
4 Remove the primary piston (see **FIG 11 : 4**). Do not dismantle this any further since a new one is supplied ready assembled in the repair kit.
5 Tap the cylinder very gently on a block of soft wood or apply low pressure air to the front outlet port until the secondary piston emerges from the cylinder.

Inspection:

Clean the parts thoroughly in brake fluid or denatured alcohol and dry with lint free rag or absorbent paper. Inspect the cylinder bore for corrosion, scores or other damage. Reject it if these conditions are found. See that the bypass and compensating ports are clear and unrestricted and that no foreign matter is present in any part. If the replaceable outlet port pipe seatings are damaged they can be renewed as described in the next paragraph. Discard all rubber items and the primary piston assembly.

Renewing pipe seatings:

1 Drill the seating bore oversize with a $\frac{13}{64}$ inch drill then tap the bore $\frac{1}{4}$ inch x 20 TPI. Fit a $\frac{3}{4}$ inch long $\frac{1}{4}$ inch x 20 TPI bolt with a thick washer and screw into the seating. Tighten the bolt against the washer until the seating is extracted.
2 Carefully remove every particle of swarf from the cylinder then place a new seat insert in the port. See that it has started squarely in the port bore then fit a spare piece of hydraulic pipe into the bore and tighten the union nut until the pipe forces the seat insert right home. Again check carefully to see that no burrs or swarf are present.

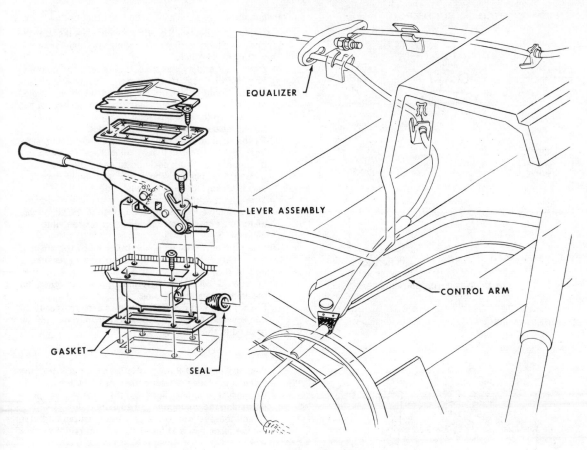

EQUALIZER

LEVER ASSEMBLY

CONTROL ARM

GASKET

SEAL

FIG 11:2   Parking brake details

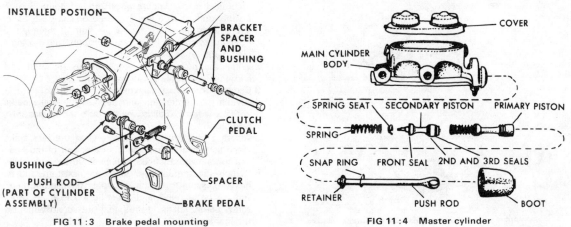

INSTALLED POSTION

BRACKET
SPACER
AND
BUSHING

CLUTCH
PEDAL

BUSHING

PUSH ROD
(PART OF CYLINDER
ASSEMBLY)

SPACER

BRAKE PEDAL

FIG 11:3   Brake pedal mounting

COVER

MAIN CYLINDER
BODY

SPRING SEAT   SECONDARY PISTON   PRIMARY PISTON

SPRING

SNAP RING   FRONT SEAL   2ND AND 3RD SEALS

RETAINER   PUSH ROD   BOOT

FIG 11:4   Master cylinder

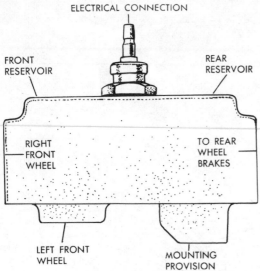

FIG 11:5   Distribution unit

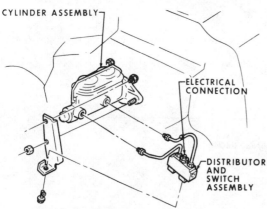

FIG 11:6   Distribution unit pipe connections

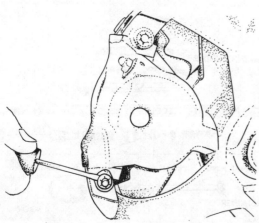

FIG 11:7   Removing caliper retainers

Reassembly:

Carefully compare the identification marks on the secondary piston with the markings on the repair kit. They must be identical.

1 Dip the secondary piston seals in new, clean fluid and fit the front seal to the piston. The seal with the smallest bore is the front seal and when assembled the lip of this seal must face the closed end of the cylinder. Fit the seal protector.
2 Install the seal retainer and spring seat.
3 Fit the second and third seal to the secondary piston. The second (middle) seal must face in the same direction as the front seal and towards the small holes around the piston. The third seal must face the opposite way; towards the pushrod.
4 Liberally coat the cylinder bore with clean fluid and then assemble the spring to the nose of the secondary piston. Gently insert spring and piston into the cylinder.
5 Insert the new primary piston followed by the pushrod and retainer. Install the new snap ring in its groove and fit the rubber boot. The inside of the boot may be coated with special rubber grease designed for use with hydraulic systems.
6 Put a quantity of new clean fluid in each reservoir and depress and release the pushrod to remove any air trapped in the cylinder.

Refitting:

1 Pass the pushrod through the bulkhead and bolt the cylinder in place tightening the nuts to 24 lb ft.
2 Connect the brake lines to their respective ports tightening the union nuts to 140 lb inch.
3 Attach the pushrod to the pedal with its pin and clip.
4 Fill the reservoirs and bleed the system (see **Section 11 : 7**).

11 : 4 The distribution unit and switch assembly

This is illustrated in **FIG 11 : 5** and its pipe connections and mounting detail in **FIG 11 : 6**. It cannot be repaired so that in the event of failure it must be renewed.

Testing switch unit:

1 Disconnect the electrical cable at the switch and reconnect it to a known good ground point. Switch on the ignition. The warning bulb on the dash panel should light up. If not, renew the bulb. If there is still no light trace the fault back through the electrical circuit and repair the circuit.
2 When the bulb lights, switch off the ignition and reconnect the cable to the switch unit.
3 See that both brake reservoirs are full of fluid.
4 Switch the ignition on and depress the brake pedal with some force. If all is well the bulb should not light. Switch off.
5 Attach a bleed hose to either one of the rear brake bleed screws and immerse the other end of the hose in a container partly filled with clean fluid.
6 Switch the ignition on while an assistant applies heavy pressure to the brake pedal. Release the bleed screw. The warning lamp must light. Close the bleed screw before releasing the pedal pressure. Switch off the ignition.

7 Transfer the bleed hose to one of the front brake bleed screws and repeat steps 5 and 6. Again the lamp must light.

   If the bulb lights when the cable is connected to ground but does not light at steps 5, 6 and 7 then the distribution unit and switch must be renewed.

   Remove the unit by first disconnecting the battery, then the switch cable and hydraulic pipes. Unbolt from the bracket. Take care not to spill fluid on the bodywork or allow dirt to enter the pipes.

   Make certain that the new unit is perfectly clean and install by reversing the removal process. Bleed the hydraulic system and reconnect the battery.

11 : 5 The disc brake

Fitting new friction pads:

1 It is not necessary for the hydraulic hose to be disconnected provided no strain is applied to it. Do not let the caliper hang from the hose when the caliper is removed from the steering knuckle. Tie it up to the suspension with a piece of wire or strong cord. When worn, thin pads are replaced with new ones of correct thickness the piston will be forced into the cylinder thus displacing up to half the volume of fluid in the master cylinder reservoir. It is wise to release the reservoir lid and pack old rag below the reservoir to mop up this spillage before beginning the operation of pad renewal.

2 Raise the car and safely support it so that the front wheels can be removed.

3 Refer to **FIG 11 : 7**. Lever off and discard the retainers then pull out the mounting pins (see **FIG 11 : 8**).

4 Lift the caliper from the disc, slide the pads to the mounting sleeve opening and lift out from the caliper (see **FIG 11 : 9**). Remove the mounting sleeve and bushing assembly.

5 Examine the caliper for signs of fluid leakage. If these are present the caliper must be overhauled. See that the piston boot is not damaged. Wipe the caliper clean with dry rag and then push the piston home in the cylinder.

6 Fit new sleeves and bushings with the shouldered ends as shown in **FIG 11 : 9**.

7 Insert the friction pads and install the caliper on the steering knuckle.

8 Push the mounting pins in from the direction of the outside of the car and press new retainers over their ends. A socket spanner which just presses on the circumference is ideal for this.

9 Top up the reservoir if necessary and refit the lid.

10 Apply pressure to the brake pedal two or three times to seat the pads and bring them to the correct position against the disc. This is all the brake adjustment needed.

11 Replace the road wheels and lower the car to the ground.

Overhauling the caliper:

   If any sign of fluid leakage is present in the caliper it must be dismantled and the cause found. Only two areas for leakage exist, one at the hose union and the other at the piston seal. Leakage at the hose union is unlikely but can be cured by fitting a new copper washer and

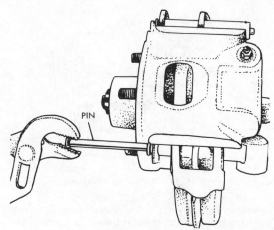

FIG 11 : 8   Extracting the mounting pins

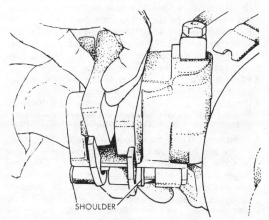

FIG 11 : 9   Removing or installing pads

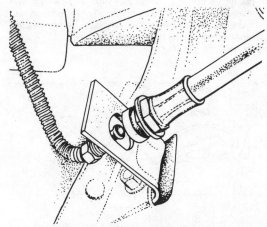

FIG 11 : 10   Hydraulic hose and pipe connection

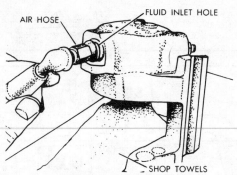

FIG 11:11 Removing a piston

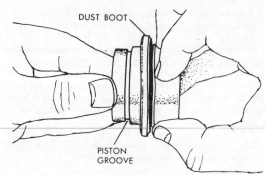

FIG 11:13 Assembling the piston and dust boot

tightening the bolt to 22 lb ft provided the hose is itself undamaged. Inspect carefully. If leakage is evidenced at the piston dust boot, proceed as follows:

1 Remove the caliper as described under 'Fitting new friction pads'.

2 Undo the union nut attaching the steel pipe to the flexible hose, remove the hose retainer and release the hose from the support bracket (see **FIG 11:10**). Be careful not to twist either the pipe or the hose. Use wrenches on both the union nut and the hose hexagons as a precaution although the bracket hole is so shaped that the hose should not turn.

3 Plug the pipe and hose ends and lift the caliper complete with hose away from the car.

4 Clean the exterior of the caliper and remove the hose. Discard the copper washer, these are never used twice.

5 Drain the fluid from the caliper then protect the casting with a pad of rag and blow the piston out with low pressure air as shown in **FIG 11:11**. Keep the fingers away from the piston while doing this. If no air-line is available, the piston can be removed by having an assistant pump the brake pedal before disconnecting the hydraulic hose thus using the hydraulic fluid pressure of the brake system.

6 Remove the dust boot as shown in **FIG 11:12** but be careful not to scratch the cylinder bore.

7 Remove the piston seal with a piece of wood or plastic, do not use a metal tool since any damage will involve renewal of the piston. These pistons are manufactured and plated to very close tolerances; no repair or refinishing is possible.

8 Remove the bleed screw.

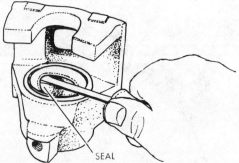

FIG 11:12 Removing the dust boot

Inspection:

Discard all rubber parts. Look for any sign of damage to the piston and discard at once if any doubt exists. Slight discolouration or corrosion of the cylinder bore can be polished out using nothing more abrasive than crocus cloth. Wash thoroughly after this.

Reassembly:

1 Coat the caliper bore and the new piston seal with clean hydraulic fluid and install the seal.

2 Coat the piston with clean fluid and assemble the dust boot as shown in **FIG 11:13**.

3 Insert the piston into the caliper bore and push it to the bottom (see **FIG 11:14**). Considerable force will be needed. Be careful not to dislodge the piston seal.

4 Seat the dust boot in the counter bore and drive home with tool J-23572 (see **FIG 11:15**).

5 Refit the hydraulic hose using a new copper washer and tighten the bolt to 22 lb ft. Refit the bleed screw.

6 Replace the caliper as described under 'Fitting new friction pads' and tighten the hose to pipe union nut to 140 lb inch.

7 Bleed the hydraulic system (see **Section 11:7**).

Refinishing the brake disc:

A badly pitted or scored disc may be reground provided the following tolerances are maintained.

1 Thickness must not be reduced below .470 inch by the refinishing process. Scrap the disc if it is worn to .440 inch.

2 Surface must be flat within .002 inch total indicator reading (TIR).

3 Faces must be parallel with each other within .003 inch (TIR).

4 Total thickness variation must not exceed .0005 inch in 360 deg.

5 Mounted on its bearings, lateral runout of disc must not exceed .005 inch (TIR).

6 No scratch marks or porosity may ve visible (surface finish must be 20 to 60 micro inch).

7 Both faces must be square with hub axis within .003 (TIR).

All discs have a dimension cast in. Scrap the disc at this figure if different from paragraph 1.

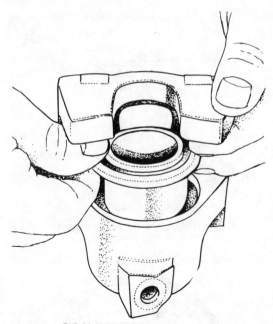

FIG 11 : 14   Inserting the piston

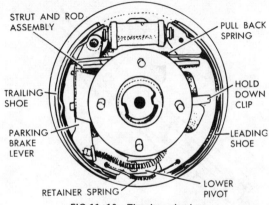

STRUT AND ROD ASSEMBLY

PULL BACK SPRING

TRAILING SHOE

HOLD DOWN CLIP

PARKING BRAKE LEVER

LEADING SHOE

RETAINER SPRING

LOWER PIVOT

FIG 11 : 16   The drum brake

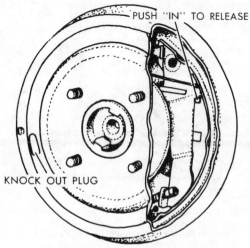

PUSH "IN" TO RELEASE

KNOCK OUT PLUG

FIG 11 : 17   Releasing a tight drum

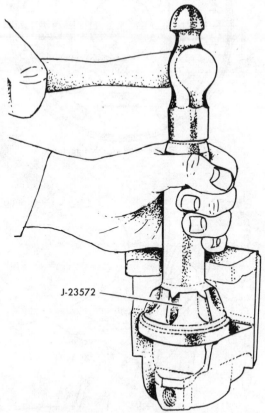

J-23572

FIG 11 : 15   Installing the dust boot

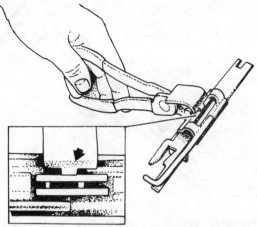

FIG 11 : 18   Releasing the strut and rod assembly

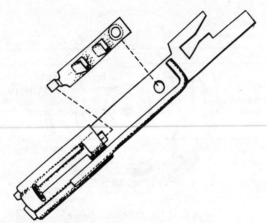

FIG 11 : 19   Components of the strut and rod assembly

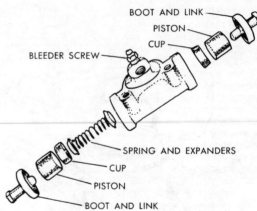

BOOT AND LINK
PISTON
CUP
BLEEDER SCREW
SPRING AND EXPANDERS
CUP
PISTON
BOOT AND LINK

FIG 11 : 22   Hydraulic slave cylinder

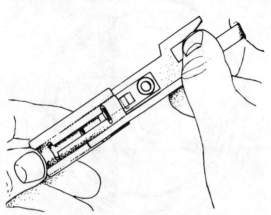

FIG 11 : 20   Reassembling the strut and rod

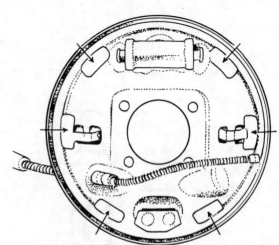

FIG 11 : 23   Brake shoe contact surfaces

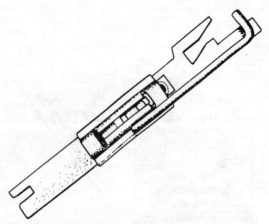

FIG 11 : 21   Strut and rod assembled for new brake shoes

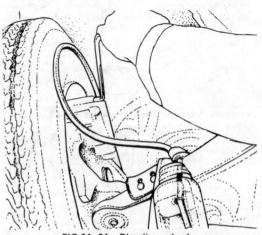

FIG 11 : 24   Bleeding a brake

11 : 6 The drum brake

FIG 11 : 16 shows the main features of the rear drum brake and illustrates the method of automatic clearance adjustment adopted for the brake shoes. This operates as follows:

When the parking brake is applied, the parking brake lever is pulled towards the hub by the brake cable; at the same time the strut and rod assembly act as a fulcrum and the top of the parking brake lever pushes the trailing shoe against the drum. The strut and rod assembly transmit the pressure of the parking brake lever to the leading shoe thus forcing this against the drum. The strut and rod assembly is so arranged that the rod can move outwards relative to the strut but cannot move inwards. Therefore the strut assembly can lengthen but not become shorter. The cranked end of the rod is fitted in a hole in the trailing shoe so that as the shoes move apart the rod is pulled out of the strut if sufficient clearance exists. When the parking brake is released the strut and rod assembly retains the length adopted when the brakes were applied and would still hold the shoes against the drum but for the fact that the hole in the trailing shoe is larger than the rod. This slackness gives the running clearance.

Dismantling:

1 Jack up and safely support the rear of the car. Remove the road wheels. Release the parking brake.
2 Remove the brake drum. If the drum will not pull away from the axle shaft it means that the shoe adjuster (strut and rod assembly) has just moved to a new position and there is insufficient shoe to drum clearance for the drum to move sideways. Refer to **FIG 11 : 17**. With a hammer and punch, knock in the plug. Turn the drum until the end of the rod in the trailing shoe can be pushed inwards away from the shoe. The pull back spring will then pull the shoes together and release the drum. Be sure to clear away all small pieces of metal and the plug from the brake mechanism. When reassembling the drum, fit the special cover obtainable from a Chevrolet Agent to the hole knocked in the drum.
3 Slacken the parking brake locknut and adjusting nut at the equalizer (see **FIG 11 : 2**), sufficiently for the brake cable to be detached from the lever (see **FIG 11 : 16**). Do not pull the lever towards the hub as this will extend the strut and rod assembly.
4 With a pair of pliers unhook and remove the pull back spring.
5 Pull the shoes from the hold down clips and remove from the backplate with the strut and rod assembly still attached. Detach the strut and rod assembly, parking brake lever and retainer spring.

If the hydraulic cylinder is not to be dismantled wind a piece of soft wire round the piston links to prevent the pistons being accidently released from the cylinder.
6 Refer to **FIG 11 : 18**. With tool J-23730 press down on the strut adjuster locks until the rod can be pushed clear of the strut. The dismantled strut and rod can be seen in **FIG 11 : 19**. Renew any worn parts then reset the assembly by starting the rod into position as shown in **FIG 11 : 29** and then pushing the rod up to the position shown in **FIG 11 : 21**. This will be the proper

length for fitting new brake shoes. If the rod is pushed too far, the shoes will be held so far apart that the brake drum cannot be installed.

The hydraulic slave cylinder:

Refer to **FIG 11 : 22**. With the brake dismantled as far as the preceding operation 5, disconnect the brake pipe from the rear of the cylinder and plug the pipe. Undo the bolts holding the cylinder to the brake backplate and remove the cylinder. Wipe the exterior clean and then dismantle on a clean bench. Observe the same rules of cleanliness that were demanded for work on the master cylinder and front brake. Pull the boots from each end of the cylinder and release the piston, seals and expander. Examine the bore of the cylinder; any scratches, scores or pitting must mean rejection. If a piston has stuck in the cylinder the whole unit should be scrapped. Slight discolouration that can be polished out with crocus cloth will not be harmful. When using crocus cloth always polish radially, never from end to end. Wash the cylinder thoroughly in clean, new fluid. Discard the seals and boots. If the pistons are scratched or corroded renew these as well.

Coat the cylinder bore with clean fluid and assemble the components as shown in **FIG 11 : 22**. Do not lubricate the seals with fluid before assembly. The flat end of each piston must be inserted first.

Bolt the cylinder to the backplate and reconnect the hydraulic pipe. When the brake drum is refitted, bleed the brakes (see **Section 11 : 7**).

The brake drums:

Use an inside micrometer and check for size and truth. Any 'out of round' or deep scoring of the friction surface must mean renewal or machining. Drums may be skimmed provided that the finished diameter does not exceed 9.030 inches.

Reassembly:

1 Smear a little high melting point grease on the surfaces indicated by arrows in **FIG 11 : 23**. Keep this grease to a minimum and away from the hydraulic cylinder and shoe friction surfaces.
2 Fit the parking brake lever and strut assembly to the trailing shoe. Connect the shoes with the retainer spring and fit to the backplate. The retainer spring must pass below the lower pivot (see **FIG 11 : 16**).
3 See that both shoes are underneath their hold down clips then guide the strut and rod assembly into position in the leading shoe. Install the pull back spring. Do not move the parking brake lever forward or the strut and rod assembly will be extended. Check that the pull back spring is over the parking brake lever.
4 Connect the parking brake cable and adjust the equalizer nut to approximately its previous position without moving the lever at the brake.
5 Refit the brake drum and road wheel.
6 Apply the parking brake two or three times to adjust the shoe clearance then adjust the parking brake at the equalizer as described in **Section 11 : 2**.
7 If necessary bleed the hydraulic system. Lower the car to the ground. Tighten the road wheel nuts.

11:7 Brake bleeding

An assistant will be needed for this operation. Clean the master cylinder reservoir surface and remove the lid. Top up with clean, new brake fluid, GM Supreme No. 11 or equivalent. Never use fluid bled from the brakes as it may contain impurities such as water or entrapped air. Keep the reservoir topped up as bleeding proceeds.

Fit a hose to a brake bleed screw and submerge its lower end in clean fluid. A glass jar as shown in **FIG 11:24** is ideal. The hose must remain below the fluid surface throughout the operation. The brakes may be bled in any sequence, it is immaterial which one is bled first.

Unscrew the bleed screw $\frac{1}{3}$ turn and slowly depress the brake pedal. Just before the pedal reaches the end of its travel, close the screw and allow the pedal to return slowly. Continue this sequence until no air bubbles are seen to issue from the hose into the jar. Tighten the bleed screw and remove the hose. Repeat for the remaining brakes. Top up the reservoirs and fit the lid.

11:8 Fault diagnosis

(a) Poor braking performance

1 Worn linings or pads
2 Oil or grease on friction surfaces
3 Water in drums
4 Hydraulic failure
5 Air in system

(b) Brakes grab

1 Contaminated friction linings or pads
2 Unevenly worn brake disc
3 Brake drum out of round

(c) Soft brakes, excessive pedal movement

1 Air in hydraulic system
2 One brake circuit leaking
3 Lack of hydraulic fluid

(d) Warning light inoperative

1 Check switch and pedal contact
2 Check electrical circuit

(e) Brake failure light inoperative

1 Check distribution switch
2 Check lamp bulb
3 Check circuit

(f) Brakes pull to one side

1 Contaminated friction pads
2 Seized piston
3 Unevenly worn disc

CHAPTER 12

THE ELECTRICAL SYSTEM

12:1 Description

A 12-volt electrical system is fitted to all models described in this manual. The circuit is of the negative ground polarity in which the battery negative connection is made to the car frame. Battery charging current is supplied by the 'Delcotron' (alternator) which has its own regulating mechanism of transistors and diodes. No separate voltage or current regulator is needed.

As a general rule, it is wiser to renew or exchange units which are mechanically or electrically faulty than to attempt to repair them. If accurate test instruments are available it is possible to carry out tests of the charging system provided that precautions are taken to protect the alternator as described in the appropriate Section.

The main wiring circuits are illustrated in **Technical Data** at the end of this manual but detail circuits are given in this **Chapter** where necessary.

12:2 The Battery (energizer)

This is of the lead/acid type and is contained in a robust case with all cell connections moulded internally to reduce electrical losses. Occasionally wipe the exterior with a cloth soaked in a dilute solution of ammonia or soda then wash off with clean water. Keep the vent plugs tight to prevent the ammonia or soda from entering the cells.

Clean the connecting lugs and cable ends with the same neutralizer, dry off and coat with petroleum jelly. Keep the cable bolts tight.

The second cell from the positive terminal has an electrolyte level indicator incorporated. When the centre of the indicator appears dark the electrolyte is at a safe level, when it appears light, distilled water or clean soft water must be added. Only one indicator is fitted since it is known that this particular cell mirrors the condition of the other cells. All must be topped up if this one is low. Never add acid to the battery. If spillage has occurred take the battery to a qualified Service Agent for refilling and charging.

The battery may be charged at any rate of amperes provided that the electrolyte temperature does not exceed 125°F and that violent gassing does not throw electrolyte from the vent holes. It is always best to remove the battery from the car when charging from an outside power source. To test the battery condition a hydrometer is required. A fully charged battery should give a specific gravity reading of 1.260 to 1.280. A reading below 1.200

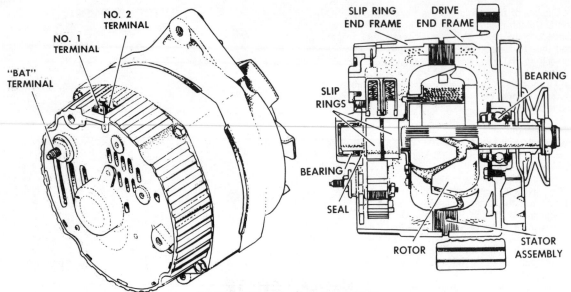

FIG 12:1 The Delcotron, Series 10-S1

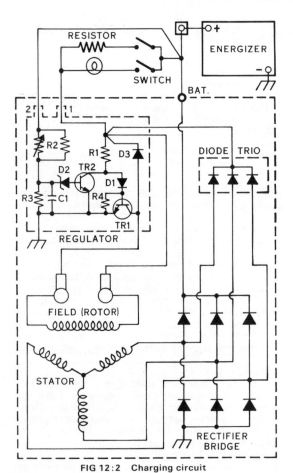

FIG 12:2 Charging circuit

shows a fully discharged, or defective battery and a reading above 1.310 indicates that the wrong mixture of acid and water was used to activate the battery when new. To obtain an accurate check on battery condition first see that the correct electrolyte level is maintained then put the battery on slow charge at 5 amps for between 10 and 15 hours. When all cells have gassed freely for 2 hours and no change in specific gravity has occurred the battery is as fully charged as its condition will allow. Never put a naked light near the vents when charging as an explosive gas is given off by the electrolute. If a quick check is required, charge the battery at a rate high enough to cause vigorous gassing for 15 minutes. Never test the electrolyte immediately after adding water.

Temperature variations will affect hydrometer readings. For every 10°F above 80°F add .004 to the specific gravity reading and subtract .004 for every 10°F below 80°F.

If hydrometer readings show a difference between cells of .050 or more, the battery must be renewed.

12:3 The Delcotron (alternator)

The current generator, rectifier and regulator are contained within the one unit; **FIG 12:1** shows the main constructional details. The regulator components are moulded in one piece and no provision is made for adjustment or repair of this part of the unit. The bearings are filled with lubricant and sealed for life. AC produced by the stator winding is converted to DC by a rectifier bridge of six diodes protected from high voltage by a capacitor. The energizing current to the field (rotor) winding is supplied through the diode trio also connected to the stator windings. The operation of the unit will be understood if the following explanation is read in conjunction with the circuit diagram (see **FIG 12:2**).

Closing of the switch allows battery current to flow to the Delcotron No. 1 terminal then through resistor R1, diode D1, the base emitter of transistor TR1 to ground and thus back to the battery. TR1 turns on and current flows from TR1 through the field winding and back to the battery. This energizes the field winding in the rotor and as the engine starts to turn the rotor, AC is generated in the stator windings. Part of this AC passes back through the diode trio, is rectified to DC and then to the field winding. The alternator is now providing its own field current independently of the battery. This field current passes through TR1, the grounded diodes in the rectifier bridge and back to the stator. The six diodes in the bridge convert the rising AC to DC which appears between ground and the 'BAT' terminal of the Delcotron.

The No. 2 terminal is always connected to the battery but the current passed is limited by the high resistances of R2 and R3. As the Delcotron speed and voltage increase so the voltage between R2 and R3 rises until the zener diode D2 conducts, TR2 then turns on and TR1 off. With TR1 off the field current is cut and the system voltage drops until D2 stops conducting. The field current is restored by TR1 again conducting and the system voltage and current again rise. This cycle is repeated many times per second to hold the output to the designed figure.

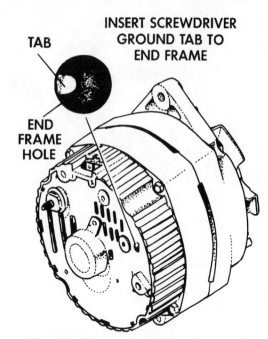

FIG 12:3   Test aperture, field winding (rotor)

Testing the Delcotron in situ:

Check that all connections are tight and clean and that the battery is fully charged. This is important.

Never polarize the Delcotron, short or ground any connection unless specifically instructed in this Section or operate the Delcotron with the 'BAT' terminal disconnected. Always see that the Delcotron and battery are of the same polarity. Proceed to test for causes of the defects as listed in the following paragraphs.

Indicator lamp on when switch is off:

Disconnect leads 1 and 2 from the Delcotron. If the lamp remains alight, these leads are shorted together. A defective rectifier bridge can also cause this fault.

Engine stationary, switch on but lamp does not light:

1 Test bulb. Check for blown fuse or fusible link.
2 Check that the leads to terminals 1 and 2 of the Delcotron are not reversed, shorted together or open circuit.
3 Connect an 0-20 voltmeter from No. 2 terminal to ground. If no reading on the voltmeter, trace the cable to the battery and find the open circuit.
4 Disconnect the leads from terminals 1 and 2, switch on and check lead No. 1 for open circuit. Do not allow lead No. 2 to ground. Momentarily ground lead No. 1.
5 If lamp now lights, reconnect the leads 1 and 2 to the terminals, then insert a screwdriver blade in the test hole (see **FIG 12:3**) and ground the winding. Do not insert the screwdriver more than $\frac{3}{4}$ inch. Reconnect the voltmeter between No. 2 terminal and ground.

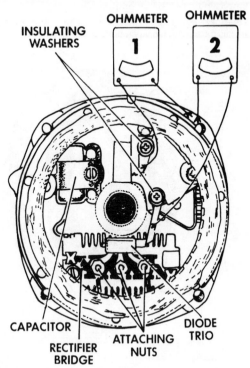

FIG 12:4   Test for defective regulator or brush lead clip

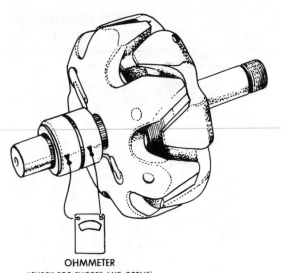

OHMMETER
(CHECK FOR SHORTS AND OPENS)

FIG 12:5   Testing rotor

A reading now means that the regulator must be renewed. If the lamp does not light at this stage, check the wiring harness connection at No. 1 terminal again then check brushes, slip rings and field winding as described later.

Lamp remains on when engine is running:

See next paragraph. The causes of this fault are the same as those which give an undercharged battery.

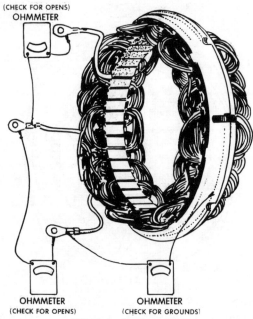

(CHECK FOR OPENS)
OHMMETER

OHMMETER
(CHECK FOR OPENS)

OHMMETER
(CHECK FOR GROUNDS)

FIG 12:6   Testing stator

Battery is continually undercharged:

1 Test battery for condition. It must be fully charged for the tests to be valid. Check cleanliness of terminal posts.
2 Check Delcotron belt tension and all wiring connections.
3 Switch on. Connect the voltmeter in turn between 'BAT' No. 1 and No. 2 terminals and ground. No reading indicates an open circuit to be traced and repaired.
4 Disconnect battery ground cable. Connect an ammeter in the circuit at the Delcotron 'BAT' terminal. Reconnect the battery. Connect a carbon pile across the battery then turn on the radio, windshield wiper, all lights on high beam and the blower motor at high speed.
5 Start and run the engine at 1500 to 2000 rev/min. Adjust the carbon pile to give the highest reading possible on the ammeter. If this reading is within 10 per cent of the rated output as stamped on the Delcotron frame, the Delcotron is not defective. Recheck the wiring. If the reading is not within 10 per cent, ground the field winding (see **FIG 12:3**). If the output now comes within the 10 per cent renew the regulator and check the field winding. If the output does not even now come within 10 per cent, check the field winding, diode trio, rectifier bridge and stator.

Battery is continually overcharged (requires constant topping up):

1 The battery must be in good condition and fully charged for the tests to be valid.
2 Connect the voltmeter between terminal 2 and ground. No reading indicates that the fault is an open circuit in this wiring putting the regulator out of action.
3 If operation 2 does not reveal the fault, remove the Delcotron and dismantle as described later. Refer to **FIG 12:4**. Set the ohmmeter to its lowest range and connect between the brush lead clip and the frame then reverse the connections. If no reading in either direction either the brush lead clip is grounded or the regulator must be renewed. Check that the insulating washers and sleeves are in position on the brush lead clip before renewing the regulator.

Overhauling the Delcotron:

Dismantling:

1 Grip the Delcotron in the vice by one of the mounting lugs. Fit a ring spanner to the pulley mounting nut and an Allen key into the end of the shaft. Hold the key and undo the nut. Slide the washers, pulley, fan and spacer from the shaft.
2 Scribe a line lengthwise on the body then remove the four through-bolts. Prise the stator and slip ring end away from the drive end by inserting a screwdriver at the stator slot. Slide the rotor from the drive end and remove the stator lead nuts so that the stator can be disconnected.
   Note: Many of the electrical tests can now be made without further dismantling. Refer to later paragraphs.

3 Remove the diode trio screw and release the diode trio from the end frame. Keep careful note of the position of insulating washers and sleeve.

4 Remove the rectifier bridge screw, the 'BAT' terminal screw, disconnect the capacitor lead and remove the rectifier bridge.

5 Remove the brush holder and regulator. Important: Note which screws have insulating washers and sleeve.

6 Remove the capacitor.

Inspection:

1 Wash all metal parts except stator and rotor assemblies in cleaning fluid.

2 Inspect the bearings for roughness or slack. Renew the slip ring end bearing if the grease supply is exhausted. Never repack this bearing.

3 Mount the rotor between centres in a lathe. Check the slip rings for truth with a dial indicator. Both must run within .001 inch maximum indicator reading. Skim with a sharp tool and polish with 400 grade polishing cloth if necessary. If badly burnt beyond the ability to clean up without a heavy cut, then the rotor must be renewed.

4 If the brushes have worn to half length, renew. See that the springs are not distorted and that the brushes move freely in the holder. Clean the brushes with trichlorethylene should they be contaminated with oil or grease.

Electrical testing of dismantled components:

Where an ohmmeter is required employ one powered by a $1\frac{1}{2}$-volt cell and use the lowest range.

Rotor field winding (see FIG 12:5):

1 Connect the ohmmeter as shown. If the reading is high the winding is open circuit.

2 Connect an ammeter and 12-volt battery in series with the slip rings. An ammeter reading above 4.5 amps indicates a shortcircuit.

Stator winding (see FIG 12:6):

1 Connect the ohmmeter between any lead and the frame. If the reading is low, the windings are shorted to ground.

2 Connect the ohmmeter between each pair of leads. If the reading is high, the windings are open circuit.

3 Windings shorted to adjacent coils are difficult to find due to the low resistance of even a good winding. If all other tests are normal but the alternator will not give the rated output, suspect a shorted winding. Sometimes the affected part shows up due to the heat discolouring the insulation.

Diode trio (see FIG 12:7):

Connect the ohmmeter as shown. Note the reading then reverse the connections. A good diode will give one high and one low reading. Repeat for the other two connectors of the three. If any one diode gives two readings the same, renew the trio.

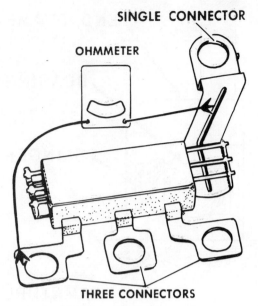

FIG 12:7   Testing diode trio

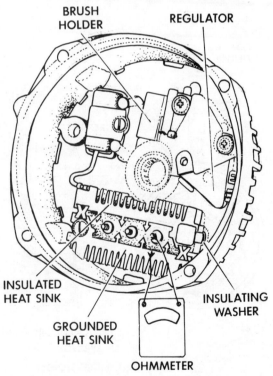

FIG 12:8   Testing the rectifier bridge

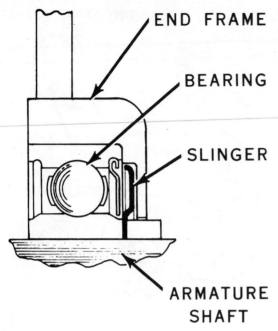

FIG 12:9   Drive end bearing

Rectifier bridge (see FIG 12:8):

Connect the ohmmeter as shown. Note the reading then reverse the connections. One reading must be high, the other low. If both are the same, renew the entire bridge. Repeat for the other two terminals then between the insulated heat sink and the three terminals. When completed, all six diodes will have been tested with two readings at each. Renew the bridge if any one diode gives the same readings in each direction.

Regulator (see FIG 12:4):

Overcharged battery (see paragraph 3):

Important: When dismantling the regulator do not interchange the screws. The brush lead clips must be fitted with insulating sleeved and washers; if not, the alternator will either give an uncontrolled or no output. The insulating washers are clearly shown in FIG 12:4.

Bearing renewal:

Drive end frame:

1 Remove the retainer bolts, retainer plate and seal. Press the bearing out.
2 Fill the new bearing one quarter full with Delco-Remy No. 1948791 grease. Do not overfill.
3 Press the bearing into the frame (see FIG 12:9). Install retainer plate, seal and bolts. Tighten bolts and stake to the frame.

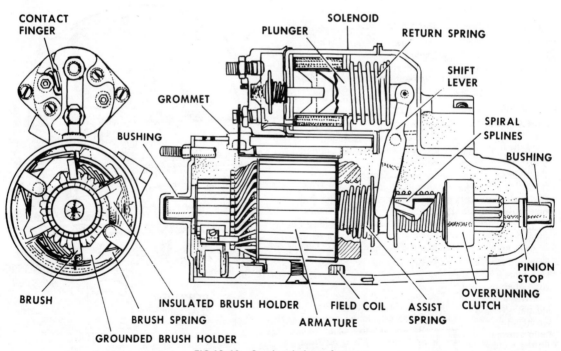

FIG 12:10   Sectional view of starter

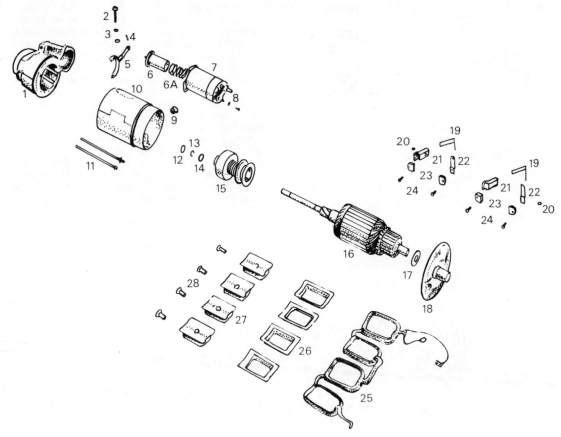

FIG 12:11   Starter dismantled

Key to Fig 12:11   1 Drive housing   2 Shift lever bolt   3 Shift lever nut and lockwasher   4 Pin   5 Shift lever   6 Solenoid plunger   6a Solenoid return spring   7 Solenoid case   8 Screw and lockwasher   9 Grommet   10 Field frame   11 Through-bolts   12 Thrust collar   13 Snap ring   14 Retainer   15 Overrunning clutch assembly   16 Armature   17 Braking washer   18 Commutator end frame   19 Brush springs   20 Washer   21 Insulated brush holders   22 Grounded brush holders   23 Brushes   24 Screws   25 Field coils   26 Insulators   27 Pole shoes   28 Screws

Slip ring end frame:

1 Press the old bearing towards the inside of the frame until it is free of the housing.

2 Press the new bearing in from the outside of the frame until it is flush with the housing.

3 Lightly cover the new seal lip with oil and press in with the seal lip towards the inside of the frame.

Reassembly:

1 Fit the rotor to the drive end frame and assemble the spacer, fan, pulley, washer and nut. Tighten the nut to 40 to 50 lb ft.

2 Refer to **FIG 12:4**. Install the capacitor in the slip ring end frame followed by the brush holder and regulator. Note that the screws holding the brush lead clips (shown nearly vertically above one another in the illustration), must have the insulating sleeves and washers fitted. Fit the top screw first, then the right-hand screw (not insulated).

3 Fit the rectifier bridge, fit the holding screw and the 'BAT' terminal. Connect the capacitor lead.

4 Fit the diode trio over the rectifier terminals and then install the third screw (insulated) through the diode trio clip and into the brush holder. The insulating washer must be on top of the clip.

5 Place the stator in the slip ring end frame. Connect the stator leads to the rectifier bridge terminals.

6 Hold the brushes up in their guides with a toothpick or similar passed through the slot in the slip ring end frame.

7 Fit the slip ring end frame and stator to the drive end frame in line with the scribed mark made when dismantling. Install and tighten the through bolts. Remove the restraint from the brushes.

12:4 The starter motor

Tests:

If the starter fails to crank the engine or only cranks slowly, first check the battery condition. If the battery is well charged proceed to the following circuit resistance checks.

1 Disconnect the distributor primary (LT) lead so that the engine cannot start.

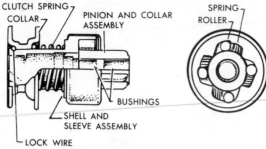

CLUTCH SPRING
COLLAR
PINION AND COLLAR
ASSEMBLY
SPRING
ROLLER
BUSHINGS
SHELL AND
SLEEVE ASSEMBLY
LOCK WIRE

FIG 12:12   Clutch in section

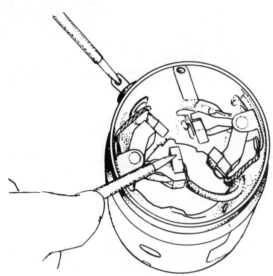

FIG 12:13   Field coil test

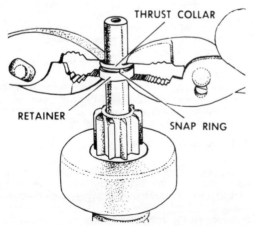

THRUST COLLAR

RETAINER

SNAP RING

FIG 12:14   Assembling snap ring and retainer

2 Connect a good 0-20 voltmeter between the battery positive terminal and the solenoid battery terminal. Operate the starter. Keep this period of operation below 30 seconds at any one time.

3 Repeat between the battery negative terminal and motor housing.

4 Repeat between the solenoid battery and motor terminals.

If the checks at steps 2, 3 and 4 show a voltage drop of more than .2 volts there is high resistance in the circuit which is affecting the motor performance.

If the solenoid will not pull in, repeat the preceding tests with the voltmeter connected between the battery and switch (S) terminals of the solenoid. If the voltage drop exceeds 3.5 volts there is high resistance in the solenoid control circuit. As a precaution check that there are at least 7.7 volts available at the S terminal. The solenoid should operate at this voltage when cold although a slightly higher voltage is needed when warm.

If the solenoid chatters but will not hold in, the hold in winding is open circuit. Renew the solenoid.

Dismantling:

Disconnect the battery ground cable and unbolt the starter from the engine. It is usually easiest to remove the starter from below the car.

Refer to **FIGS 12:10** and **12:11**.

1 Disconnect the strap connector between the solenoid and the motor field coil.

2 Remove the two screws holding the solenoid to the motor.

3 Turn solenoid clockwise and separate from motor.

4 Remove the through bolts 11 (see **FIG 12:11**).

5 Release the commutator end frame 18 and the field frame 10 from the drive housing 1. Support the brushes and extract the armature 16. Do not lose the braking washers 17.

6 Remove the overrunning clutch as follows: Slide the thrust collar 12 from the shaft; with a piece of tube drive the retainer 14 back along the shaft exposing the snap ring 13, remove the snap ring and then slide the retainer from the shaft. Pull the clutch from the shaft.

7 Dismantle the brush gear as follows: Release spring 19 from the slot in the brush holder support, remove the support pin and lift the brush holder, brush and spring away as a unit. Disconnect the lead. Repeat for the remaining brushes.

Wipe all parts clean but do not use solvent on the clutch, armature or field coils. Note that the field coils need not be removed unless defective.

Inspection and repair:

1 Check that the clutch spins freely one way but locks in the opposite direction. See that the pinion teeth are not badly worn, chipped or cracked. If the clutch spring is broken, push the collar (see **FIG 12:12** towards the pinion, extract the lock wire (snap ring) release the collar and remove the spring. Fit a new spring and reassemble the clutch with a new snap ring. It is usual for these clutches to be supplied as a unit, therefore no other repair is possible.

2 See that the brush gear is not damaged and examine the brushes. If these are worn to half their new length they must be renewed.

3 Test the fit of the armature shaft in both bearings. If the bush in the drive end housing is worn it may be pressed out and a replacement fitted. A worn bush at the commutator end necessitate a new commutator end frame.

4 Inspect the commutator. If the surface is reasonably smooth and consistent throughout the circumference it may be rotated in a lathe and polished with 00 sandpaper. Never use any other abrasive. Should it be scored more deeply all round the circumference, mount it in a lathe between centres and skim the commutator using a sharp tool, fine feed and medium speed. Remove the minimum amount of metal necessary to clean up. If one bar of the commutator is badly burnt, this is a clear sign of a 'thrown' winding. Renew the armature unless the poor connection is obviously between the commutator bar and winding. Resolder using a resin flux. If the commutator is of the built-up type, undercut the insulation between the bars. The cut must be $\frac{1}{32}$ inch deep, square bottomed and the full width of the insulation. If the commutator has moulded insulation do not undercut this or serious damage will result. After undercutting a built-up commutator, rotate in a lathe and polish with 00 sandpaper to remove burrs.

Electrical tests:

Armature:

Shortcircuit testing can only be carried out on a 'growler'. If this is available, rotate the armature on the blocks while holding a hacksaw blade above it and in the same plane as the armature axis. If the blade vibrates the armature is shorted and must be renewed.

A grounded armature can be checked with a 12-volt bulb and battery. Place one lead on the commutator and the other on the shaft. If the bulb lights the armature is grounded and must be renewed.

Field coil tests:

Use a 12-volt bulb and battery. Place one lead on an insulated brush and the other on the field coil connector (see **FIG 12:13**). No light means an open circuit. Disconnect the shunt coil. Place one lead on the connector bar and the other on a grounded brush. If the lamp lights the coils are grounded. Both defects indicate renewal of the coils.

Reassembly:

1 Assemble the brush gear and brushes.

2 Coat the drive end of the armature shaft with silicone grease, fit the clutch and pinion assembly then the retainer cupped side outwards. Fit the snap ring to the shaft groove then the thrust collar. Use two pairs of pliers and squeeze until the snap ring is forced into retainer (see **FIG 12:14**).

3 Lubricate the drive end bush with silicone grease and slide the armature into the drive end frame, engaging the clutch collar with the shift lever.

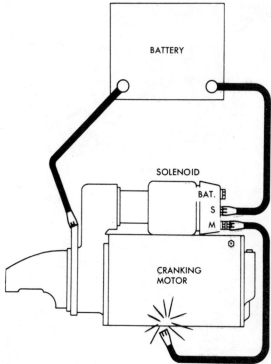

FIG 12:15 Energizing the solenoid to check pinion clearance

4 Slide the field frame over the armature, carefully seating the brushes on the commutator.

5 Fit the braking washer to the armature shaft and lubricate the end frame brush with silicone grease. Assemble the end frame, fit the through-bolts and tighten securely. If the solenoid is in place, reconnect the field coil strap to the 'motor' terminal unless the pinion clearance is to be checked.

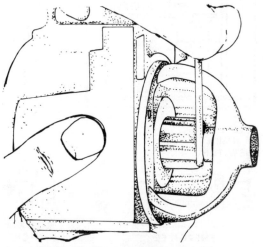

FIG 12:16 Measuring pinion clearance

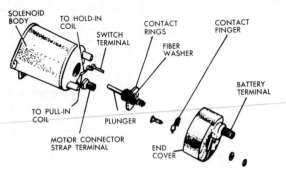

FIG 12:17 Solenoid dismantled

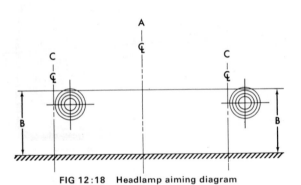

FIG 12:18 Headlamp aiming diagram

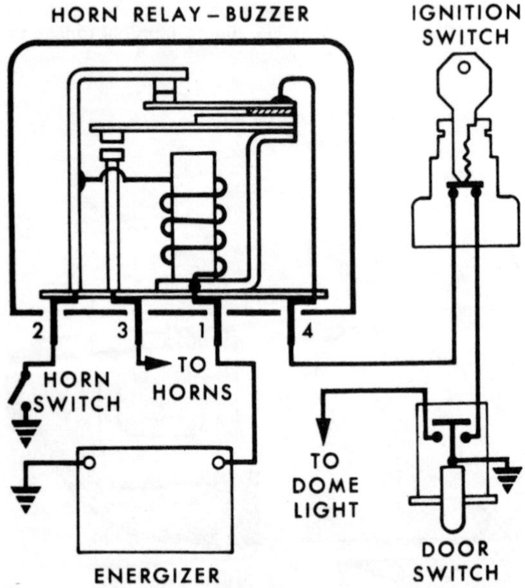

HORN RELAY – BUZZER

FIG 12:19 Horn relay buzzer circuit

Pinion clearance check:

Disconnect the motor field coil to solenoid strap. Connect motor and battery as shown in **FIG 12:15**. Flash the lead from the motor terminal to the motor case for a moment. The pinion will now move to the cranking position. Measure the clearance as illustrated in **FIG 12:16**. If the clearance is not between .010 and .140 inch find and correct the fault. No adjustment is provided so a worn part or incorrect assembly are the only causes.

Renewing solenoid contacts (see FIG 12:17):

1 Remove solenoid from motor and remove nuts and washers from 'switch' and 'motor' terminals.
2 Remove two screws and release end cover.
3 Remove battery terminal, resistor bypass terminal and contactor.
4 Remove motor strap terminal and solder new one in place.
5 Fit new battery terminal washer and nut to end cover. Fit bypass terminal and contactor.
6 Refit end cover and install screws. Fit terminal nuts and washers.
7 Replace the solenoid on the motor, turning anticlockwise to engage the flange key in the slot. Refit holding screws and reconnect motor field coil connector strap.

12:5 Fuses and fusible link

The fuse block is located inside the car just above and to the right of the headlamp dimmer switch. Each fuse holder is marked with the fuse rating and the circuit it protects. The small can plugged into the corner of the fuse block is the four-way hazard flasher unit.

The fusible link is a conductor two gauge sizes smaller than the wiring cable it has to protect. In the event of operation, the link covering will be heavily discoloured. Fit a new link by splicing and soldering into the cable. Links are fitted in the following locations: (a) In the circuit from the horn relay to the fuse block, (b) Two links in the circuit from the starter solenoid to the horn relay, in the circuit from the starter solenoid to the ammeter and from the horn relay to the heated backlight timer.

12:6 Turn direction indicator

Operation of the indicator in one direction but not in the other indicates a faulty bulb. Failure in both directions is usually a defective flasher unit. This is located behind the instrument panel at the left. Pull it from the holding clip and unplug from the cable. Fit a new unit. No signal now indicates a wiring defect.

12:7 Headlamps
Renewing a light unit:

1 Remove the headlamp bezel by unscrewing the three Philips head screws.
2 Hook the retaining spring away from the unit.
3 Rotate the righthand headlamp clockwise and the lefthand one anticlockwise to release.
4 Remove the cable plug.
5 Remove the metal retaining ring.
Fit the new unit by reversing the preceding operations.

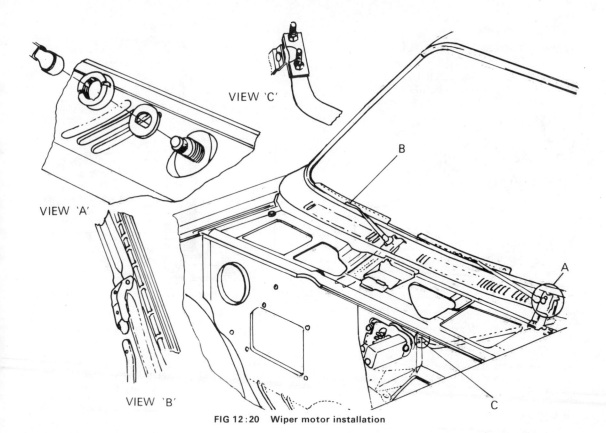

VIEW 'C'

VIEW 'A'

VIEW 'B'

B

A

C

FIG 12:20 Wiper motor installation

Headlamp aiming (see FIG 12:18):

There is no need to remove the headlamp bezel. The two aiming screws will be self-evident upon inspection.
1 If the car spends most of its time with an unusual load at the back, carry out this operation with the load installed (e.g. heavy equipment in the trunk or towing a trailer). If not, the gas tank should be half-full and the car unladen.
2 Position the car on the level 25 feet from a wall to the headlamps.
3 Measure the centre height of the headlamps and mark this height on the wall (B).
4 Mark the centre line of the car on the wall (A).
5 Mark the centres of the headlamps each side of (A). Dimension (C).
6 Switch on low beam. The brightest part of the beam should fall 4 inch to the right and below the intersection of lines (B) and (C). If the car is operated in a lefthand drive country, adjust the beam 4 inch to the left and below the intersection.
7 To raise or lower the beam, adjust the top screw; to traverse the beam, adjust the side screw.

12:8 Theft deterrent system

Refer to **FIG 12:19**.

A buzzer has been incorporated in the horn relay to warn the driver if the ignition key is inadvertently left in the lock and the drivers door is opened. To test for buzzer and horn relay operation proceed as follows.

Buzzer:

1 Insert the ignition key in the switch.
2 Open the driver's door, if both the dome lamp and the buzzer fail to work, check the door switch.
3 If the dome lamp lights but the buzzer does not sound, connect No. 4 terminal on the relay to ground. If the buzzer now works, check the ignition switch and wiring. If the buzzer still does not work connect a voltmeter between No. 1 terminal and ground. No reading indicates an open circuit; a voltage reading shows that the relay is at fault.

Horn relay:

1 Connect No. 2 terminal to ground. If the horn now operates, check the circuit to the terminal and the horn switch.
2 If the horn still does not sound, leave No. 2 terminal grounded and connect a voltmeter between terminal 3 and ground. No reading indicates a faulty relay, a reading shows that the defect lies in the horn or its circuit from the relay.

12:9 Windshield wiper motor servicing

The motor is a two-speed compound wound unit driving a gear train and transmission links. **FIG 12:20** shows the location of the motor and also the correct position for the wiper blades when parked. A cam on the output shaft opens the park switch contacts at each

LO SPEED - AS SHOWN

HI SPEED - DISCONNECT JUMPER WIRE FROM
TERMINAL NO. 3.

OFF - LEAVE JUMPER CONNECTED TO NOS. 1 & 3 BUT
DISCONNECT IT FROM GRD. STRAP. WIPER SHOULD
STOP WITH GEAR SHAFT FLATS AS SHOWN.

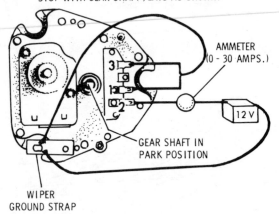

FIG 12:21   Wiper motor test circuit

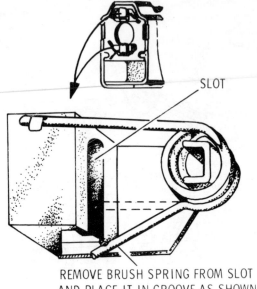

REMOVE BRUSH SPRING FROM SLOT
AND PLACE IT IN GROOVE AS SHOWN

FIG 12:23   Brush spring detail

revolution; if the dash panel switch is in the 'OFF'
position, then the blades should stop as shown in **FIG
12:20**.

Testing the motor:

Before dismantling the motor, carry out the following
tests to determine the reason for unsatisfactory operation.
(a) See that all connections are clean and sound, that
current is reaching the motor (check fuse) and that the
dash panel switch and motor are properly connected
to ground.

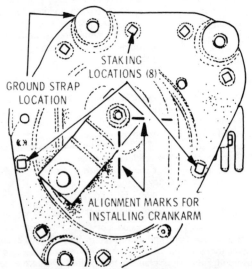

FIG 12:22   Wiper motor gearbox end cover

(b) Refer to **FIG 12:21**, remove the wiring harness from
the motor and connect temporary leads as shown.
Connect the battery to ground strap last. The motor
should now operate at low speed. Disconnect
terminal number 3, the wiper should now operate at
high speed. Reconnect terminal number 3 and disconnect the jumper lead from the ground strap but
leave 1 and 3 coupled. The wiper should run until it
reaches the park position then stop.
(c) If the motor still fails to operate or runs sluggishly
disconnect the link from the crank arm and repeat
step (b). If there is still no improvement the motor
must be removed. If the motor now runs at correct
speed, suspect a seized spindle and housing.
(d) If the motor runs correctly when connected as at step
(b) then the trouble will lie in either the dash panel
switch or the wiring connections.

Removing and refitting the motor:

1 Refer to **FIG 12:20**. Disconnect the wiring harness
from the motor then release the two bolts 'C' and free
the link from the crank.
2 Undo the three bolts holding the motor to the panel
and lift it out through the cowl opening.
Refitting is a reversal of the removal process.

Removing and replacing wiper arms and blades:

Use a forked tool to prise the arms from the spindle
bosses and make sure when refitting that the blades are
positioned as shown in **FIG 12:20**. Blades are disconnected from the wiper arms by pressing the arm back
against the spring in the blade socket until the indent is
free of the blade socket face (see view 'B' of **FIG 12:20**).

Dismantling the motor:

1 Grip the crank arm in a vice and remove the nut, crank arm, sealing cap and washers.
2 Refer to **FIG 12:22.** With a $\frac{9}{32}$ inch drill, remove the staking that secures the end cover. Mark the position of the ground strap.
3 Remove the gears.
4 Note the position of the motor leads on the terminals of the parking switch board then unsolder the leads.
5 Drill out the parking switch board and ground strap rivets with a $\frac{7}{64}$ inch drill.
6 Remove the two long tie bolts which pass through the motor, hold the end cap against the motor and disengage the motor from the gearbox.
7 Release the brush springs from the brushes, move the brushes clear of the commutator then release the armature from the frame and field assembly. Remove the end cap from the armature. Do not lose the plastic thrust plug from the end of the shaft. Remove the end float washers.

Testing the motor:

Use a twelve-volt battery and test lamp.

Armature:

(a) Apply the probes to adjacent bars of the commutator. The lamp should light. If not, the winding is open circuit.
(b) Apply the probes between the commutator bars and the armature shaft. The light must not light, if it does, the armature is grounded.

Failure at either step (a) or (b) involves renewal of the armature.

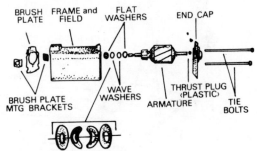

WASHER ARRANGEMENT

FIG 12:24   Wiper motor dismantled

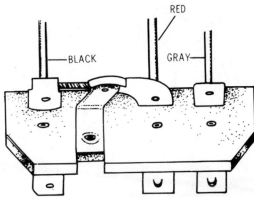

FIG 12:25   Terminal board connections

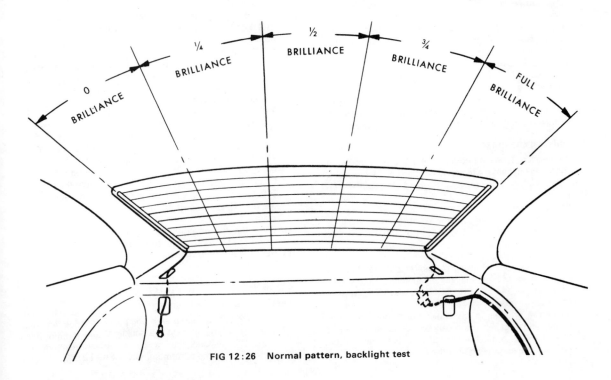

FIG 12:26   Normal pattern, backlight test

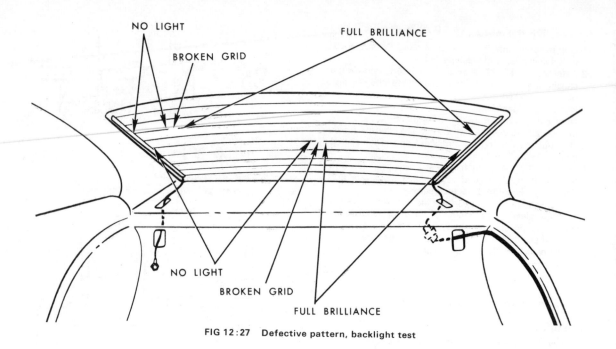

NO LIGHT

BROKEN GRID

FULL BRILLIANCE

NO LIGHT

BROKEN GRID

FULL BRILLIANCE

FIG 12:27   Defective pattern, backlight test

Field coils:

(a) Apply one probe to the grey lead normally connected to terminal 2 and the other probe to the brush lead of the brush in the centre of the motor end plate. The lamp should light, if not, the series winding is open circuit.

(b) Apply one probe to the grey lead and the other to a jumper lead connecting the brush lead of step (a) and the black lead. The lamp should light, if not, the shunt winding is open circuit.

(c) Connect a jumper lead between the brush lead of step (a) and the motor body. Apply one probe to the grey lead and the other to the motor body. The lamp should not light, if it does, the coils are grounded. Failure at any test involves renewal of the motor.

Rebuilding the motor:

The Service Repair Kit contains all parts (except major components) necessary to service the motor. Screws and nuts are included to replace rivets drilled out when dismantling.

Proceed as follows:

1 Examine the commutator for burning and pitting. It should not be skimmed except in an emergency but should be capable of being cleaned with fine sandpaper. Wipe off all abrasive dust.

2 Fit new brushes by cutting the leads from the old ones $\frac{1}{4}$ inch from the spliced joint. Crimp the new brush lead to the $\frac{1}{4}$ inch of the old lead using the crimping collar supplied.

3 Insert the brushes in the brush boxes but hook the spring ends against the brush box sides as shown in **FIG 12:23**, until the armature is in place then position the springs against the brushes.

4 Continue to rebuild the motor by reversing the dismantling process. Refer to **FIG 12:24** for the correct assembly sequence.

5 Lubricate all gears and the inside of the seal cap with Multifak No. 2 (Texaco) or equivalent.

6 Resolder the leads to the terminal board as shown in **FIG 12:25**. Fit the terminal board using screws and nuts.

7 Fit the wave washer then the helical gear to the intermediate shaft. Install the output gear with the cam well clear of the park switch.

8 Refit the gearbox cover using screws and nuts. Replace the washers and seal cap ensuring that .005 inch end float exists at the output shaft.

9 Connect the motor as described at the commencement of this Section under 'Testing the motor', step (b), for checking the park position (see **FIG 12:21**). The motor should start up and run until the cam contacts the park switch. Disconnect the battery and fit the crank arm to the alignment marks shown in **FIG 12:22**. Grip the arm in the vice when tightening the nut. This is important, otherwise the gears may be stripped.

10 Carry out the complete sequence of tests described under the heading 'Testing the motor', step (b).

11 Refit the motor to the car.

12:10 Heated backlight repair

Testing the backlight grid:

1 Use a 12-volt test lamp with one probe grounded.

2 Start the engine, turn on the backlight and very lightly contact each grid line with the probe. The lamp should light in the pattern shown in **FIG 12:26**.

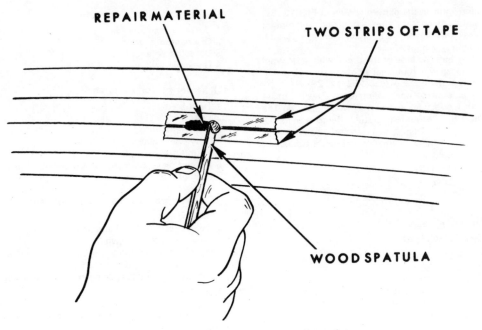

FIG 12 : 28 Repairing broken grid in backlight

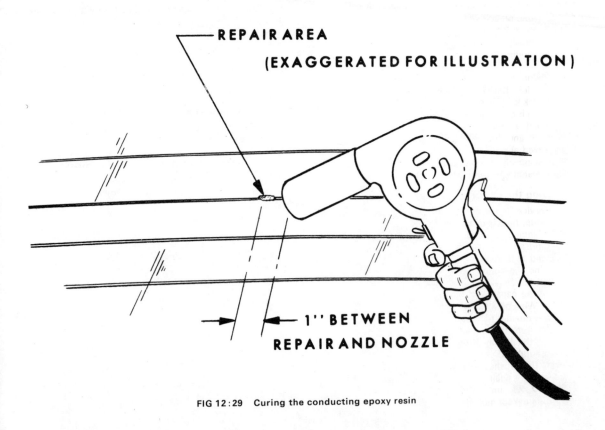

FIG 12 : 29 Curing the conducting epoxy resin

3 If the lamp lights in the pattern shown in **FIG 12:27**, make sufficient contact with the probe to pinpoint each break then mark the spot with crayon. Switch off backlight and engine.

4 Very lightly buff the area of the break with steel wool and wipe clean with industrial alcohol.

5 Apply two strips of tape (see **FIG 12:28**). Mix the required amount of conducting epoxy resin (Bliss-Bond 200) or similar and apply with a spatula. The glass must be at room temperature. Remove the tape.

6 Blow air at 500°F from a heat gun for 2 minutes (see **FIG 12:29**), then leave undisturbed for 24 hours.

7 Retest to check continuity.

12:11 Fault diagnosis

(a) Battery discharged

1 Loose or dirty connections
2 Alternator belt slipping
3 Alternator not charging
4 Battery internally defective
5 Lighting circuit grounded

(b) Alternator not charging

1 Break in circuit
2 Break in rotor winding
3 Defective diode in regulator or rectifier bridge
4 Stator coil open circuit
5 Drive belt slipping

(c) Battery overcharged

1 Regulator circuit broken
2 Brush lead clip grounded (alternator)
3 Regulator defective

(d) Starter motor lacks power

1 Discharged battery
2 High resistance connections
3 Worn brushes
4 Commutator burnt

(e) Starter will not operate

1 Overrunning clutch failed
2 Discharged battery
3 Defective solenoid
4 Defective switch

(f) Wiper motor sluggish

1 Tight linkage
2 Poor electrical connection
3 Faulty armature
4 Dirty commutator
5 Worn brushes
6 No end play to armature shaft or output gear
7 Lack of lubrication

(g) Wiper inoperative or intermittent

1 Blown fuse
2 Open circuit to No. 1 terminal
3 Loose or defective switch
4 Open circuit, switch to motor No. 2 terminal

(h) Wiper will not stop, operates at both speeds

1 No. 1 terminal to switch lead grounded

(j) Wiper operates at low speed only and will not stop

1 Defective switch
2 No. 3 terminal to switch lead grounded

(k) Wiper operates at high speed only and will not stop

1 Defective switch
2 No. 3 terminal to switch lead open circuit

(l) Wiper operates at high speed only

1 No. 3 terminal to switch lead open circuit

(m) Wiper operates at low speed only

1 No. 3 terminal to switch lead grounded
2 Defective switch

(n) Blades will not return to 'park' position

1 Loose wiper motor ground strap
2 Cam and switch in gearbox defective

CHAPTER 13

THE BODYWORK

13:1 Removing door trim

1 Refer to **FIG 13:1**. With one hand, press the trim away from the window regulator handle and then push the slotted tool behind the handle to release the spring clip. The slotted tool can easily be made up from a strip of flat steel or brass.

2 Refer to **FIG 13:2**. Remove the screw from the inside handle cup and the two screws from the door arm rest.

3 Commence at the lower corner and insert the tool used at step (1) between the flanges of a retainer clip. Lever the clip out of the door and repeat for all the retainers at the locations shown in **FIG 13:2**.

4 Pull the inside handle as though unlocking the door and ease the trim pad over the handle and away from the door.

To refit the trim pad, reverse the dismantling process. Seat the trim retainers by tapping gently with a clean rubber mallet. Fit the spring clip to the door window regulator handle then push the handle onto the spindle until the spring seats in its groove.

13:2 Door lock servicing

Adjusting the striker (see **FIG 13:3**):

Observe whether the door needs to be held more closely to the body or if it is too tight and difficult to close. If the former then the striker must be moved towards the car centre line and if the latter, away. Mark round the striker bolt with pencil then loosen the bolt and move in the required direction. Retighten and check. If the striker bolt is not central in the lock latch, the spacer (see **FIG 13:3**) may be changed for a thicker or thinner one as necessary.

Inside locking rod and button:

Refer to **FIG 13:4**. Remove the door trim pad (see **Section 13:1**), peel back the top corner of the water deflector panel, reach through the aperture and release the spring clip from the lower end of the rod. The rod will now lift out. Replace by reversing the removal procedure.

Remote control assembly:

Refer to **FIG 13:4**. Remove the trim pad and pull the water deflector panel downwards. Release the control handle assembly mounting bolts then rotate the assembly rearwards to disconnect the rod. Remove the rod anti-rattle clip and spring clip at the lock end. Lift the rod out. Replace by reversing the removal procedure.

Door lock assembly:

The door lock cannot be repaired, in the event of any difficulty in operation, it must be renewed. Wind the window right up, disconnect the inside locking rod and

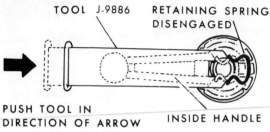

TOOL J-9886 RETAINING SPRING
DISENGAGED

**PUSH TOOL IN
DIRECTION OF ARROW**   **INSIDE HANDLE**

FIG 13:1   Releasing window regulator handle

remote control assembly, undo the lock mounting bolts and lift the lock out through the door aperture. Fit the new lock by reversing this process.

Door lock cylinder:

Wind the window right up. Remove the trim pad and water deflector panel. Refer to **FIG 13:5.** With a screwdriver, prise the retainer from the lock cylinder and remove the cylinder. Refit by reversing this procedure.

13:3 Servicing the window regulator

Refer to **FIG 13:4.** It will be seen that the regulator mechanism consists of a gear and toothed quadrant connected to a link which engages with a channel at the window glass lower edge. In addition a cross link acts in

scissors fashion between the channel and the inner panel cam (see item 7). This cam can be raised or lowered at either end to correct a window glass which is not parallel to the door upper edge.

To remove the regulator, detach the door trim pad and water deflector panel, raise the window and release the inner panel cam bolts. Slide the cam from the link roller and withdraw from the door. The window must be propped up in the raised position. The regulator is welded to the door panel therefore the spot welds must be drilled away. Slide the link roller from the window glass channel and lift the regulator out through the door aperture.

The regulator cannot be repaired. A new regulator will be supplied complete with bolts and nuts to fit holes already punched in the door panel. There is no need for spot welding. Assemble the rest of the mechanism by reversing the removal sequence not forgetting to apply a little thin grease to moving parts. If the window does not lie flush with the door edge when fully lowered, loosen the stop which is situated just beside the winding handle spindle and adjust as necessary. Tighten the stop.

13:4 Removing the door window glass

The window is a frameless piece of tempered safety plate glass pressed into the lower sash channel. The window and channel are supplied as one unit.

To remove the window, release the door trim pad, and water deflector panel. Loosen the window down travel

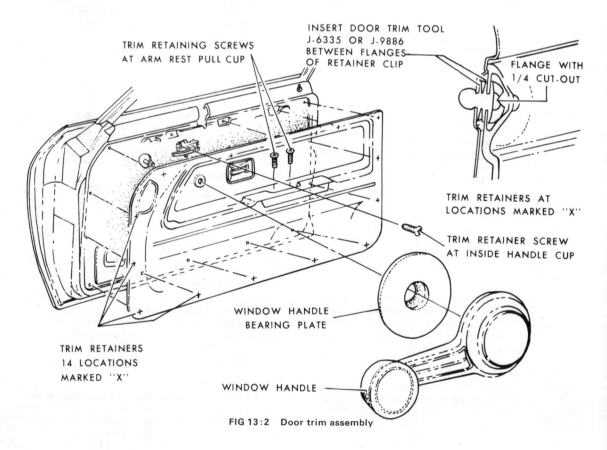

TRIM RETAINING SCREWS
AT ARM REST PULL CUP

INSERT DOOR TRIM TOOL
J-6335 OR J-9886
BETWEEN FLANGES
OF RETAINER CLIP

FLANGE WITH
1/4 CUT-OUT

TRIM RETAINERS AT
LOCATIONS MARKED "X"

TRIM RETAINER SCREW
AT INSIDE HANDLE CUP

WINDOW HANDLE
BEARING PLATE

TRIM RETAINERS
14 LOCATIONS
MARKED "X"

WINDOW HANDLE

FIG 13:2   Door trim assembly

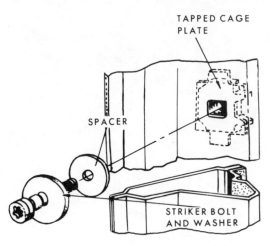

TAPPED CAGE
PLATE

SPACER

STRIKER BOLT
AND WASHER

FIG 13:3   Door lock striker

SEALING
GASKET

LOCK CYLINDER
(REMOVED)

RETAINER

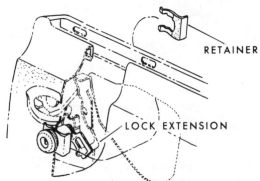

LOCK EXTENSION

FIG 13:5   Lock cylinder installation

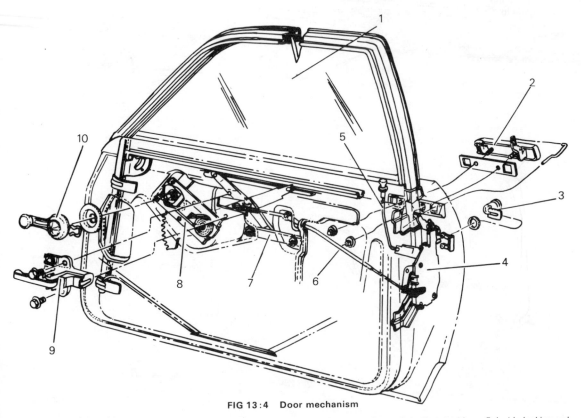

FIG 13:4   Door mechanism

Key to Fig 13:4   1 Window assembly   2 Door outside handle   3 Lock cylinder   4 Lock assembly   5 Inside locking rod
6 Remote control to lock rod   7 Inner panel cam   8 Window regulator   9 Remote control handle assembly   10 Window
regulator handle

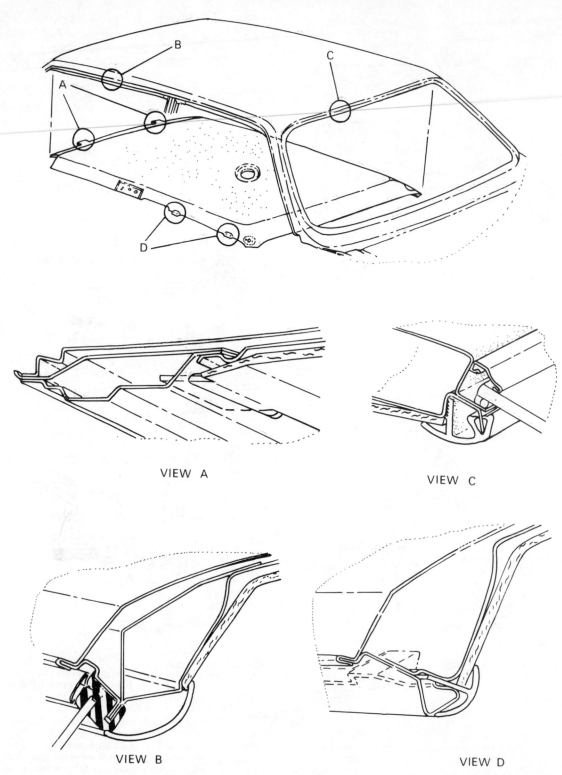

VIEW A

VIEW C

VIEW B

VIEW D

FIG 13:6   Headlining, Models 11 and 77

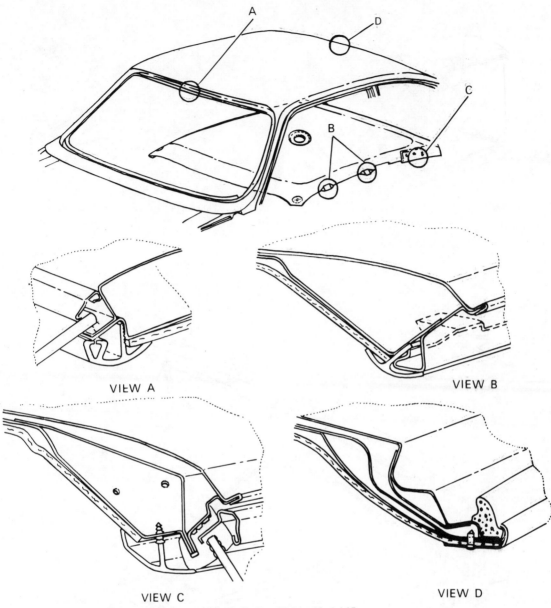

FIG 13:7 Headlining. Model 15

stop (see **Section 13:3**), and lower the window to the bottom of the door. Apply protective tape to the door adjacent to the sealing strips at the door aperture through which the glass moves. Use a flat bladed slotted tool to spring the sealing strip clips from the door flanges. Remove both inner and outer strips. Raise the window and remove the inner panel cam. Lower the front of the glass and free the regulator arm roller from the channel. Lift the window upwards and slightly inwards when it will pass clear of the door upper frame. Refit by reversing this sequence.

13:5 Renewing the headlining

If the headlining is accidentally damaged or discoloured it is a simple job to renew it. Reference to **FIGS 13:6** and **13:7** will show that it is a one-piece glass fibre moulding held in place by decorative trim and tabs.

Protect the seats then remove the following: Sunshade visors, windshield side and upper trim, dome lamp, coat hooks, seat belt fixings, centre pillar trim, quarter upper trim, side roof rail trim, back window upper trim. On the station waggon remove the tailgate torque rod cover then disengage the tabs at both sides and rear of

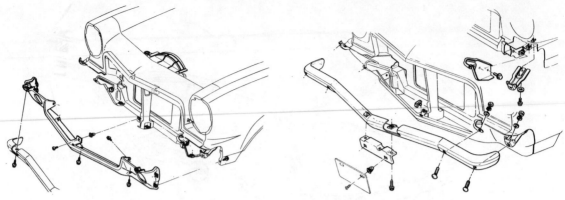

FIG 13 : 8   Removing the valance

FIG 13 : 9   Removing the bumper

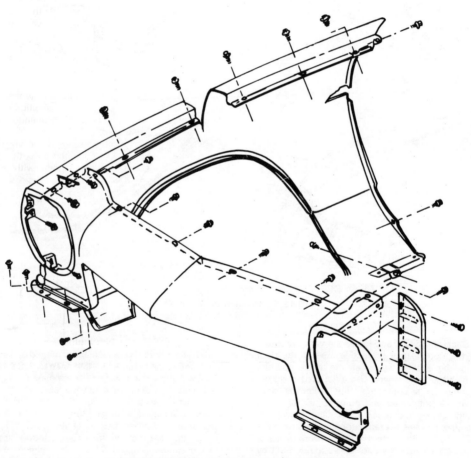

FIG 13 : 10   Removing the fenders and filler panel

the headlining and remove the complete assembly through the tailgate aperture.

On car body styles, release the two tabs at each side then move the assembly to the rear enough to give clearance above the windshield. Lower the assembly and remove it diagonally through the front door opening.

Fit the new headlining by reversing this process but take care not to flex the assembly more than necessary.

13:6 Renewing front body panels

In the event of minor damage to the front of the car, the grille, valance, filler panel and fenders can be un-bolted and replaced as new. Proceed as follows:

1 Remove the neadlamp assemblies complete.
2 Undo the Phillips screws and lift the grille up and forwards.
3 Remove the valance as shown in **FIG 13:8.**
4 Remove the bumper as shown in **FIG 13:9.**
5 Attach adhesive tape to the door edges to protect them from damage as the fenders are lifted away. Refer to **FIG 13:10** and undo the bolts along the top of the fender, at the rear and lower edges then across the filler panel. Both fenders and the filler panel will then be released from the main panels of the car.

To fit new components reverse the preceding instructions but apply a layer of approved sealant between mating panel edges.

13:7 Hood latch, emergency unlocking

If the hood latch cable breaks or the hood is distorted due to an accident, it is possible to release the hood without further damage. Refer to **FIG 13:11** and insert tool J.23581 through the vent grille and to the left of the hood latch bolt. Press down on the hood and rotate the tool towards the right to release the latch.

13:8 Windshield and backlight glass

These glasses are held in position by an adhesive caulk method. Renewal of broken glasses is a job for a Chevrolet dealer due to the specialized technique necessary

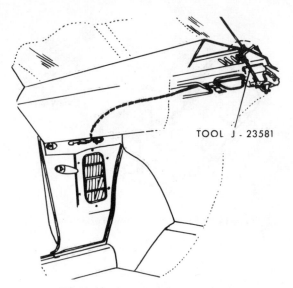

TOOL J - 23581

FIG 13:11   Releasing the hood latch

for a satisfactory result. Suffice it to say that two operators are required and since the adhesive cures in 15 minutes, a high degree of skill is needed.

13:9 The heater

Controls:

The heater blower motor is running whenever the ignition is switched on, there is no 'off' position of the fan switch, only high or low. It is not recommended that the circuit be modified to give an 'off' position.

Refer to **FIG 13:12** for a diagrammatic view of the components and the air flow through the heater. Operation of the controls may be studied with reference to **FIG 13:12.**

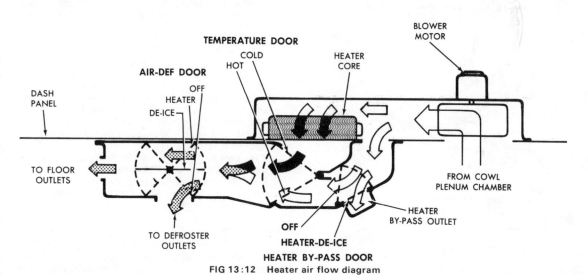

FIG 13:12   Heater air flow diagram

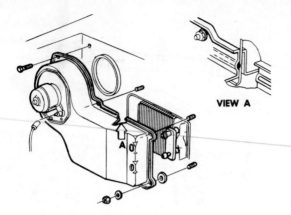

VIEW A

FIG 13:13   Heater to bulkhead attachment

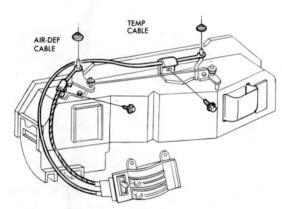

TEMP CABLE

AIR-DEF CABLE

FIG 13:14   Heater control cables

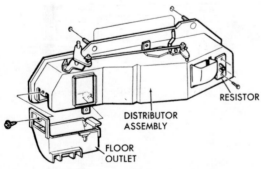

RESISTOR

DISTRIBUTOR ASSEMBLY

FLOOR OUTLET

FIG 13:15   Removing the floor outlet

The uppermost sliding lever controls the air/defrost door and the heater bypass outlet. These two doors are connected by the non-adjustable spring wire link at the top of the heater casing. When the control lever is at 'OFF' (and the lower lever at 'COLD'), air at ambient temperature enters the car through the bypass outlet. At the 'HEATER' position, the bypass outlet is closed, the air/defrost door is open and most of the air enters the car at the floor outlets, although some reaches the windshield. At the 'DE-ICE' position, the air/defrost door moves further over and directs most of the air to the windshield although some still passes to the floor outlets.

The lower sliding lever controls the temperature door and, depending on the position in which it is placed, more or less air passes into the car via the heater radiator core. Intermediate temperatures are obtained by the mixing of hot and ambient temperature air.

Servicing the heater:

Blower motor:

To remove the motor, proceed as follows:
1 Disconnect both the battery ground lead and the motor lead.
2 Pencil round the blower motor flange so that the flange can be refitted in the same position.
3 Undo the screws and gently pull the motor from the case. Remove the fan nut and fan. Note that the open side of the fan is away from the motor.
4 The motor cannot be repaired satisfactorily so that if electrical tests show it to be defective it must be renewed. Fit the new motor by reversing steps 1 to 3.

Heater core:

If the core leaks or it is suspected that an obstruction to the circulation of water has occurred, the core may be removed as follows:
1 Place a tray below the engine to catch any coolant spilt as the hoses are released.
2 Disconnect the battery and blower motor leads.
3 Disconnect the hoses and quickly raise and tie the ends so that coolant loss is minimized. When releasing the hoses, do not use excessive force in case the core connections are damaged (see 'Hose renewal').
4 Refer to **FIG 13:13**, undo the retaining nuts and ease the cover away from the dash panel.
5 Release the core retaining strap screws and lift the core from the panel.

If it is necessary to flush the core to remove an obstruction, apply a low pressure hose to the upper connection. This will introduce water into the core in the reverse direction to normal. Should the core be furred up with scale deposit, use a chemical de-scaler and follow the makers instructions exactly.

If the core is leaking it must be exchanged for a new or reconditioned unit at a Chevrolet dealer.

Refit the core by reversing the removal process, topping up the engine coolant system with coolant of the correct proportions of antifreeze and water.

Hose renewal:

Refer to **Chapter 4, FIG 4:1** for correct hose routing. Drain the coolant system to avoid coolant loss and then release the hose clips. If the hoses will not release from the

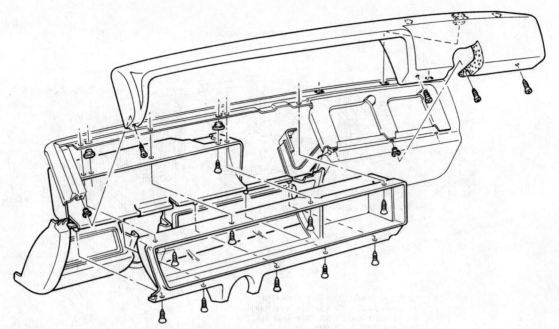

FIG 13:16   Facia panel and pad

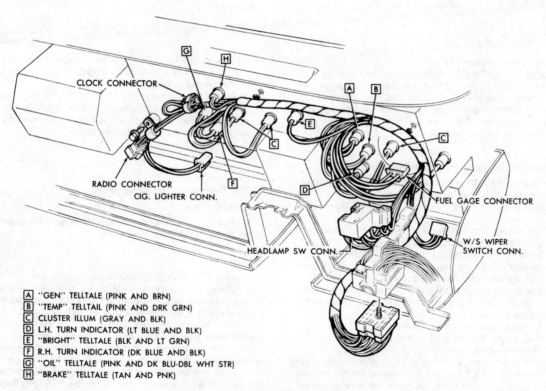

CLOCK CONNECTOR

RADIO CONNECTOR
CIG. LIGHTER CONN.

HEADLAMP SW CONN.

FUEL GAGE CONNECTOR

W/S WIPER
SWITCH CONN.

A "GEN" TELLTALE (PINK AND BRN)
B "TEMP" TELLTAIL (PINK AND DRK GRN)
C CLUSTER ILLUM (GRAY AND BLK)
D L.H. TURN INDICATOR (LT BLUE AND BLK)
E "BRIGHT" TELLTALE (BLK AND LT GRN)
F R.H. TURN INDICATOR (DK BLUE AND BLK)
G "OIL" TELLTALE (PINK AND DK BLU-DBL WHT STR)
H "BRAKE" TELLTALE (TAN AND PNK)

FIG 13:17   Standard panel cable harness

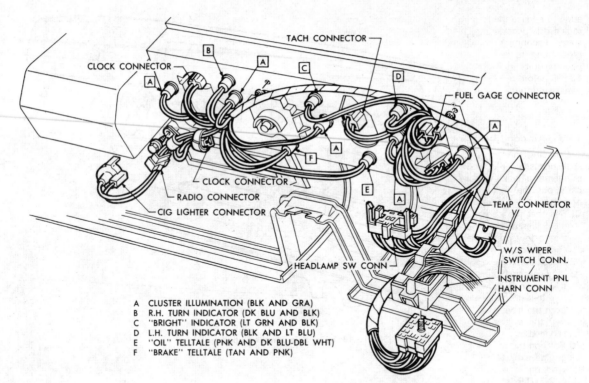

A CLUSTER ILLUMINATION (BLK AND GRA)
B R.H. TURN INDICATOR (DK BLU AND BLK)
C "BRIGHT" INDICATOR (LT GRN AND BLK)
D L.H. TURN INDICATOR (BLK AND LT BLU)
E "OIL" TELLTALE (PNK AND DK BLU-DBL WHT)
F "BRAKE" TELLTALE (TAN AND PNK)

FIG 13:18   GT panel cable harness

heater core connections without force, cut them until they can be split and peeled away from the connections. Force applied to the connections can easily strain the core and induce a leak. To assist the new hoses to slip over the connections smear a very small quantity of soap over the outside of the connections. Tighten the clips and refill the cooling system.

Control cable renewal and adjustment:

Refer to **FIG 13:14**. The cables are not adjustable but if necessary, the position of the doors inside the heater can be changed. To renew control cables proceed as follows:

1 Disconnect the battery and remove the instrument panel bezel (see **Section 13:10**).
2 Release the control panel screws, push the panel forwards, then downwards. Release the cable clips and screws and remove the cables.
3 Check that the new cables move freely then assemble them to the heater and control panel by reversing the removal sequences.

Carry out adjustments as follows:

1 Remove the floor outlet (see **FIG 13:15**).
2 Place the upper control lever to 'HEATER'.
3 The air/defrost door should be parallel to the dash panel (see **FIG 13:12**). If not, loosen the two screws at the top of the heater and move the door as necessary. Tighten the screws and check by moving the

control to 'DE-ICE'. The door should now seal at the rear of the heater and have a gap of $\frac{1}{8}$ to $\frac{1}{4}$ inch at the forward edge.
4 Place the lower lever at 'COLD'. The door should seal at the forward side of the heater. If it does not, loosen the two screws at the top of the heater and move the door as necessary. Retighten the screws.
5 Refit the floor outlet.

13:10 Removing the facia panel
Standard panel:

Undo the 9 screws and remove the instrument cluster bezel. Remove the clock stem knob.

GT panel:

Undo the 6 screws and remove the cluster bezel.

To obtain access to the instruments, remove the lens light shield and lens. On both GT and standard panels these are held in by screws which are self-evident when the bezel is removed. All instruments, including the speedometer and cable, are removed from the front of the panel, whereas all indicator and panel lighting bulbs are removed from the rear. Refer to **FIG 13:16**. The protective pad can be removed by releasing one screw at the left and three screws at the right lower edge. Rap upwards sharply with the hands below the righthand edge to release the pad from the three spring clips at the top. If it is necessary to dismantle the facia beyond this stage, disconnect the battery and the instruments before proceeding to remove the screws shown holding the various units in **FIG 13:16**. Refer to **FIGS 13:17** or **13:18** before reconnecting the wiring harness when the panel is refitted.

13:11 Air conditioning

Servicing the air conditioning systems is a job for a specialist since most troubles stem from contaminated refrigerant or lack of refrigerant. The owner can, however, carry out the following inspections and maintenance operations.

1 See that the condenser is not obstructed by leaves, dead flies or other foreign matter. If it is obstructed play a low pressure water hose through it from the engine side.

2 Check that the evaporator drain tube is clear.

3 If necessary, adjust the compressor belt tension so that it can be deflected $\frac{3}{8}$ to $\frac{1}{2}$ inch at its longest run.

4 See that no more than a slight film of oil has exuded from the front of the compressor. Any more than this and the system must not be run until it has been serviced by a Chevrolet agent.

5 Position the car out of doors or otherwise see that the engine exhaust is discharged outside the building if working in a workshop. Gears must be in 'PARK' or 'NEUTRAL', parking brake hard on. Start the engine, set the air conditioner controls to maximum cold, blower full on and then run the engine at 2000 rev/min for 10 minutes.

Watch the clutch pulley bolt to see that the compressor is running at the same speed as the pulley. If not, the clutch is slipping.

6 Remove the cover from the sight glass on the receiver dehydrator in the engine compartment. The following facts can be established by watching the sight glass.

Engine running:

(a) Bubbles in glass. System low on refrigerant. Recharge by a Chevrolet agent.

(b) Sight glass clear. System either fully charged or empty. Feel compressor hoses, high pressure hose should be warm, low pressure hose cold.

(c) If there is no appreciable temperature difference at step (b), the system is empty. Recharge by a Chevrolet agent.

(d) If there is an appreciable temperature difference at step (b) the system may be overfilled.

(e) To see if the system is overfilled, disconnect the electrical connection to the compressor clutch thus stopping the compressor. Keep the hands clear of all moving parts while doing this. Watch the sight glass. If the glass remains clear for more than 45 seconds before foam appears and settles away, the system is overfilled. If foam appears and settles away in less than 45 seconds, the system is correctly charged with refrigerant.

7 Replace the sight glass cover, stop the engine.

There is no more that the owner can do with the refrigerant system, but in any case, it should be checked by a Chevrolet Service Station at least once a year. In case of electrical failure, refer to the wiring diagram in the **Technical Data** section of this Manual.

APPENDIX

TECHNICAL DATA

Engine   Fuel system   Ignition system   Cooling system
Clutch   Transmission   Suspension   Steering   Brakes
Electrical system   Capacities   Torque wrench settings

WIRING DIAGRAMS

METRIC CONVERSION TABLE

HINTS ON MAINTENANCE AND OVERHAUL

GLOSSARY OF TERMS

INDEX

TECHNICAL DATA

Dimensions are in inches unless otherwise stated

ENGINE

Bore and stroke:
Standard ...	3.5 x 3.625
L11 ...	3.5 x 3.625

Compression ratio:
Standard ...	8.5:1
L11 ...	8.5:1
Firing order ...	1-3-4-2
Cylinder diameter limits ...	3.4996 to 3.5024

Cylinder out of round:
New ...	.0005 max.
Worn ...	.002 max.

Cylinder taper:
New—thrust side ...	.0005 max.
New—relief side ...	.0005 max.
Worn—total measurement ...	.005 max.

Pistons:

Clearance in bore:
New ...	.0018 to .0028
Worn ...	.005 max.

Piston rings:

Compression rings:
Clearance in groove, top ring, new ...	.0012 to .0027
Clearance in groove, top ring, worn ...	.0037
Clearance in groove, second ring, new ...	.0012 to .0027
Clearance in groove, second ring, worn ...	.0037
Ring gap—top ...	.009 to .019
Ring gap—second ...	.009 to .019

Oil control ring:
Clearance in groove, new ...	Nil to .005
Clearance in groove, worn ...	.006
Ring gap ...	.010 to .030

Piston pin:
Diameter ...	.9270 to .9273
Clearance, new ...	.0003 to .0004
Clearance, worn ...	.001 max.
Interference in rod ...	.0008 to .0021

Crankshaft:
Main journal diameter ...	2.2983 to 2.2993
Main journal taper, new ...	.0002 max.
Main journal taper, worn ...	.001 max.
Main journal out of round, new ...	.0002 max.
Main journal out of round, worn ...	.001 max.
End play of shaft ...	.002 to .007
Crankpin diameter ...	1.999 to 2.000
Crankpin taper, new ...	.0003 max.
Crankpin taper, worn ...	.001 max.
Crankpin, out of round, new ...	.0002 max.
Crankpin, out of round, worn ...	.001 max.

Connecting rod:

Bearing clearance, new	.0007 to .0027
Bearing clearance, worn	.004 max.
End play	.0085 to .0135

Camshaft:

Lift, standard engine,	Intake	...	...	.4199
	Exhaust	...	...	.4301
L11 engine,	Intake	...	...	.4365
	Exhaust	...	...	.4365

All lift figures ± .002

Journal diameter	2.2812 to 2.2822
Camshaft runout	.0015 max.
Camshaft end play	.004 to .012

Valves:

Valve lash (cold)	Intake		.014 to .016
	Exhaust		.029 to .031
Face angle, all valves			45 deg.
Cylinder head seat angle, all valves ...			46 deg.
Valve face runout, all valves			.002 max.
Seat width, intake			$\frac{3}{64}$ to $\frac{1}{16}$
Seat width, exhaust			$\frac{3}{64}$ to $\frac{5}{64}$
Clearance, stem to guide, intake and exhaust ...			.001 to .0027

Valve springs:

Outer, free length	2.03
installed length	1.75
Damper, free length	1.84
Coils	$4\frac{1}{2}$

Oil pump:

Type	Ring gear on crankshaft
Bypass valve lifts at	9 to 11 p.s.i.
Oil pressure switch operates at	2 to 6 p.s.i.
Pressure relief valve operates at	40 p.s.i.

FUEL SYSTEM

Carburetter:

Type:		
Standard engine	Rochester	MV monojet
L11	Rochester	2 GV
	MV	2 GV
Float level	$\frac{1}{16}$	$\frac{5}{8}$
Float drop	—	$1\frac{3}{4}$
Pump rod	—	$1\frac{3}{8}$
Fast idle	.110	—
Choke rod Auto	.080	.080
Synchro	.120	.080
Vacuum break Auto	.140	.120
Synchro	.200	.120
Unloader	.350	.180
Idle rev/min Synchro 3-speed	850	
Synchro 4-speed	1200	
Auto (in drive)	650	

Fuel pump:

Type	AG electric, submersible
Pressure	3 to 4.5 p.s.i.
Volume	1 pint in 30 to 45 seconds

IGNITION SYSTEM

Distributor:

Type:

    Manual transmission ... ... Model No. 1110492

    Automatic transmission ... ... Model No. 1110435

Centrifugal advance in crankshaft angle:

	Automatic	*Manual*
	Nil at 945 rev/min	Nil at 1185 rev/min
	2 deg. at 1455 rev/min	2 deg. at 1615 rev/min
	22 deg at 4000 rev/min	24 deg at 4000 rev/min

Vacuum advance in crankshaft angle:

	Nil at 7 inch Hg	Nil at 7 inch Hg
	24 deg. at 15 inch Hg	24 deg. at 15 inch Hg
Point dwell setting	31 deg. to 34 deg.	31 deg. to 34 deg.
Ignition timing BTDC	Engine idling and vacuum advance dis-connected	
Standard engine	6 deg.	6 deg.
L11 engine	10 deg.	6 deg.
Point gap	.016 inch used contacts	.019 inch new contacts
Contact spring tension	19 to 23 oz	
Condensor	.18 to .23 mfd	
Spark plugs Standard	AC R42 TS	
Cold	AC R41 RS	

COOLING SYSTEM

Pump type	Centrifugal impeller
Thermostat open temperature	192° to 198°F
Radiator pressure cap	15 psi

CLUTCH

Type	Dry plate, diaphragm spring
Operation	Mechanical
Pedal free travel	.90±.25
Friction plate diameter	Standard 8.0 L11 9.1

SYNCHROMESH TRANSMISSION

Type	3 and 4-speed, floor shift
Ratios	3-speed 3.24, 1.68, 1.00
	4-speed 3.43, 2.16, 1.37, 1.00

AUTOMATIC TRANSMISSION

Types	Torque Drive and Powerglide
Ratios Torque converter	2.6:1 multiplication
Planetary gear	1.82:1, 1:1
Stall speed Standard engine	1800 rev/min
L11 engine	2400 rev/min

SUSPENSION

Castor angle	$-\frac{3}{4}$ deg.±1 deg.
Camber angle	$+\frac{1}{4}$ deg.±1 deg.
Toe-in	$\frac{3}{16}$ to $\frac{5}{16}$
Roll centre, front	2.4 above surface
Roll centre, rear	14 above surface

STEERING

Manual steering:

	Gear installed	Gear at bench
Ratio	20.9:1	
Thrust bearing preload	5 to 8 inch lb	7 inch lb
Over centre preload	4 to 10 inch lb	14 inch lb
Total preload	16 inch lb max.	21 inch lb max.

Power steering:

Ratio	16:1
Pump pressure	900 to 1000 p.s.i.
Valve drag	3 inch lb max.
Thrust bearing preload	½ to 2 inch lb in excess of valve drag
Over centre preload	3 to 6 inch lb in excess of valve drag

BRAKES

Type	Front disc
Type	Rear drum
Swept area (friction material)	228 sq inch
Disc diameter	9.64
Drum diameter	9.00
Drum width	1.18
Hydraulic fluid type	GM Supreme No. 11

ELECTRICAL SYSTEM

Battery:

Type	Y86 or Y86A
Capacity	45 a.h. at 20 hour rate

Alternator:

	Full current	Output at 5000 rev/min
Type C4531	4 to 4.5 amps	31 amps
C4520	4 to 4.5 amps	50 amps

Fuses	
TCS, idle stop solenoid	10 amp
Turn flasher, fuel gauge, panel warning bulbs, back-up light, heat gauge, tachometer	20 amp
Radio	10 amp
Wiper	25 amp
Heater or air conditioning	25 amp
Panel illumination, radio dial light	4 amp
Hazard flasher, brake lights	20 amp
Tail lights, marker lights, park lights	20 amp
Clock, dome light, lighter	20 amp
Fuel pump	20 amp
In-line air conditioning blower	30 amp

(Headlamps protected by circuit breaker in switch)

CAPACITIES

Fuel	11.0 gallons US
Oil	3.0 quarts US
Radiator	6.5 quarts US
Automatic transmission fluid	2.0 quarts US

TORQUE WRENCH SETTINGS

Engine:

Front cover	50 inch lb
Cam cover	35 inch lb
Oil screen to support	50 inch lb
Clutch dust cover	80 inch lb
Oil screen to baffle	50 inch lb
Oil drain tube	50 inch lb
Fan blade bolts	20 ft lb
Clutch pressure plate to flywheel $\frac{5}{16}$ bolt	20 ft lb
Clutch pressure plate to flywheel $\frac{3}{8}$ bolt	35 ft lb
Oil pick up tube	25 ft lb
Crankshaft damper to sprocket	15 ft lb
Oil pump holding bolt	15 ft lb
Oil pump holding stud	30 ft lb
Water pump bolt	15 ft lb
Oil pan bolts	15 ft lb
Cam retainer	15 ft lb
Connecting rod bearing cap	35 ft lb
Distributor clamp	25 ft lb
Water outlet	30 ft lb
Manifold bolts	30 ft lb
Manifold studs	30 ft lb
Clutch housing to engine	25 ft lb
Main bearing cap	65 ft lb
Cylinder head	60 ft lb
Flywheel to crankshaft	60 ft lb
Cam sprocket	80 ft lb
Damper to crankshaft	80 ft lb
Oil pan drain plug	20 ft lb
Oil filter connector	30 ft lb
Oil filter	Hand pressure
Spark plug	15 ft lb

Front suspension:

Upper ball joint	30 ft lb
Lower ball joint	60 ft lb
Upper control arm pivot	60 ft lb
Lower control arm cam	125 ft lb
Shock absorber lower	22 lb ft
Shock absorber top	116 inch lb
Stabilizer bracket	30 ft lb
Stabilizer bar to control arm	120 inch lb

Rear suspension:

Upper control arm, front	60 ft lb
Upper control arm, rear	60 ft lb
Lower control arm, front	80 ft lb
Lower control arm, rear	80 ft lb
Shock absorber, upper	18 ft lb
Shock absorber, lower	80 inch lb
Universal joint bolts	14 ft lb
Stabilizer bolts	36 ft lb

Brakes:

Main cylinder	24 ft lb
Front hose to pipe	140 inch lb
Front hose to caliper	22 ft lb
Rear hose to pipe	140 inch lb
Rear pipe to cylinders	140 inch lb

Transmission:

Clutch fork cover...	80 inch lb
Gearbox to clutch housing	24 ft lb
Clutch fork ball stud locknut	25 ft lb
Crossmember to frame	28 ft lb
Crossmember mount	26 ft lb
Rear extension mounting...	30 ft lb
Rear extension mounting to case	31 ft lb
Gearbox cover screws	48 inch lb

Automatic:

Case to engine	35 ft lb
Oil pan	8 ft lb
Oil cooler plugs	5 ft lb
Low band locknut	15 ft lb
Converter to engine	35 ft lb
Drain plug	20 ft lb

Steering:

Pitman arm to relay rod	35 ft lb
Tie rod end stud nuts	35 ft lb
Tie rod clamp bolts	132 inch lb
Idler arm to relay rod	35 ft lb
Idler to frame	30 ft lb
Steering wheel nut	30 ft lb
Dash bracket to column	19 ft lb
Pot joint clamp	55 ft lb
Flexible coupling pinch bolt	30 ft lb
Flexible coupling flange bolts	18 ft lb

Manual:

Mounting bolts	70 ft lb
Adjuster plug locknut	75 ft lb
Side cover	18 ft lb
Lash adjuster locknut	15 ft lb
Pitman shaft nut	93 ft lb

Power:

Mounting bolts	70 ft lb
Adjuster locknut	80 ft lb
Side cover	30 ft lb
Lash adjuster locknut	32 ft lb
Pitman shaft nut	140 ft lb

Pump:

Pulley nut	60 ft lb
Mounting studs	33 ft lb
Outlet union	33 ft lb
Bracket	25 ft lb
Brace to engine	18 ft lb
Brace to pump	25 ft lb

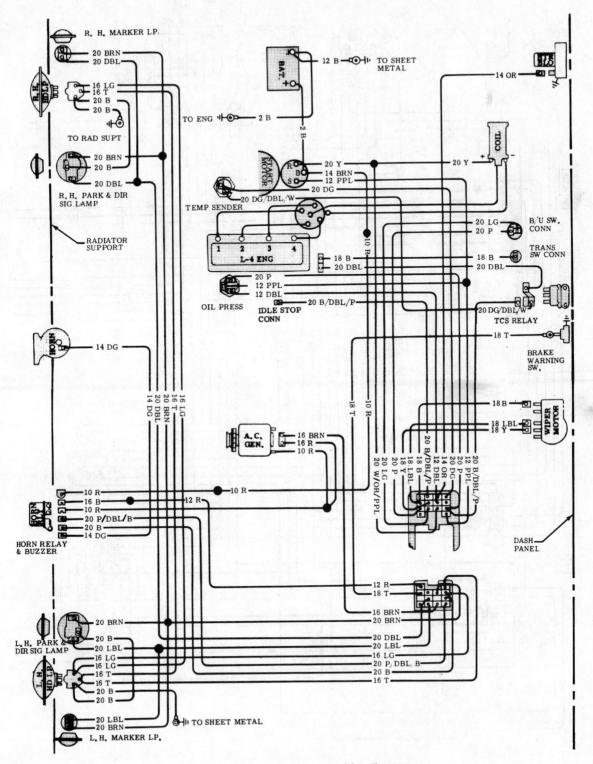

FIG 14:1 Engine compartment wiring diagram

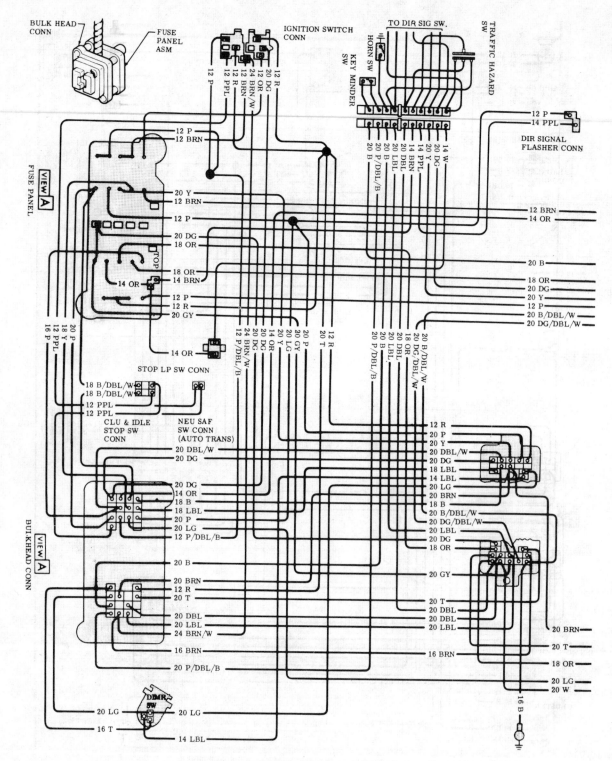

FIG 14:2   Instrument panel, wiring diagram, part 'A'

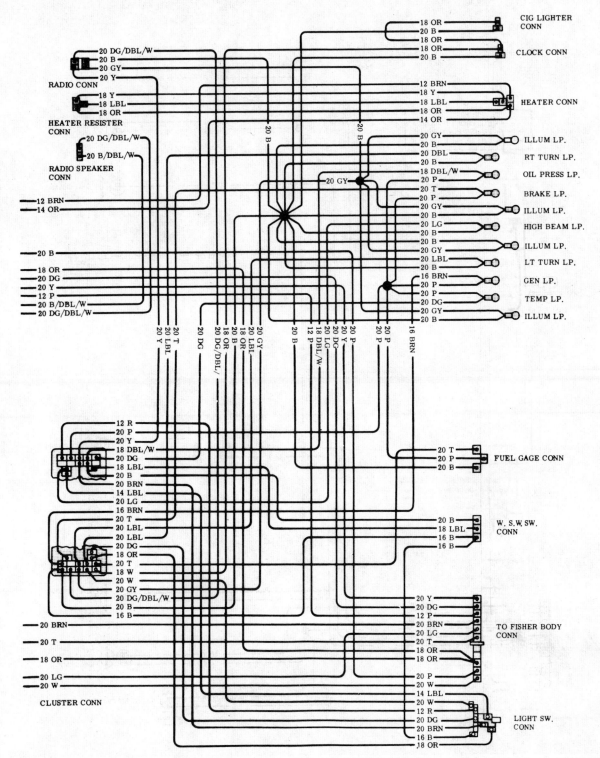

FIG 14:3   Instrument panel, wiring diagram, part 'B'

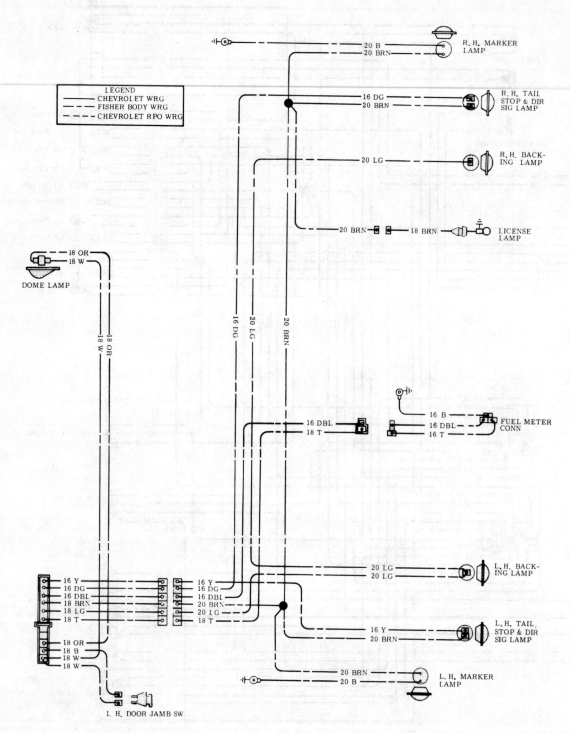

FIG 14:4   Body and rear lamp circuit wiring diagram

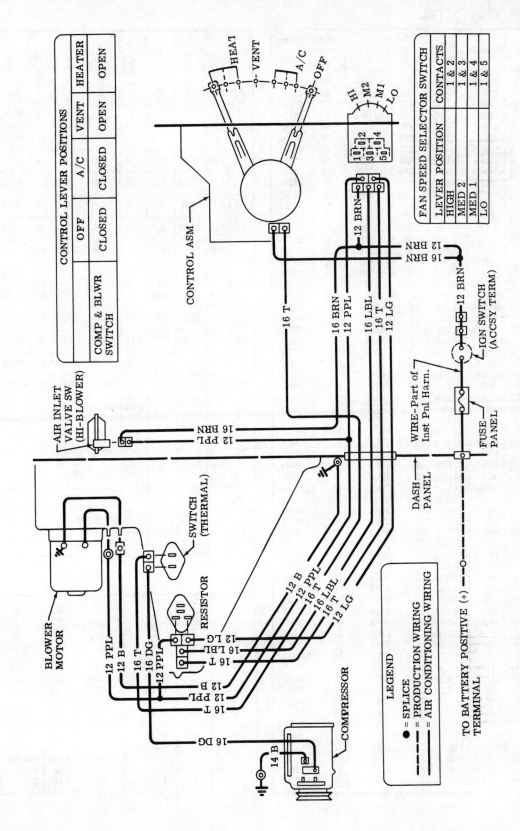

FIG 14:5   Air conditioning system wiring diagram

Inches		Decimals	Milli-metres	Inches to Millimetres		Millimetres to Inches	
				Inches	mm	mm	Inches
	1/64	.015625	.3969	.001	.0254	.01	.00039
1/32		.03125	.7937	.002	.0508	.02	.00079
	3/64	.046875	1.1906	.003	.0762	.03	.00118
1/16		.0625	1.5875	.004	.1016	.04	.00157
	5/64	.078125	1.9844	.005	.1270	.05	.00197
3/32		.09375	2.3812	.006	.1524	.06	.00236
	7/64	.109375	2.7781	.007	.1778	.07	.00276
1/8		.125	3.1750	.008	.2032	.08	.00315
	9/64	.140625	3.5719	.009	.2286	.09	.00354
5/32		.15625	3.9687	.01	.254	.1	.00394
	11/64	.171875	4.3656	.02	.508	.2	.00787
3/16		.1875	4.7625	.03	:762	.3	.01181
	13/64	.203125	5·1594	.04	1.016	.4	.01575
7/32		.21875	5.5562	.05	1.270	.5	.01969
	15/64	.234375	5.9531	.06	1.524	.6	.02362
1/4		.25	6.3500	.07	1.778	.7	.02756
	17/64	.265625	6.7469	.08	2.032	.8	.03150
9/32		.28125	7.1437	.09	2.286	.9	.03543
	19/64	.296875	7.5406	.1	2.54	1	.03937
5/16		.3125	7.9375	.2	5.08	2	.07874
	21/64	.328125	8.3344	.3	7.62	3	.11811
11/32		.34375	8.7312	.4	10.16	4	.15748
	23/64	.359375	9.1281	.5	12.70	5	.19685
3/8		.375	9.5250	.6	15.24	6	.23622
	25/64	.390625	9.9219	.7	17.78	7	.27559
13/32		.40625	10.3187	.8	20.32	8	.31496
	27/64	.421875	10.7156	.9	22.86	9	.35433
7/16		.4375	11.1125	1	25.4	10	.39370
	29/64	.453125	11.5094	2	50.8	11	.43307
15/32		.46875	11.9062	3	76.2	12	.47244
	31/64	.484375	12.3031	4	101.6	13	.51181
1/2		.5	12.7000	5	127.0	14	.55118
	33/64	.515625	13.0969	6	152.4	15	.59055
17/32		.53125	13.4937	7	177.8	16	.62992
	35/64	.546875	13.8906	8	203.2	17	.66929
9/16		.5625	14.2875	9	228.6	18	.70866
	37/64	.578125	14.6844	10	254.0	19	.74803
19/32		.59375	15.0812	11	279.4	20	.78740
	39/64	.609375	15.4781	12	304.8	21	.82677
5/8		.625	15.8750	13	330.2	22	.86614
	41/64	.640625	16.2719	14	355.6	23	.90551
21/32		.65625	16.6687	15	381.0	24	.94488
	43/64	.671875	17.0656	16	406.4	25	.98425
11/16		.6875	17.4625	17	431.8	26	1.02362
	45/64	.703125	17.8594	18	457.2	27	1.06299
23/32		.71875	18.2562	19	482.6	28	1.10236
	47/64	.734375	18.6531	20	508.0	29	1.14173
3/4		.75	19.0500	21	533.4	30	1.18110
	49/64	.765625	19.4469	22	558.8	31	1.22047
25/32		.78125	19.8437	23	584.2	32	1.25984
	51/64	.796875	20.2406	24	609.6	33	1.29921
13/16		.8125	20.6375	25	635.0	34	1.33858
	53/64	.828125	21.0344	26	660.4	35	1.37795
27/32		.84375	21.4312	27	685.8	36	1.41732
	55/64	.859375	21.8281	28	711.2	37	1.4567
7/8		.875	22.2250	29	736.6	38	1.4961
	57/64	.890625	22.6219	30	762.0	39	1.5354
29/32		.90625	23.0187	31	787.4	40	1.5748
	59/64	.921875	23.4156	32	812.8	41	1.6142
15/16		.9375	23.8125	33	838.2	42	1.6535
	61/64	.953125	24.2094	34	863.6	43	1.6929
31/32		.96875	24.6062	35	889.0	44	1.7323
	63/64	.984375	25.0031	36	914.4	45	1.7717

UNITS	Pints to Litres	Gallons to Litres	Litres to Pints	Litres to Gallons	Miles to Kilometres	Kilometres to Miles	Lbs. per sq. In. to Kg. per sq. Cm.	Kg. per sq. Cm. to Lbs. per sq. In.
1	.57	4.55	1.76	.22	1.61	.62	.07	14.22
2	1.14	9.09	3.52	.44	3.22	1.24	.14	28.50
3	1.70	13.64	5.28	.66	4.83	1.86	.21	42.67
4	2.27	18.18	7.04	.88	6.44	2.49	.28	56.89
5	2.84	22.73	8.80	1.10	8.05	3.11	.35	71.12
6	3.41	27.28	10.56	1.32	9.66	3.73	.42	85.34
7	3.98	31.82	12.32	1.54	11.27	4.35	.49	99.56
8	4.55	36.37	14.08	1.76	12.88	4.97	.56	113.79
9		40.91	15.84	1.98	14.48	5.59	.63	128.00
10		45.46	17.60	2.20	16.09	6.21	.70	142.23
20				4.40	32.19	12.43	1.41	284.47
30				6.60	48.28	18.64	2.11	426.70
40				8.80	64.37	24.85		
50					80.47	31.07		
60					96.56	37.28		
70					112.65	43.50		
80					128.75	49.71		
90					144.84	55.92		
100					160.93	62.14		

UNITS	Lb ft to kgm	Kgm to lb ft	UNITS	Lb ft to kgm	Kgm to lb ft
1	.138	7.233	7	.967	50.631
2	.276	14.466	8	1.106	57.864
3	.414	21.699	9	1.244	65.097
4	.553	28.932	10	1.382	72.330
5	.691	36.165	20	2.765	144.660
6	.829	43.398	30	4.147	216.990

HINTS ON MAINTENANCE AND OVERHAUL

There are few things more rewarding than the restoration of a vehicle's original peak of efficiency and smooth performance.

The following notes are intended to help the owner to reach that state of perfection. Providing that he possesses the basic manual skills he should have no difficulty in performing most of the operations detailed in this manual. It must be stressed, however, that where recommended in the manual, highly-skilled operations ought to be entrusted to experts, who have the necessary equipment, to carry out the work satisfactorily.

Quality of workmanship:

The hazardous driving conditions on the roads to-day demand that vehicles should be as nearly perfect, mechanically, as possible. It is therefore most important that amateur work be carried out with care, bearing in mind the often inadequate working conditions, and also the inferior tools which may have to be used. It is easy to counsel perfection in all things, and we recognize that it may be setting an impossibly high standard. We do, however, suggest that every care should be taken to ensure that a vehicle is as safe to take on the road as it is humanly possible to make it.

Safe working conditions:

Even though a vehicle may be stationary, it is still potentially dangerous if certain sensible precautions are not taken when working on it while it is supported on jacks or blocks. It is indeed preferable not to use jacks alone, but to supplement them with carefully placed blocks, so that there will be plenty of support if the car rolls off the jacks during a strenuous manoeuvre. Axle stands are an excellent way of providing a rigid base which is not readily disturbed. Piles of bricks are a dangerous substitute. Be careful not to get under heavy loads on lifting tackle, the load could fall. It is preferable not to work alone when lifting an engine, or when working underneath a vehicle which is supported well off the ground. To be trapped, particularly under the vehicle, may have unpleasant results if help is not quickly forthcoming. Make some provision, however humble, to deal with fires. Always disconnect a battery if there is a likelihood of electrical shorts. These may start a fire if there is leaking fuel about. This applies particularly to leads which can carry a heavy current, like those in the starter circuit. While on the subject of electricity, we must also stress the danger of using equipment which is run off the mains and which has no earth or has faulty wiring or connections. So many workshops have damp floors, and electrical shocks are of such a nature that it is sometimes impossible to let go of a live lead or piece of equipment due to the muscular spasms which take place.

Work demanding special care:

This involves the servicing of braking, steering and suspension systems. On the road, failure of the braking system may be disastrous. Make quite sure that there can be no possibility of failure through the bursting of rusty brake pipes or rotten hoses, nor to a sudden loss of pressure due to defective seals or valves.

Problems:

The chief problems which may face an operator are:
1 External dirt.
2 Difficulty in undoing tight fixings
3 Dismantling unfamiliar mechanisms.
4 Deciding in what respect parts are defective.
5 Confusion about the correct order for reassembly.
6 Adjusting running clearances.
7 Road testing.
8 Final tuning.

Practical suggestion to solve the problems:

1 Preliminary cleaning of large parts—engines, transmissions, steering, suspensions, etc.,—should be carried out before removal from the car. Where road dirt and mud alone are present, wash clean with a high-pressure water jet, brushing to remove stubborn adhesions, and allow to drain and dry. Where oil or grease is also present, wash down with a proprietary compound (Gunk, Teepol etc.,) applying with a stiff brush—an old paint brush is suitable—into all crevices. Cover the distributor and ignition coils with a polythene bag and then apply a strong water jet to clear the loosened deposits. Allow to drain and dry. The assemblies will then be sufficiently clean to remove and transfer to the bench for the next stage.

On the bench, further cleaning can be carried out, first wiping the parts as free as possible from grease with old newspaper. Avoid using rag or cotton waste which can leave clogging fibres behind. Any remaining grease can be removed with a brush dipped in paraffin. If necessary, traces of paraffin can be removed by carbon tetrachloride. Avoid using paraffin or petrol in large quantities for cleaning in enclosed areas, such as garages, on account of the high fire risk.

When all exteriors have been cleaned, and not before, dismantling can be commenced. This ensures that dirt will not enter into interiors and orifices revealed by dismantling. In the next phases, where components have to be cleaned, use carbon tetrachloride in preference to petrol and keep the containers covered except when in use. After the components have been cleaned, plug small holes with tapered hard wood plugs cut to size and blank off larger orifices with grease-proof paper and masking tape. Do not use soft wood plugs or matchsticks as they may break.

2 It is not advisable to hammer on the end of a screw thread, but if it must be done, first screw on a nut to protect the thread, and use a lead hammer. This applies particularly to the removal of tapered cotters. Nuts and bolts seem to 'grow' together, especially in exhaust systems. If penetrating oil does not work, try the judicious application of heat, but be careful ot starting a fire. Asbestos sheet or cloth is useful to isolate heat.

Tight bushes or pieces of tail-pipe rusted into a silencer can be removed by splitting them with an open-ended hacksaw. Tight screws can sometimes be started by a tap from a hammer on the end of a suitable screwdriver. Many tight fittings will yield to the judicious use of a hammer, but it must be a soft-faced hammer if damage is to be avoided, use a heavy block on the opposite side to absorb shock. Any parts of the steering system which have been damaged should be renewed, as attempts to repair them may lead to cracking and subsequent failure, and steering ball joints should be disconnected using a recommended tool to prevent damage.

3 If often happens that an owner is baffled when trying to dismantle an unfamiliar piece of equipment. So many modern devices are pressed together or assembled by spinning-over flanges, that they must be sawn apart. The intention is that the whole assembly must be renewed. However, parts which appear to be in one piece to the naked eye, may reveal close-fitting joint lines when inspected with a magnifying glass, and, this may provide the necessary clue to dismantling. Left-handed screw threads are used where rotational forces would tend to unscrew a right-handed screw thread.

Be very careful when dismantling mechanisms which may come apart suddenly. Work in an enclosed space where the parts will be contained, and drape a piece of cloth over the device if springs are likely to fly in all directions. Mark everything which might be reassembled in the wrong position, scratched symbols may be used on unstressed parts, or a sequence of tiny dots from a centre punch can be useful. Stressed parts should never be scratched or centre-popped as this may lead to cracking under working conditions. Store parts which look alike in the correct order for reassembly. Never rely upon memory to assist in the assembly of complicated mechanisms, especially when they will be dismantled for a long time, but make notes, and drawings to supplement the diagrams in the manual, and put labels on detached wires. Rust stains may indicate unlubricated wear. This can sometimes be seen round the outside edge of a bearing cup in a universal joint. Look for bright rubbing marks on parts which normally should not make heavy contact. These might prove that something is bent or running out of truth. For example, there might be bright marks on one side of a piston, at the top near the ring grooves, and others at the bottom of the skirt on the other side. This could well be the clue to a bent connecting rod. Suspected cracks can be proved by heating the component in a light oil to approximately 100°C, removing, drying off, and dusting with french chalk, if a crack is present the oil retained in the crack will stain the french chalk.

4 In determining wear, and the degree, against the permissible limits set in the manual, accurate measurement can only be achieved by the use of a micrometer. In many cases, the wear is given to the fourth place of decimals; that is in ten-thousandths of an inch. This can be read by the vernier scale on the barrel of a good micrometer. Bore diameters are more difficult to determine. If, however, the matching shaft is accurately measured, the degree of play in the bore can be felt as a guide to its suitability. In other cases, the shank of a twist drill of known diameter is a handy check.

Many methods have been devised for determining the clearance between bearing surfaces. To-day the best and simplest is by the use of Plastigage, obtainable from most garages. A thin plastic thread is laid between the two surfaces and the bearing is tightened, flattening the thread. On removal, the width of the thread is compared with a scale supplied with the thread and the clearance is read off directly. Sometimes joint faces leak persistently, even after gasket renewal. The fault will then be traceable to distortion, dirt or burrs. Studs which are screwed into soft metal frequently raise burrs at the point of entry. A quick cure for this is to chamfer the edge of the hole in the part which fits over the stud.

5 **Always check a replacement part with the original one before it is fitted.**

If parts are not marked, and the order for reassembly is not known, a little detective work will help. Look for marks which are due to wear to see if they can be mated. Joint faces may not be identical due to manufacturing errors, and parts which overlap may be stained, giving a clue to the correct position. Most fixings leave identifying marks especially if they were painted over on assembly. It is then easier to decide whether a nut, for instance, has a plain, a spring, or a shakeproof washer under it. All running surfaces become 'bedded' together after long spells of work and tiny imperfections on one part will be found to have left corresponding marks on the other. This is particularly true of shafts and bearings and even a score on a cylinder wall will show on the piston.

6 Checking end float or rocker clearances by feeler gauge may not always give accurate results because of wear. For instance, the rocker tip which bears on a valve stem may be deeply pitted, in which case the feeler will simply be bridging a depression. Thrust washers may also wear depressions in opposing faces to make accurate measurement difficult. End float is then easier to check by using a dial gauge. It is common practice to adjust end play in bearing assemblies, like front hubs with taper rollers, by doing up the axle nut until the hub becomes stiff to turn and then backing it off a little. Do not use this method with ballbearing hubs as the assembly is often preloaded by tightening the axle nut to its fullest extent. If the splitpin hole will not line up, file the base of the nut a little.

Steering assemblies often wear in the straight-ahead position. If any part is adjusted, make sure that it remains free when moved from lock to lock. Do not be surprised if an assembly like a steering gearbox, which is known to be carefully adjusted outside the car, becomes stiff when it is bolted in place. This will be due to distortion of the case by the pull of the mounting bolts, particularly if the mounting points are not all touching together. This problem may be met in other equipment and is cured by careful attention to the alignment of mounting points.

When a spanner is stamped with a size and A/F it means that the dimension is the width between the jaws and has no connection with ANF, which is the designation for the American National Fine thread. Coarse threads like Whitworth are rarely used on cars to-day except for studs which screw into soft aluminium or cast iron. For this reason it might be found that the top end of a cylinder head stud has a fine thread and the lower end a coarse thread to screw into the cylinder block. If the car has mainly UNF threads then it is likely that any coarse threads will be UNC, which are not the same as Whitworth. Small sizes have the same number of threads in Whitworth and UNC, but in the $\frac{1}{2}$ inch size for example, there are twelve threads to the inch in the former and thirteen in the latter.

7 After a major overhaul, particularly if a great deal of work has been done on the braking, steering and suspension systems, it is advisable to approach the problem of testing with care. If the braking system has been overhauled, apply heavy pressure to the brake pedal and get a second operator to check every possible source of leakage. The brakes may work extremely well, but a leak could cause complete failure after a few miles.

Do not fit the hub caps until every wheel nut has been checked for tightness, and make sure the tyre pressures are correct. Check the levels of coolant, lubricants and hydraulic fluids. Being satisfied that all is well, take the car on the road and test the brakes at once. Check the steering and the action of the handbrake. Do all this at moderate speeds on quiet roads, and make sure there is no other vehicle behind you when you try a rapid stop.

Finally, remember that many parts settle down after a time, so check for tightness of all fixings after the car has been on the road for a hundred miles or so.

8 It is useless to tune an engine which has not reached its normal running temperature. In the same way, the tune of an engine which is stiff after a rebore will be different when the engine is again running free. Remember too, that rocker clearances on pushrod operated valve gear will change when the cylinder head nuts are tightened after an initial period of running with a new head gasket.

Trouble may not always be due to what seems the obvious cause. Ignition, carburation and mechanical condition are interdependent and spitting back through the carburetter, which might be attributed to a weak mixture, can be caused by a sticking inlet valve.

For one final hint on tuning, never adjust more than one thing at a time or it will be impossible to tell which adjustment produced the desired result.

GLOSSARY OF TERMS

Allen key   Cranked wrench of hexagonal section for use with socket head screws.

Alternator   Electrical generator producing alternating current. Rectified to direct current for battery charging.

Ambient temperature   Surrounding atmospheric temperature.

Annulus   Used in engineering to indicate the outer ring gear of an epicyclic gear train.

Armature   The shaft carrying the windings, which rotates in the magnetic field of a generator or starter motor. That part of a solenoid or relay which is activated by the magnetic field.

Axial   In line with, or pertaining to, an axis.

Backlash   Play in meshing gears.

Balance lever   A bar where force applied at the centre is equally divided between connections at the ends.

Banjo axle   Axle casing with large diameter housing for the crownwheel and differential.

Bendix pinion   A self-engaging and self-disengaging drive on a starter motor shaft.

Bevel pinion   A conical shaped gearwheel, designed to mesh with a similar gear with an axis usually at 90 deg. to its own.

bhp   Brake horse power, measured on a dynamometer.

bmep   Brake mean effective pressure. Average pressure on a piston during the working stroke.

Brake cylinder   Cylinder with hydraulically operated piston(s) acting on brake shoes or pad(s).

Brake regulator   Control valve fitted in hydraulic braking system which limits brake pressure to rear brakes during heavy braking to prevent rear wheel locking.

Camber   Angle at which a wheel is tilted from the vertical.

Capacitor   Modern term for an electrical condenser. Part of distributor assembly, connected across contact breaker points, acts as an interference suppressor.

Castellated   Top face of a nut, slotted across the flats, to take a locking splitpin.

Castor   Angle at which the kingpin or swivel pin is tilted when viewed from the side.

cc   Cubic centimetres. Engine capacity is arrived at by multiplying the area of the bore in sq cm by the stroke in cm by the number of cylinders.

Clevis   U-shaped forked connector used with a clevis pin, usually at handbrake connections.

Collet   A type of collar, usually split and located in a groove in a shaft, and held in place by a retainer. The arrangement used to retain the spring(s) on a valve stem in most cases.

Commutator   Rotating segmented current distributor between armature windings and brushes in generator or motor.

Compression   The ratio, or quantitative relation, of the total volume (piston at bottom of stroke) to the unswept volume (piston at top of stroke) in an engine cylinder.

Condenser   See capacitor.

Core plug   Plug for blanking off a manufacturing hole in a casting.

Crownwheel   Large bevel gear in rear axle, driven by a bevel pinion attached to the propeller shaft. Sometimes called a 'ring gear'.

'C'-spanner   Like a 'C' with a handle. For use on screwed collars without flats, but with slots or holes.

Damper   Modern term for shock-absorber, used in vehicle suspension systems to damp out spring oscillations.

Depression   The lowering of atmospheric pressure as in the inlet manifold and carburetter.

Dowel   Close tolerance pin, peg, tube, or bolt, which accurately locates mating parts.

Drag link   Rod connecting steering box drop arm (pitman arm) to nearest front wheel steering arm in certain types of steering systems.

Dry liner   Thinwall tube pressed into cylinder bore

Dry sump   Lubrication system where all oil is scavenged from the sump, and returned to a separate tank.

Dynamo   See Generator.

Electrode   Terminal, part of an electrical component, such as the points or 'Electrodes' of a sparking plug.

Electrolyte   In lead-acid car batteries a solution of sulphuric acid and distilled water.

End float   The axial movement between associated parts, end play.

EP   Extreme pressure. In lubricants, special grades for heavily loaded bearing surfaces, such as gear teeth in a gearbox, or crownwheel and pinion in a rear axle.

Fade	Of brakes. Reduced efficiency due to overheating.
Field coils	Windings on the polepieces of motors and generators.
Fillets	Narrow finishing strips usually applied to interior bodywork.
First motion shaft	Input shaft from clutch to gearbox.
Fullflow filter	Filters in which all the oil is pumped to the engine. If the element becomes clogged, a bypass valve operates to pass unfiltered oil to the engine.
FWD	Front wheel drive.
Gear pump	Two meshing gears in a close fitting casing. Oil is carried from the inlet round the outside of both gears in the spaces between the gear teeth and casing to the outlet, the meshing gear teeth prevent oil passing back to the inlet, and the oil is forced through the outlet port.
Generator	Modern term for 'Dynamo'. When rotated produces electrical current.
Grommet	A ring of protective or sealing material. Can be used to protect pipes or leads passing through bulkheads.
Grubscrew	Fully threaded headless screw with screwdriver slot. Used for locking, or alignment purposes.
Gudgeon pin	Shaft which connects a piston to its connecting rod. Sometimes called 'wrist pin', or 'piston pin'.
Halfshaft	One of a pair transmitting drive from the differential.
Helical	In spiral form. The teeth of helical gears are cut at a spiral angle to the side faces of the gearwheel.
Hot spot	Hot area that assists vapourisation of fuel on its way to cylinders. Often provided by close contact between inlet and exhaust manifolds.
HT	High Tension. Applied to electrical current produced by the ignition coil for the sparking plugs.
Hydrometer	A device for checking specific gravity of liquids. Used to check specific gravity of electrolyte.
Hypoid bevel gears	A form of bevel gear used in the rear axle drive gears. The bevel pinion meshes below the centre line of the crownwheel, giving a lower propeller shaft line.
Idler	A device for passing on movement. A free running gear between driving and driven gears. A lever transmitting track rod movement to a side rod in steering gear.
Impeller	A centrifugal pumping element. Used in water pumps to stimulate flow.
Journals	Those parts of a shaft that are in contact with the bearings.
Kingpin	The main vertical pin which carries the front wheel spindle, and permits steering movement. May be called 'steering pin' or 'swivel pin'.
Layshaft	The shaft which carries the laygear in the gearbox. The laygear is driven by the first motion shaft and drives the third motion shaft according to the gear selected. Sometimes called the 'countershaft' or 'second motion shaft.'
lb ft	A measure of twist or torque. A pull of 10 lb at a radius of 1 ft is a torque of 10 lb ft.
lb/sq in	Pounds per square inch.
Little-end	The small, or piston end of a connecting rod. Sometimes called the 'small-end'.
LT	Low Tension. The current output from the battery.
Mandrel	Accurately manufactured bar or rod used for test or centring purposes.
Manifold	A pipe, duct, or chamber, with several branches.
Needle rollers	Bearing rollers with a length many times their diameter.
Oil bath	Reservoir which lubricates parts by immersion. In air filters, a separate oil supply for wetting a wire mesh element to hold the dust.
Oil wetted	In air filters, a wire mesh element lightly oiled to trap and hold airborne dust.
Overlap	Period during which inlet and exhaust valves are open together.
Panhard rod	Bar connected between fixed point on chassis and another on axle to control sideways movement.
Pawl	Pivoted catch which engages in the teeth of a ratchet to permit movement in one direction only.
Peg spanner	Tool with pegs, or pins, to engage in holes or slots in the part to be turned.
Pendant pedals	Pedals with levers that are pivoted at the top end.
Phillips screwdriver	A cross-point screwdriver for use with the cross-slotted heads of Phillips screws.
Pinion	A small gear, usually in relation to another gear.
Piston-type damper	Shock absorber in which damping is controlled by a piston working in a closed oil-filled cylinder.
Preloading	Preset static pressure on ball or roller bearings not due to working loads.
Radial	Radiating from a centre, like the spokes of a wheel.

Radius rod	Pivoted arm confining movement of a part to an arc of fixed radius.
Ratchet	Toothed wheel or rack which can move in one direction only, movement in the other being prevented by a pawl.
Ring gear	A gear tooth ring attached to outer periphery of flywheel. Starter pinion engages with it during starting.
Runout	Amount by which rotating part is out of true.
Semi-floating axle	Outer end of rear axle halfshaft is carried on bearing inside axle casing. Wheel hub is secured to end of shaft.
Servo	A hydraulic or pneumatic system for assisting, or, augmenting a physical effort. See 'Vacuum Servo'.
Setscrew	One which is threaded for the full length of the shank.
Shackle	A coupling link, used in the form of two parallel pins connected by side plates to secure the end of the master suspension spring and absorb the effects of deflection.
Shell bearing	Thinwalled steel shell lined with anti-friction metal. Usually semi-circular and used in pairs for main and big-end bearings.
Shock absorber	See 'Damper'.
Silentbloc	Rubber bush bonded to inner and outer metal sleeves.
Socket-head screw	Screw with hexagonal socket for an Allen key.
Solenoid	A coil of wire creating a magnetic field when electric current passes through it. Used with a soft iron core to operate contacts or a mechanical device.
Spur gear	A gear with teeth cut axially across the periphery.
Stub axle	Short axle fixed at one end only.
Tachometer	An instrument for accurate measurement of rotating speed. Usually indicates in revolutions per minute.

TDC	Top Dead Centre. The highest point reached by a piston in a cylinder, with the crank and connecting rod in line.
Thermostat	Automatic device for regulating temperature. Used in vehicle coolant systems to open a valve which restricts circulation at low temperature.
Third motion shaft	Output shaft of gearbox.
Threequarter floating axle	Outer end of rear axle halfshaft flanged and bolted to wheel hub, which runs on bearing mounted on outside of axle casing. Vehicle weight is not carried by the axle shaft.
Thrust bearing or washer	Used to reduce friction in rotating parts subject to axial loads.
Torque	Turning or twisting effort. See 'lb ft'.
Track rod	The bar(s) across the vehicle which connect the steering arms and maintain the front wheels in their correct alignment.
UJ	Universal joint. A coupling between shafts which permits angular movement.
UNF	Unified National Fine screw thread.
Vacuum servo	Device used in brake system, using difference between atmospheric pressure and inlet manifold depression to operate a piston which acts to augment brake pressure as required. See 'Servo'.
Venturi	A restriction or 'choke' in a tube, as in a carburetter, used to increase velocity to obtain a reduction in pressure.
Vernier	A sliding scale for obtaining fractional readings of the graduations of an adjacent scale.
Welch plug	A domed thin metal disc which is partially flattened to lock in a recess. Used to plug core holes in castings.
Wet liner	Removable cylinder barrel, sealed against coolant leakage, where the coolant is in direct contact with the outer surface.
Wet sump	A reservoir attached to the crankcase to hold the lubricating oil.

INDEX

THE AUTOBOOK SERIES OF WORKSHOP MANUALS

Alfa Romeo Giulia
1962 on
Aston Martin 1921-58
Audi 100 1969 on
(Austin, Morris etc.)
1100 Mk. 1 1962-67
(Austin, Morris etc.) 1100
Mk. 2, 1300 Mk. 1, 2,
America 1968 on
Austin A30, A35, A40
Farina
Austin A55 Mk. 2, A60
1958-69
Austin A99, A110 1959-68
Austin J4 1960 on
Austin Maxi 1969 on
Austin, Morris 1800
1964 on
BMC 3 (Austin A50,
A55 Mk. 1, Morris
Oxford 2. 3 1954-59)
Austin Healey 100/6, 3000
1956-68
(Austin Healey, MG)
Sprite, Midget 1958 on
BMW 1600 1964 on
BMW 1800 1964-68
BMW 2000, 2002 1966 on
Chevrolet Corvair 1960-69
Chevrolet Corvette V8
1957-65
Chevrolet Vega 2300
1970-71
Chevrolet Corvette V8
1965-71
Chrysler Valiant V8
1965 on
Chrysler Valiant Straight
Six 1966-70
Citroen DS 19, ID 19
1955-66
Citroen ID 19, DS 19, 20,
21 1966-70
Datsun 1200 1970 on
Datsun 1300, 1600
1968 on
Datsun 240Z Sport
1970 on
De Dion Bouton
1899-1907
Fiat 124 1966 on
Fiat 124 Sport 1966 on
Fiat 125 1967 on
Fiat 500 1957 on
Fiat 600, 600D 1955-69
Fiat 850 1964 on
Fiat 1100 1957-69
Fiat 1300, 1500 1961-67
Ford Anglia Prefect 100E
1953-62
Ford Anglia 105E,
Prefect 107E 1959-67
Ford Capri 1300, 1600
1968 on
Ford Capri 2000 GT,
3000 GT 1969 on
Ford Classic, Capri
1961-64
Ford Consul, Zephyr,
Zodiac, 1, 2 1950-62
Ford Corsair Straight
Four 1963-65

Ford Corsair V4 1965-68
Ford Corsair V4 1969 on
Ford Cortina 1962-66
Ford Cortina 1967-68
Ford Cortina 1969-70
Ford Cortina Mk. 3
1970 on
Ford Escort 1967 on
Ford Falcon V8 1964-69
Ford Thames 10, 12,
15 cwt 1957-65
Ford Transit 1965 on
Ford Zephyr Zodiac
Mk. 3 1962-66
Ford Zephyr V4, V6,
Zodiac 1966 on
Hillman Avenger 1970 on
Hillman Hunter 1966 on
Hillman Imp 1963-68
Hillman Imp 1969 on
Hillman Minx 1 to 5
1956-65
Hillman Minx 1965-67
Hillman Minx 1966-70
Hillman Super Minx
1961-65
Holden Straight Six
1948-66
Holden Straight Six
1966 on
Jaguar XK120, 140, 150,
Mk. 7, 8, 9 1948-61
Jaguar 2.4, 3.4, 3.8
Mk. 1, 2 1955-69
Jaguar 'E' Type 1961 on
Jaguar 'S' Type 420
1963-68
Jaguar XJ6 1968 on
Jowett Javelin Jupiter
1947-53
Landrover 1, 2 1948-61
Landrover 2, 2a, 3 1959 on
Mercedes-Benz 190b,
190c 200 1959-68
Mercedes-Benz 220
1959-65
Mercedes-Benz 220/8
1968 on
Mercedes-Benz 230
1963-68
Mercedes-Benz 250
1965-67
Mercedes-Benz 250
1968 on
Mercedes-Benz 280
1968 on
MG TA to TF 1936-55
MGA MGB 1955-68
MG MGB 1969 on
Mini 1959 on
Mini Cooper 1961 on
Morgan 1936-69
Morris Marina 1971 on
Morris Minor 2, 1000
1952-71
Morris Oxford 5, 6 1959-71
NSU 1000 1963 on
NSU Prinz 1 to 4
1957 on
Opel Ascona, Manta
1970 on
Opel G.T. 1900 1968 on

Opel Kadett, Olympia
993 cc, 1078 cc
1962 on
Opel Kadett, Olympia
1492, 1698, 1897 cc
1967 on
Opel Rekord C 1966 on
Peugeot 204 1965 on
Peugeot 404 1960 on
Peugeot 504 1968-70
Porsche 356a, 356b, 356c
1957-65
Porsche 911 1964-69
Porsche 912 1965-69
Reliant Regal 1962 on
Renault R4, R4L, 4
1961 on
Renault 6 1968 on
Renault 8, 10, 1100
1962 on
Renault 12 1969 on
Renault R16 1965 on
Renault Dauphine
Floride 1957-67
Renault Caravelle 1962-68
Rover 60 to 110 1953-64
Rover 2000 1963 on
Rover 3 Litre 1958-67
Rover 3500, 3500S
1968 on
Saab 95, 96, Sport
1960-68
Saab 99 1969 on
Saab V4 1966 on
Simca 1000 1961 on
Simca 1100 1967 on
Simca 1300, 1301, 1500,
1501 1963 on
Skoda One (440, 445, 450)
1957-69
Sunbeam Rapier Alpine
1955-65
Toyota Corolla 1100
1967 on
Toyota Corona 1500
Mk. 1 1965-70
Toyota Corona 1900 Mk. 2
1969 on
Triumph TR2, TR3,
TR3A 1952-62
Triumph TR4, TR4A
1961-67
Triumph TR5, TR250,
TR6 1967 on
Triumph 1300, 1500
1965 on
Triumph 2000 Mk. 1, 2.5 PI
Mk. 1 1963-69
Triumph 2000 Mk. 2, 2.5
PI Mk. 2 1969 on
Triumph Herald 1959-68
Triumph Herald 1969-71
Triumph Spitfire Vitesse
1962-68
Triumph Spitfire Mk. 3
1969 on
Triumph GT6, Vitesse 2
Litre 1969 on
Triumph Toledo 1970 on
Vauxhall Velox, Cresta
1957 on

Vauxhall Victor 1, 2, FB
1957-64
Vauxhall Victor 101
1964-67
Vauxhall Victor FD 1600,
2000 1967 on
Vauxhall Viva HA 1963-66
Vauxhall Viva HB 1966-70
Vauxhall Viva, HC Firenza
1971 on
Vauxhall Victor 3300,
Ventura 1968 on
Volkswagen Beetle
1954-67
Volkswagen Beetle
1968 on
Volkswagen 1500 1961-66
Volkswagen 1600
Fastback 1965 on
Volkswagen Transporter
1954-67
Volkswagen Transporter
1968 on
Volvo P120 1961-70
Volvo P140 1966 on
Volvo 160 series 1968 on
Volvo 1800 1961 on

NOTES